Great
DESSERTS
OF THE AMERICAN WEST

Raspberry Chocolate-Pecan Torte, see page 13.

Great DESSERTS

OF THE AMERICAN WEST

Sweet Endings and Treats from the West Coast to the Lone Star State

Frances Towner Giedt

Lone Star Books®

An imprint of Gulf Publishing Company

Houston, Texas

To David,
for 34 years of shared happy times,
with love

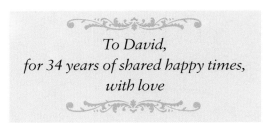

Great
DESSERTS
OF THE AMERICAN WEST

Lone Star Books®
An imprint of Gulf Publishing Company
Book Division
P.O. Box 2608 □ Houston, Texas 77252-2608

10   9   8   7   6   5   4   3   2   1

Library of Congress Cataloging-in-Publication Data

Giedt, Frances Towner.
    Great desserts of the American West : sweet endings and treats from the West Coast to the Lone Star State / Frances Towner Giedt.
    p.   cm.
ISBN 0-87719-346-0 (alk. paper)
1. Desserts–(West (U.S.)   I. Title.
TX773.G44   1999
641.8´6–dc21   99-27283
                                                 CIP

Printed in Hong Kong.
Printed on acid-free paper (∞).

Photography by Mary Herrmann.
Food styling by Lee Stanyer.
Art direction/cover and book design by Roxann L. Combs.

Contents

Acknowledgments

Usually doing a book of this magnitude involves a year or so in the dreaming stage. It happened quite differently for me, starting with an e-mail to Cheryl Smith, a publicist at Gulf Publishing, on an entirely different subject. Cheryl recognized my name as she owns several of my previous books, and within a day or two, I received a phone call from Kim Kilmer, acquisitions editor at Gulf, requesting a proposal for a dessert cookbook that featured, in part, recipes from our Lone Star State of Texas. Thus, *Great Desserts of the American West* was born in our heads and soon, in several test kitchens. For Cheryl and Kim's insight and trust, I will always be grateful.

First, extra thanks to Debra and Chesley Sanders, who proved to be invaluable recipe testers, and to all of the fire fighters of Fort Worth (Texas) Station 12, who so willingly tasted and commented on most of the recipes. And, extra thanks to Debra, who raided her family recipe files, and to Chesley, a recognized authority on wine in Texas, for his help in compiling and writing the section on dessert wines. I will always treasure their talent, friendship, and commitment to the book. Others who graciously tested and re-tested recipes are Jackie Davidson, my daughter-in-law Kimberly Giedt, my sister Eileen Ryberg, and my sister-in-law Ruth Towner. They all worked hard and long to get the testing done on time. A million thanks.

This book never would have come to be if it weren't for my husband David and his love and unending support, as well as his "volunteering" to be a critical taste-tester. Also indispensable are my editors at Gulf Publishing, Joyce Alff and Kelly Perkins. Gratitude also to Roxann Combs, creative director; Mary Herrmann, photographer, who brought many of my recipes to life with her beautiful photographs; Lee Stanyer, food stylist; Laura Dion, graphic artist; Beth Cunningham, typesetter; and Kathy Veale, proofreader—all of whom contributed their unique talents.

Last, but not least, to the many people who contributed recipes for the book: Selma Andrews, Los Angeles, CA; Betty Barns, Anaheim Hills, CA; Billie Brown, Kennedale, TX; Lucia Deichmann of Bite-Size Bakery, Moriarity, NM; Pat Eby, Incline Village, NV; Dean Fearing of Mansion on Turtle Creek, Dallas, TX; Gloria Giedt, Rancho Palos Verdes, CA; Helen Giedt, Granada Hills, CA; Estelle Goldman, Palm Springs, CA; Hadley Date Gardens, Indio, CA; Ann Hite, Laguna Niguel, CA; Diane Joy, Las Vegas, NV; Martha Kimball, Redondo Beach, CA; Brenda Owens, Salem, OR; Sheila and Amanda Parker, Golden, TX; Nancy Parks, Palm Springs, CA; Pat Pierringer, Anaheim Hills, CA; the late Vincent Price, Hollywood Hills, CA; the late Elaine Rogers, Hollywood, CA; Eileen Ryberg, Phoenix, AZ; Chesley Sanders, Burleson, TX; Debra Sanders, Burleson, TX; Peggy Sanders, Burleson, TX; Ninnie Sanders, Burleson, TX; Shields Date Farm, Indio, CA; Laile Towner, Bellevue, WA; Ruth Towner, Bellevue, WA; Helen Weissman, Los Angeles, CA; and the late Robert Young, Los Angeles, CA. I thank you one and all.

In my first cookbook, published thirteen years ago, I wrote that writing a cookbook was a group effort. Never has this been a more true statement. My eternal gratitude to everyone who worked on this book and to those who will hopefully purchase and enjoy it.

Frances Towner Giedt

Introduction

Desserts are an emotional experience for most everyone. If you've ever shared a truly decadent dessert with a loved one or created a fabulous dessert for a special person, you know what I mean. When we dine out, our Western obsession with sweet sauce-laced, chocolaty, to-die-for desserts is reflected by the dramatic increase in dessert sales, whether at the corner diner or the most fashionable restaurant. At the same time, home baking is experiencing a resurgence, and baking classes by the nation's top bakers are sold out well before classes in other categories.

Surprisingly in this age of concern about cutting back on protein, while eating more fruits, vegetables, and healthy grains, desserts in the western part of our country haven't changed all that much from those of our mothers or grandmothers. If one works and plays hard, as most westerners do, what's the harm in an occasional indulgence of a luscious chocolate cake, a fruit cobbler "like Mom use to make," a fresh peach baked with spices and splashed with cream, a spoonful of smooth, melt-in-the-mouth Mexican flan, a scoop of Texas ruby red grapefruit sorbet, or a slice of pie piled high with the season's best fruits and berries and baked in a flaky pie crust that dissolves on the tongue? Desserts can raise our spirits, provide us a respite from the tedium of daily life, comfort us on a cold winter night, satisfy a hunger, cool us off after a lazy summer supper, and delight our senses from the first bite to the last.

While it is true that most of us can't eat dessert every day without seeing some unhealthy changes in our body, one of the most important results of the wave of health consciousness sweeping across the plains and mountains of the American West is the realization that with increased exercise and physical activity, we can indulge occasionally and still stay fit.

Although we may not grow or produce every food of the world, we in the West are truly blessed with climatic and fertile soil conditions to grow the most luscious fruits, the juiciest berries, the plumpest and meatiest nuts. We've been wine country since the 1500s. Much of the early West was populated by the Spanish, Mexicans, and Native Americans whose lives revolved around the Franciscan monks who devoted their lives to prayer and tilling the soil. The friars brought European grape and fig cuttings to the California valleys and other parts of the Southwest where the climate is so like the Mediterranean, producing sun-drenched table and wine grapes, raisins, figs, and pistachios.

By the mid-19th century, Conestoga wagons filled with apple and pear seedlings rumbled over the plains to the Pacific Northwest; today, the quality of apples and pears in that region is legendary. Germans, Frenchmen, and Englishmen sailed to Panama and then up the Pacific coast to seek their fortune and till the soil. Native berries in all shapes, colors, and flavors grew abundantly, awaiting cultivation by the farmers who emigrated from the eastern United States, Europe, and Asia. In the arid south, citrus and semitropical fruits including limes, grapefruits, oranges, mangoes, papayas, apricots, peaches, and plums thrived.

The chuckwagons that followed the cowboys were veritable pantries on wheels stocked with flour, cornmeal, salt, lard, sugar, coffee, molasses, and cane sugar syrup. The cook would manage to put forth a dessert to counter the coffee, made black and strong—perhaps a pie sweetened with molasses or sugar and filled with wild berries picked near the campsite. The Southwest took its clue from its Mexican neighbors and adopted flan and other Mexican sweets as its own. The pralines and pecan pies of Texas reflect a southern influence. The lower Rio Grande Valley grows some of the finest citrus, pecans, and melons in the world.

New Mexico has pockets of micro-climates perfect for growing the sweetest figs and fat, meaty pistachios. The Sonoran desert that stretches from Yuma, Arizona, to Indio, California, is blessed with sunshine and long growing seasons for citrus and dates. In the higher elevations, apples, pears, and dozens of other fruits and several varieties of nuts flourish. As the West has grown in size, it has also grown in awareness that dessert is a food category that transcends history, resonating in the pleasures and pageantry of our lives.

My own passion for making desserts began in my mother's kitchen, when at age 10 I volunteered a batch of chocolate chip cookies for a school bake sale, not remembering that my parents were going to be away and that I would be staying with a sitter. Undaunted, I begged the sitter to let me make the cookies, using the basic ingredients that we always had on hand—margarine, flour, sugar, and imitation vanilla. I rode my bike to the corner store for chocolate chips, but didn't take enough money for nuts, so I convinced myself I wouldn't need them. I baked the cookies, and although many were of different sizes and shapes, my chocolate chip cookies quickly sold at the bake sale. I couldn't have been more proud.

Luckily my mother shared my interest in baking and was well known in her church and social circles as the lady who makes the lightest cakes, the creamiest puddings, and the best pies—an instinctive baker who never measured. She'd just dump in the ingredients by sight and always came up with a winner. Just watching her bake as we talked about my day taught me a lot. Later I learned the finer techniques of baking in cooking classes in school while earning a university degree in foods and nutrition. As a graduate student, I even did the final testing on a major brand of pie crust mix, baking twenty pies a day, six days a week for six months. In my after-college test kitchen work, I was fortunate to be working with most every fruit advisory board in California, and desserts were often on my assignment list of recipes to develop for national magazines and newspapers.

As a working wife, mother, and now grandmother with a busy career, I've always felt that one of life's finest pleasures is sharing excellent, homemade food around the kitchen or dining room table with loved ones and friends. For my family, the meal is not complete without a sweet at the end. It may be something as simple as a perfect poached pear or a couple of crisp homemade cookies and a few strawberries, but dessert is always there.

Some of my recipes are very contemporary, using fruits or nuts that only a few years ago were considered exotic. Others are old-style family recipes that came into use only at holiday times or family gatherings. Several are contributed by others—people from all walks of life who are the trusted "keepers" of their family's recipes. Many are based on desserts I've sampled in my extensive travels throughout the West, and my own experiences in professionally developing dessert recipes, combined with my acquired knowledge as a caterer and hostess in both California and Texas. For those of you who are armchair cooks, this book is rich with vignettes of western lore and history of the native ingredients used to create the recipes. Hopefully the recipes' down-home quality may actually encourage you to try out your own cooking abilities.

Keeping in mind that we all live busy lives, I've tried to keep the recipes straightforward and easy for the most inexperienced cook to follow. If you can take shortcuts or want to tinker with the recipes, substituting ingredients, and so forth, please do. The point of a dessert is to enjoy the making as well as the eating. And, "customizing" recipes to suit one's preference is what pleasurable cooking is all about. I hope that this book will inspire you to get into the kitchen and start on a delicious excursion of the desserts of the American West.

Frances Towner Giedt
Arlington, Texas

Chocolate

Chocolate Mousse Tostada, see page 39.

Bittersweet Chocolate Mini-Cakes

These superb little cakes are inspired by a recipe that delighted diners at La Provence in Austin, Texas, where my friend Carole Peck, now one of the country's leading woman chefs, was combining her French training with ingredients from the Southwest. At the restaurant, these little cakes were sitting in a puddle of rich chocolate sauce and garnished with sugar-crusted pecans. I like them plain, just sprinkled with a bit of powdered sugar, making them perfect for lunch boxes and hot weather picnics.

Makes 24 servings

12 ounces bittersweet chocolate
5   ounces (1¼ stick) unsalted butter
¾   cup granulated sugar
5   large eggs, separated
⅓   cup unbleached all-purpose flour
⅓   cup chopped pecans
½   cup powdered sugar

Preheat oven to 350°. Lightly butter two 2-inch mini-muffin tins.

Place chocolate, butter, and sugar in a stainless steel bowl and set over a pot of simmering water (Do not let water actually touch the bottom of the bowl.) Stir mixture until melted and smooth. Set aside to cool to room temperature.

Using an electric mixer, add egg yolks, one at a time, beating well after each addition. Toss together the flour and pecans. Stir into chocolate mixture.

In a separate bowl, whip egg whites until they form stiff peaks. Gently stir ⅓ of the egg whites into the chocolate mixture, then fold in remaining egg whites. Spoon into prepared tins, filling ¾ full.

Bake 15 minutes. Remove from oven and let stand 20 minutes. Unmold onto a baking sheet and cool completely. Using a fine mesh strainer, sprinkle generously with powdered sugar.

Devil's Food Cake with Peanut Butter Frosting

My family dearly loves this combination of chocolate and peanut butter. Throughout the years, this has been a frequently requested cake at our house, especially for a birthday.

One of the best devil's food cakes I've ever eaten was made at The Lake Creek Inn in the redwoods of Marin County, California, owned by chef Bradley Ogden. After talking with his pastry chef, I came up with this similar recipe.

Cake

2   cups sugar

3   large eggs

1¼ cups canola oil

4   teaspoons pure vanilla extract

1⅓ cups boiling water

1   cup unsweetened cocoa powder

1½ teaspoons baking powder

1½ teaspoons baking soda

½   teaspoon salt

2⅓ cups unsifted unbleached all-purpose flour

Makes 10 to 12 servings

Peanut Butter Frosting

½   cup creamy peanut butter

¼   cup (½ stick) unsalted butter, softened

3   ounces cream cheese

¼ to ⅓ cup heavy cream

1   teaspoon vanilla extract

1   pound powdered sugar, sifted

⅓   cup coarsely chopped peanuts, for garnish

Preheat oven to 350°. Lightly grease and flour two 9-inch cake pans. Set aside.

In a large mixing bowl and using an electric mixer, beat sugar and eggs until thick and lemon colored. Blend in oil and vanilla. Continue to beat for 2 minutes. Combine boiling water and cocoa, blending thoroughly. Add to egg mixture, mixing well. Stir in baking powder, baking soda, and salt. Add flour and beat until mixture is well-blended and smooth.

Pour batter into prepared pans and bake 25 to 30 minutes, until a tester inserted in the center comes out clean. Remove from oven and let stand 5 minutes in pans before turning out onto racks to cool. Turn cakes right side up and cool completely.

TO MAKE FROSTING

In a medium mixing bowl, cream peanut butter, butter, and cream cheese until very smooth. Mix together ¼ cup cream and vanilla. Add powdered sugar, a fourth at a time, alternating with the cream mixture, beginning and ending with powdered sugar. Mix until smooth and creamy. If frosting is too thick, add additional drops of cream to achieve desired spreading consistency.

TO ASSEMBLE CAKE

Place one layer, top side down, on a cake plate and spread top with ⅔ cup of the frosting. Top with second cake layer, top side up, aligning the layers evenly and making the sides of the cake straight. Smoothly spread top and sides with remaining frosting. Garnish top with chopped peanuts. Chill for at least 30 minutes for frosting to set. Cut into wedges to serve.

Fallen Chocolate Soufflé Cake

The Princess Resort in Scottsdale, Arizona, used to serve flourless chocolate cakes that were incredibly rich with a warm, gooey center. Garnished with a drift of softly whipped cream and a few fresh raspberries, the cakes were baked in individual tartlet pans with removable bottoms. Alas, the chef wouldn't part with the recipe, but after several attempts I've come up with a close copy. The little cakes need to chill before they're baked so they make a great make-ahead dessert and can be baking while the after-dinner coffee perks.

½ cup (1 stick) unsalted butter, cut into 1-inch pieces
8   ounces semisweet chocolate, chopped
     pinch salt
⅓ cup sugar
6   large egg yolks
1¼ teaspoons vanilla extract
2   large egg whites
½ cup heavy whipping cream, chilled

Makes 6 servings

Garnish

Fresh raspberries

Butter six small tartlet pans that are 4½ inches in diameter with ¾-inch high sides and removable bottoms. Place the pans on a large baking sheet.

In a heavy saucepan over low heat, stir remaining butter and chocolate until melted and smooth. Remove from heat and sir in salt. Cool to lukewarm, stirring occasionally.

Measure and reserve 1 tablespoon of the sugar. Using an electric mixer, beat remaining sugar, egg yolks, and vanilla extract in a large bowl until mixture is pale yellow and thick, about 5 minutes. Fold one-fourth of the egg mixture into the cooled chocolate mixture, then fold the chocolate mixture into the egg mixture.

In another large bowl, beat egg whites until soft peaks form. Add reserved tablespoon of sugar and continue to beat until stiff peaks form. Gently stir one-fourth of the beaten egg whites into the chocolate mixture, then carefully fold in remaining egg whites. Divide batter between prepared pans. Cover and chill for at least 6 hours.

When ready to bake, preheat oven to 400°. Position rack in the center of the oven. Bake cakes until edges are set and centers still soft, about 11 minutes. Remove from oven and cool in pans on a rack for 2 to 3 minutes. Meanwhile, beat cream until soft peaks form.

Loosen cakes by running a small knife around pan sides. Transfer cakes to six dessert plates, slipping out the removable bottoms. Place a drift of whipped cream at one edge of each cake and garnish the cake and plate with raspberries. Serve warm.

Beating and Folding Egg Whites

Beaten egg whites contribute a light and fluffy texture to many desserts. To beat egg whites to maximum volume, start with egg whites (without even a speck of yolk) at room temperature in a clean and dry, totally grease-free mixing bowl. For soft peaks, using an electric mixer, beat the whites without sugar at medium to high speed until they barely hold a peak, still look foamy, and easily slide around the bowl. To whip egg whites to stiff peaks, beat on high speed until they form stiff peaks when the beaters are lifted, adding cream of tartar and sugar as directed in the recipe.

Usually a third of the beaten egg whites is stirred into the batter to lighten it, then the remaining egg whites can be folded in using a rubber scrapper, cutting down to the center of the bowl and scooping the whites up and over. Continue to fold, turning the bowl after each fold, preserving as much of the volume as possible.

Some dessert recipes call for uncooked egg whites that are no longer considered safe by the United States Department of Agriculture because uncooked egg whites have been found to be a possible carrier of food-borne illness. Although I could have called for Italian meringue (made by pouring a hot sugar syrup into the cold egg whites while whipping) in some recipes, I find this sometimes difficult for an inexperienced baker to achieve the desired volume. Instead, I have opted for pasteurized dried egg whites that are reconstituted with water before whipping or pasteurized liquid egg whites. This eliminates any possibility of contamination and produces an end product of equal quality as when using fresh egg whites. This dried product is distributed nationwide and should be available in almost any supermarket. If you don't readily find this product, ask your grocer. At my stores, the powdered egg is usually displayed above the sugar; the liquid egg whites are near the refrigerated egg substitute.

Mexican Chocolate Sheet Cake

Peggy Sanders of Burleson, Texas, has made this family recipe for more than 50 years for birthdays and family celebrations. In keeping with the Mexican heritage of much of Texas, I've added optional cinnamon and instant coffee to her basic recipes, for a complex flavored Mexican chocolate cake that's delightfully simple to make.

Chocolate Sheet Cake

2	cups sugar
2	cups sifted unbleached all-purpose flour
1	teaspoon baking soda
1	teaspoon ground cinnamon (optional)
1	teaspoon powdered instant espresso or instant coffee (optional)
½	cup (1 stick) butter
1	cup solid shortening
1	cup water
¼	cup unsweetened cocoa
½	cup buttermilk
2	large eggs, slightly beaten

Makes fifteen 3-inch squares

Icing

½	cup (1 stick) butter, melted
¼	cup unsweetened cocoa
1	1-pound box powdered sugar
1	teaspoon ground cinnamon (optional)
1	teaspoon powdered instant espresso or instant coffee (optional)
1	teaspoon pure vanilla extract

Preheat oven to 400°. Grease and flour a 15½-inch × 10½-inch jelly roll pan.

In a large bowl, sift together sugar, flour, baking soda, cinnamon (if using), and instant coffee (if using). In a heavy saucepan, combine the butter, shortening, water, and cocoa. Bring to a boil and remove from heat. Stir mixture until butter and shortening melt. Cool slightly, then stir in buttermilk and eggs. Pour the cocoa mixture over the dry ingredients. Mix well. Pour batter into prepared pan and bake for 20 minutes.

While cake is baking, combine icing ingredients, mixing well. As soon as the cake comes out of the oven, ice the cake. Cool in the pan on a rack. Cut into squares to serve.

Preacher's Chocolate Pecan Cake with Chocolate Glaze

I found the recipe for this scrumptious cake tucked into an old cookbook that I purchased from a garage sale near Tyler, Texas. The recipe, written on the back of a gas bill dated May 1951, called for a burnt sugar icing, but gave no clue as to the origin or author of the recipe. I've made several modifications over the years and added a chocolate glaze that you'll find versatile for all kinds of cakes, cupcakes, and cookies. The result is a rich cake with a fine, moist crumb. The chocolate glaze hardens nicely so the cake can be eaten out-of-hand at picnics and barbecues when it's baked in a sheet cake pan.

To whoever left the recipe in the cookbook, we're all much obliged. According to a notation on the original recipe, the cake was being made in honor of a preacher's visit. Hence, its name.

Chocolate Layer Cake

Makes 12 to 14 servings

4	cups unbleached all-purpose flour
1	cup good-quality unsweetened cocoa powder
2	teaspoons baking soda
¾	cup chopped pecans
1	cup (2 sticks) unsalted butter, at room temperature
2	cups sugar
2	large eggs
2	teaspoons pure vanilla extract
1	cup buttermilk
1	cup sour cream
¾	cup hot water

Chocolate Glaze

1	cup heavy cream
16	ounces semisweet chocolate chips
½	cup (1 stick) unsalted butter, cut into 6 pieces

Preheat oven to 350°. Lightly grease two 10-inch metal cake pans and line with parchment paper. Lightly oil and flour the paper.

In a medium bowl, combine flour, cocoa powder, and baking soda. Sift together twice. Add pecans and toss. In a large bowl and using an electric mixer, beat butter until fluffy. Gradually add the sugar while still beating until the mixture is light and pale yellow. Add the eggs, one at a time, continuing to beat until well mixed. Add vanilla and continue to beat until mixed.

Add the dry ingredients, a third at a time, alternating with a third of the buttermilk, sour cream, and hot water, beginning and ending with dry ingredients. Evenly spread the batter in the prepared cake pans, tapping each pan once sharply on the counter top.

Bake for 45 to 50 minutes, until cake springs back when lightly touched or a tester inserted near the middles comes out clean. Remove from oven and cool in the pans on a rack for 10 minutes while you prepare the glaze. Remove cakes from pans and transfer to a wire rack to cool, discarding the parchment paper.

TO MAKE GLAZE

Scald the cream in a 2-quart saucepan. Add the chocolate chips to the hot cream and using an electric mixer, blend until chocolate is melted and mixture is smooth. Gradually add the cold butter, beating constantly, until all butter is incorporated and glaze is smooth and creamy. Set aside to cool to lukewarm.

Trim the domed top off one cake layer so that it is flat. Place that layer, cut side down, on a large serving plate. Spread some of the cool glaze over the top and sides of the bottom layer. Place the frosted cake layer in the refrigerator for 10 minutes to allow the glaze to harden some. Then, top with the second cake layer and continue to spread on the a thin layer of glaze. Refrigerate for 10 minutes, then cover top and sides of the cake with remaining glaze. Let stand for a least 1 hour before serving. Refrigerate leftovers.

Pumpkin Surprise Cake
with Cocoa Glaze

This is a terrific cake for children's school lunch boxes sent to me by my friend Pat Eby of Incline Village, Nevada. The youngsters will love the flavor; you will feel great that the cake has a boost of fiber and good nutrition through the "surprise" ingredient—a cup of bran cereal.

Cake

Makes 12 to 14 servings

2	cups unbleached all-purpose flour
2	cups granulated sugar
2	teaspoons baking powder
1	teaspoon baking soda
1½	teaspoons ground cinnamon
1	teaspoon ground cloves
½	teaspoon ground ginger
½	teaspoons salt
4	large eggs
1	cup canola oil
2	cups canned pumpkin puree
1	cup bran cereal
1	cup chopped walnuts or pecans
1	cup chocolate chips

Cocoa Glaze

1	cup unsifted powdered sugar
3	tablespoons unsweetened cocoa powder
½	teaspoon pure vanilla extract
3	tablespoons whole milk, or as needed

Preheat oven to 350°. Lightly butter a bundt pan.

Onto waxed paper, sift together flour, granulated sugar, baking powder, baking soda, cinnamon, cloves, ginger, and salt. Set aside.

In a large bowl and using an electric mixer, beat eggs until foamy. Beat in oil and pumpkin puree. Stir in bran cereal. Gradually add flour mixture, mixing well. Stir in nuts and chocolate chips.

Pour mixture into prepared pan. Bake for 70 minutes, or until a tester inserted in the middle comes out clean. Cool in pan for 10 minutes, then turn onto a serving plate. Turn cake right side up and cool completely.

TO MAKE GLAZE

Sift together the powdered sugar and cocoa into a medium bowl. Whisk in vanilla and milk, adding a drop or two of additional milk if needed for the glaze to drip from a spoon. Spread in a thin layer over the cooled cake, using the back of a spoon, and letting the glaze drip down the sides of the cake. Glaze will harden as it air-dries.

Storing Berries

Berries are quite fragile, but if you follow a few simple steps once the hand-picked or store-bought berries are home, you can extend their shelf life.

Immediately turn the berries out onto a large piece of paper toweling and sort through them, discarding any moldy ones so they don't ruin the others. Do not wash the berries. Instead, put them in a paper-towel-lined basket or dish and store, uncovered, in the coldest part of the refrigerator. Gently rinse berries just before using and drain briefly on paper towels.

If you won't be using the berries within two days, lay in a single layer and freeze firm. Again, do not wash the berries. Once frozen, pack in freezer bags or airtight freezer containers. Do not defrost before using. Gently rinse berries just before using and drain briefly on paper towels.

Raspberry Chocolate-Pecan Torte

Although most of our raspberries come from Oregon and Washington, there are pockets of raspberry-growing areas in the other western states. Here I've combined raspberries with chocolate for a virtually flourless dessert that tastes as wonderful as it looks.

½ cup (1 stick) butter, at room temperature

3 ounces semisweet chocolate, chopped

1⅓ cups granulated sugar

1 cup pecan halves, toasted

2 large eggs, lightly beaten

1 teaspoon pure vanilla extract

⅓ cup unbleached all-purpose flour

3 cups fresh raspberries, rinsed and drained on paper towels

powdered sugar

Makes 8 to 10 servings

Preheat oven to 350°. Lightly butter a 9-inch round tart pan.

In the top of a double boiler or a large stainless-steel bowl suspended over a pot of simmering water (don't let water actually touch bottom of the bowl), combine butter and chocolate. Cook over low heat, stirring constantly, until chocolate melts and mixture is smooth. Remove from heat and stir in sugar.

In a food processor or nut grinder, process pecans until they form a fine powder. Stir into chocolate mixture along with eggs and vanilla extract. Add flour and stir to mix well. Pour batter into prepared pan.

Set aside 1 cup of the raspberries. Gently place remaining berries on top of cake batter, gently pressing each berry slightly into the batter. Bake for 45 to 50 minutes, until a tester inserted 1 inch from the edge comes out clean. Cool in pan on a rack for 10 minutes; invert out onto a rack, turn torte right side up, and cool.

When cool, sprinkle powdered sugar from a shaker or sieve onto the top of the torte and pile the remaining raspberries in the center. To serve, cut into wedges.

Chocolate Hazelnut Truffles

For years I bought chocolate truffles from a little shop on Rodeo Drive in Beverly Hills. The variety was always changing, each one seemingly more addictive than the last. It wasn't until my colleague Mary Goodbody, editor of *Chocolatier Magazine,* showed me just how easy truffles are to make that I began making my own. I'm particularly fond of this version.

Makes about 3 dozen

½ cup hazelnuts
½ pound milk chocolate, chopped
6 tablespoons heavy cream
¼ cup Frangelico (hazelnut) liqueur
3 tablespoons unsalted butter, cut into small bits
sifted unsweetened cocoa, for dusting

Preheat oven to 350°. Spread hazelnuts in a single layer in a large baking pan and toast for about 15 minutes, turning nuts after 8 minutes to toast evenly. Cool. Working with a few nuts at a time and using a clean kitchen towel, rub the nuts with the towel to remove as much of the skin as possible. Finely chop the nuts and set aside.

In the top of a double boiler or in a medium stainless-steel bowl set over simmering water (do not let the water actually touch the bottom of the bowl), melt chocolate. When almost melted, turn off the heat, and let stand until completely melted, stirring occasionally.

In a small saucepan, heat the cream and Frangelico. Remove chocolate from stove and whisk in cream mixture. Dot with butter, but do not stir. Once butter is completely melted, add hazelnuts and stir to combine well. Cool completely. Cover with plastic wrap and refrigerate overnight.

TO FORM TRUFFLES

Fill a small bowl with hot water and line a large baking sheet with parchment paper. Dip a melon baller, 1 inch in diameter, into the hot water and shake off excess water. Scoop out a truffle and quickly roll into a ball between the palms of your hands. Place formed truffle on prepared baking sheet. Repeat forming the remaining truffles, changing the bowl of hot water as needed and washing and drying your hands to prevent chocolate from sticking to your hands. (If chocolate mixture becomes too soft, refrigerate or freeze until firm.) Once all truffles are formed, refrigerate or freeze firm. Just before serving, roll each truffle in sifted cocoa. Refrigerate for 10 minutes before serving.

Almond Ecstasy Cookies

A personal favorite that I've made year after year for Christmas cookie trays, this recipe is particularly suited for the diminutive mini-chips that are now readily available.

Makes 4 dozen

1   cup (2 sticks) unsalted butter, at room temperature
¾   cup sugar, plus extra for sprinkling
1   teaspoon pure vanilla extract
2   cups sifted unbleached all-purpose flour
1   teaspoon salt
1   cup chocolate mini-chips
1   cup slivered almonds, toasted (see page 22) and coarsely chopped

Preheat oven to 375°. Place a large sheet of waxed paper under cooling racks to be used after baking cookies.

In a large bowl, cream together butter, ¾ cup sugar, and vanilla extract. Stir in flour and salt. Add chocolate chips and almonds. Mix well.

Using your hands, form dough into 1-inch balls. At first, the dough may seem crumbly, but as you work with it, it will soften and smooth out. Place balls at least 2 inches apart on an ungreased baking sheet. With a fork, press balls to flatten, making a crisscross pattern. Dip the fork in water as needed to prevent sticking. Bake for 12 to 15 minutes, until firm to touch. Let cool on pans about 1 minute before transferring to racks. Immediately sprinkle the top of each cookie with sugar. Cool, then serve, or store up to 4 days.

Chile Chocolate Pecan Cookies

Chocolate and New Mexican chiles? The flavor combination found in Mexican *mole* makes these cookies delicious. Dried New Mexican chiles are readily found in western supermarkets, already ground, or you can process the whole dried chiles into a fine powder in a food processor or spice grinder.

Makes about 3 dozen

2	cups semisweet chocolate chips
6	tablespoons (¾ stick) unsalted butter, at room temperature
1	cup plus 2 tablespoons sugar
2	large eggs, lightly beaten
2	teaspoons vanilla extract
1	cup plus 2 tablespoons unbleached all-purpose flour
1	teaspoon ground cinnamon
½	teaspoon baking powder
½	teaspoon salt
¼	cup crushed dried New Mexican red chiles
⅔	cup chopped pecans

Place 1½ cups of the chocolate chips in a 1-quart microwave-safe glass bowl. Microwave, uncovered, on MEDIUM (50 percent) power for 2 to 3 minutes, stirring after 2 minutes, until chocolate is melted and smooth. Let cool.

Preheat oven to 350°. Line a large baking sheet with parchment paper.

In a large bowl, cream together butter and sugar until lightly and fluffy. Beat in eggs, one at a time. Beat in vanilla and cooled chocolate.

In a bowl, combine flour, cinnamon, baking powder, and salt. Gradually stir into egg mixture, mixing well. Stir in ground chiles, pecans, and remaining ½ cup chocolate chips.

Drop by rounded tablespoon onto prepared baking sheet, about 2 inches apart. Bake for 8 to 10 minutes. Cool cookies on a rack.

Chocolate Rugelach

Over the years I've sampled countless versions of this traditional Hanukkah crescent-shaped cookie—some filled with fruit, others with nuts, poppy seed paste, or jam. This version was given to me by my friend, Helen Weissman, a cantor for her Los Angeles synagogue.

Cream Cheese Dough

2½ cups unbleached all-purpose flour

½ teaspoon salt

1 cup (2 sticks) cold unsalted butter

1 8-ounce package cream cheese, chilled

¼ cup sour cream

Chocolate Filling

¾ cup sugar

2 teaspoons ground cinnamon

¼ cup (½ stick) unsalted butter, melted

1 8-ounce package miniature chocolate chips

1 cup chopped pecans

½ cup dark raisins

Cinnamon Topping

2 large egg whites, beaten with 2 tablespoons water

⅓ cup sugar

1½ teaspoons ground cinnamon

Makes about 2½ dozen

In the workbowl of a food processor fitted with the metal blade, combine flour and salt. Cut butter and cream cheese into tiny pieces and scatter over the flour. Dot with sour cream. Using the on/off pulse function, process the mixture until a ball of dough forms. Divide the dough into quarters and flatten each portion into a flat, round disk. Wrap each disk in plastic wrap. Refrigerate overnight.

Preheat oven to 375°. Line a baking sheet with parchment paper. Remove one dough disk and let stand at room temperature for 10 minutes. In a small bowl, combine sugar and cinnamon.

Working on a lightly floured work surface, roll out dough to form a 10-inch circle. Brush dough with a tablespoon of the melted butter. Sprinkle with one-fourth of the sugar mixture, one-fourth of the chocolate chips, one-fourth of the pecans, and one-fourth of the raisins. Using a rolling pin, lightly press the ingredients into the dough. Using a sharp knife, cut the dough circle into 8 pie-shaped wedges. Starting at the wide end, roll up each wedge toward the point to form a crescent shape. Place 1 apart, point side down, on prepared pan.

Brush unbaked cookies with a little of the egg white mixture. Combine topping sugar and cinnamon. Sprinkle some on top of each cookie. Bake until golden brown, about 15 minutes. Cool for 5 minutes, then transfer cookies to wire racks to cool. Repeat shaping and baking process with remaining dough and remaining filling.

Five-Minute Boiled Cookies

Boiled cookies are quite popular in Texas, with several community cookbooks offering a more simple recipe. I added some extras to the basic recipe—not making them more difficult to make, just more delicious to eat.

Bertram, northwest of Austin, is the heart of Texas oat-growing country. On the first weekend in September the residents hold an annual oatmeal contest with a cook-off, oatmeal sculpture contest, and other oat-related activities.

2	cups sugar
3	tablespoons cocoa powder
½	cup (1 stick) unsalted butter
½	cup whole milk
2	ounces semisweet chocolate, finely chopped
1	cup creamy peanut butter
½	cup coarsely chopped salted peanuts
½	cup dark raisins
3	cups rolled oats

Makes about 5 dozen

In a large saucepan, bring sugar, cocoa powder, butter, and milk to a full boil. Remove from heat and immediately stir in remaining ingredients.

Drop by teaspoonfuls onto parchment or waxed paper. Cool until firm.

Hazelnut Biscotti with Chocolate Drizzle

Seattle and other western cities are known for their many coffee and espresso bars. Often a biscotti or two is served alongside for dunking. Be careful, these can become addictive.

Makes about 4 dozen

½ cup (1 stick) unsalted butter, at room temperature
¾ cup sugar
  juice and finely grated rind of 1 lemon
3 large eggs
1 teaspoon pure vanilla extract
3 cups unbleached all-purpose flour
1 tablespoon baking powder
1 teaspoon ground cinnamon
½ teaspoon salt
1 cup hazelnuts, toasted and skins removed (see page 22)
⅓ cup semisweeet chocolate baking chips

Preheat oven to 350°. Lightly grease two large baking sheets.

In a large bowl, beat butter, sugar, lemon juice, and lemon zest until fluffy. Add eggs, one at a time, beating well after each addition. Stir in vanilla. In a separate bowl, thoroughly combine flour, baking powder, cinnamon, and salt. Coarsely chop hazelnuts and toss with the flour mixture. Add to butter mixture and mix thoroughly.

Divide dough into three pieces. Shape each piece into a long roll, about 1½ inches in diameter. Place rolls 2 inches apart on one of the prepared pans and flatten each roll with your hands to about ½-inch thickness. Bake for 15 minutes.

Remove from oven and cut rolls crosswise into ¼-inch thick slices. Arrange slices, cut side up, on baking sheets (at this point, you'll be using both pans). Return to oven and continue to bake until biscotti appear dry and are lightly browned, about 15 minutes. Transfer to racks to cool.

Place chocolate chips in a self-sealing plastic bag. Microwave on HIGH for 1 to ½ minutes, until chips are melted. Snip one corner of the bag and drizzle the chocolate onto each biscotti with a zigzag motion. When chocolate firms, serve or store in an airtight container for up to 2 days. Freeze for longer storage.

Maui Macaroons Dipped in Chocolate

We were served these delicious little cookies when we ordered afternoon tea from room service at the Maui Sheraton on Ka'anapali Beach. Fortunately the pastry chef was willing to share the recipe. It brings back memories of a spectacular sunset painting the sky as we sipped tea and watched the nightly torch procession to Black Rock where a young cliff diver plunged into the rolling surf of the Pacific, 100 feet below.

3 cups sweetened flaked coconut

1 cup unsalted macadamia nuts, chopped

⅔ cup sweetened condensed milk

1 teaspoon pure vanilla extract

2 large egg whites

pinch salt

6 ounces semisweet chocolate, chopped

2 tablespoons light rum

Makes 2 dozen

Preheat oven to 350°. Line a baking sheet with parchment paper. Spread coconut and macadamia nuts on the prepared pan. Toast for about 12 minutes, stirring frequently. Remove from oven and let cool to room temperature. Transfer mixture to a large bowl. Replace parchment paper; also line a second baking sheet with parchment paper.

Maintain oven heat. In a large bowl, combine condensed milk and vanilla. Using an electric mixer, whip egg whites and salt until stiff peaks form. Carefully fold beaten egg whites into coconut mixture. Drop batter by rounded tablespoons onto prepared baking sheets. Bake until macaroons just turn golden, about 14 to 15 minutes. Transfer to a wire rack to cool.

Again line a baking sheet with parchment paper. In a 1-quart microwave-safe bowl, microwave chocolate on MEDIUM power for 2 to 5 minutes, stirring after 2 minutes and adding the rum. Continue until chocolate is completely melted and smooth.

Dip the macaroons sideways into the melted chocolate to cover half of each cookie. Place dipped cookies on prepared baking sheet. Refrigerate until chocolate is set, about 15 minutes, before serving.

Mexican Coconut–White Chocolate Cookies

These cookies remind me of the sweet, sticky coconut concoctions we used to buy from the sweet shops on Olvera Street in downtown Los Angeles.

Makes about 2 dozen

1   cup pecans, toasted and coarsely chopped
2½ cups shredded coconut
½   cup chopped dried cherries
3   ounces white chocolate, finely chopped
7   ounces canned sweetened condensed milk

Preheat oven to 325°. Line a large baking sheet with parchment paper.

In a large bowl, combine pecans, coconut, dried cherries, and white chocolate. Mix well. Add sweetened condensed milk and mix until evenly moistened.

Spoon a heaping tablespoon of batter for each cookie on the prepared baking sheet. Flatten to form small circles with the flat bottom of a glass. (Occasionally wash and dry bottom of glass to prevent sticking.) Bake 13 to 15 minutes, until edges are golden and coconut lightly browns. Do not overbake. Transfer cookies to a rack to cool.

Toasting Nuts

Toasting nuts brings out their flavor and aroma. Spread nuts, chopped or whole, in a single layer in a baking pan. Toast in a preheated 350° oven until golden brown and fragrant, about 3 to 5 minutes, shaking the pan once or twice to evenly toast. As soon as they start to color, they will toast very quickly. Be sure to not let them burn.

Mocha
Chocolate Chunk Brownies

My California neighbor Nancy Parks was truly a "chocoholic"—dessert to her meant something with chocolate. I loved being on the receiving end of many of her experiments, such as these fudgy brownies.

1   cup (2 sticks) unsalted butter

8   ounces bittersweet chocolate, chopped

3   ounces unsweetened chocolate, chopped

½   cup unbleached all-purpose flour

½   tablespoon baking powder

½   teaspoon salt

3   large eggs

1   cup plus 2 tablespoons sugar

3½ teaspoons instant coffee or instant espresso powder

1   tablespoon pure vanilla extract

1½ cups chopped pecans, toasted

6   ounces semisweet chocolate, chopped

powdered sugar

Makes about 1½ dozen

Preheat oven to 350°. Butter a 9-inch by 13-inch baking dish. Set aside.

In a medium saucepan, melt butter, bittersweet chocolate, and unsweetened chocolate, whisking until smooth. Remove from heat and set aside to cool completely.

Onto a sheet of waxed paper, sift together the flour, baking powder, and salt. Set aside.

In a large bowl and using an electric mixer, beat eggs until light and frothy. Gradually beat in sugar, instant coffee powder, and vanilla extract. Add the melted chocolate mixture and beat until well blended. By hand, stir in flour mixture, mixing until just blended. Fold in pecans and semisweet chocolate.

Pour batter into prepared pan and bake for 30 to 35 minutes, until a tester inserted in the center comes out clean. Cool in pan on a rack. Once cool, dust with sifted powdered sugar and cut into squares. Serve at room temperature.

Texas Bourbon Balls

A Christmas season in Texas wouldn't be complete without Bourbon Balls. You can count on them at most every holiday party. One noted Dallas hostess sends a small box of these confections home with every guest. What a lovely gesture! I also love these made with a good-quality brandy, instead of bourbon.

Makes about 3 dozen

1 cup ground pecans

2 cups powdered sugar

1½ tablespoons unsweetened cocoa powder

3½ cups crushed vanilla wafers

½ cup bourbon or brandy

3 tablespoons light corn syrup

In a large bowl, combine pecans, 1 cup powdered sugar, cocoa powder, and vanilla wafer crumbs. Stir in bourbon and corn syrup.

Form mixture into 1-inch balls. Roll in remaining powdered sugar. Store in a tightly covered container until ready to serve.

Warm Brownies
with Honey Vanilla
Crème Fraîche

When I worked in west Los Angeles, one of my favorite restaurants when I felt like splurging for lunch was the original Hollywood Brown Derby, just a quick 10 minutes from my office. My frequent lunch companion and I would split a salad or sandwich, then celebrate our "lean" lunch with the Derby's fabulous hot brownie. This scrumptious dessert was baked in an individual soufflé dish so that the center stayed warm and fudgy. The waiter would poke a hole in the center to add a heavenly cooked vanilla sauce. After several attempts to duplicate their recipe, I came up with this close match. Adding honey and vanilla to crème fraîche is a lot less work than the cooked vanilla sauce, and quite delicious.

Makes 4 servings

4	*ounces semisweet chocolate, chopped*
½	*cup (1 stick) unsalted butter, cut into pieces*
½	*cup unbleached all-purpose flour*
½	*cup cocoa powder*
½	*teaspoon baking powder*
⅛	*teaspoon salt*
4	*large eggs, at room temperature*
1	*teaspoon vanilla extract*
1	*cup superfine sugar*
⅓	*cup chopped walnuts*

Honey Vanilla Crème Fraîche

1	*cup Créme Fraîche (page 156)*
2	*tablespoons honey*
1	*tablespoon pure vanilla extract*

Preheat oven to 350°. Lightly butter four 8-ounce soufflé dishes or custard cups. Set in a large baking pan that is at least 3 inches deep.

In the top of a double boiler or a stainless-steel pan suspended over gently simmering water (do not let bottom of pan actually touch the water), combine chocolate and butter. Stir until almost melted. Remove from heat and whisk until smooth. Set aside to cool, whisking occasionally.

Onto a piece of waxed paper, sift together flour, cocoa powder, baking powder, and salt. Set aside.

In a large bowl and using an electric mixer, beat eggs until thick and pale yellow. Beat in vanilla extract. Gradually beat in sugar until mixture is light and fluffy. Add flour mixture in three batches, beating well after each addition. Stir in cooled chocolate mixture. Fold in walnuts. Spoon mixture into prepared soufflé dishes, filling nearly to the rim. Pour boiling water in the baking pan to come halfway up the sides of the soufflé dishes. Bake for 30 minutes, until firm around the edge, but not completely firm in the center. Remove from oven and cool on a rack for 10 minutes.

In a small bowl, combine Crème Fraîche, honey, and vanilla extract.

To serve, set each soufflé dish on individual dessert plates. Using a spoon, poke a hole in the center of each brownie and spoon in some of the Crème Fraîche mixture. Serve at once.

Mint Chocolate and Dried Fruit Tartlets

My mint garden in California was extensive—actually the mint was used as a dense, fragrant ground cover for my large camellia, gardenia, and tree fern garden. Thankfully my neighbors also adored mint and were very willing to help me keep it clipped and under control.

Mint and chocolate are an irresistible combination, even more so when combined with dried western fruits. These tiny two-bite size confections are perfect with a bracing cup of tea or after-dinner coffee. Here, I've called for peppermint, but you could use spearmint, applemint, pineapple mint, or any of the citrus mints—orange or grapefruit.

Mint Chocolate Cups

9 ounces semisweet chocolate, chopped

32 small fresh peppermint leaves

32 2½-inch paper muffin cup liners

Makes 16 servings

Dried Fruit Filling

16 dried apricots, finely chopped

16 pitted dates, finely chopped

16 dried figs, finely chopped

1 cup walnuts, finely chopped

3 tablespoons white crème de menthe

TO MAKE CHOCOLATE CUPS

Place chocolate and 16 of the mint leaves in the top of a double boiler or in a stainless steel bowl suspended over simmering water. (Do not let the water actually touch the bottom of the bowl.) Stir until chocolate melts. Remove from heat. Remove and discard mint leaves.

Stack two paper muffin cups together. With a ½-inch wide brush, paint the inside bottom and about ½ inch up the inside of each muffin cup with melted chocolate. Repeat process until 16 muffin cups have been painted with chocolate. Set cups in muffin pans and refrigerate until chocolate is hard, about 1 hour. (May be made ahead to this point, wrapped airtight, and refrigerated for up to 3 weeks.)

TO MAKE FILLING

Finely chop the remaining 16 mint leaves and combine with dried fruits and walnuts. Pour on the crème de menthe and lightly toss to evenly coat. Fill each chocolate cup with mint-fruit mixture. Refrigerate until ready to serve. Peel away paper liners before serving.

....

Chocolate Flourishes

Chocolate Leaves. Rinse and pat dry 10 to 15 small, sturdy nontoxic leaves (rose, citrus, mint, or camellia are good choices). In the top of double boiler or in a stainless-steel bowl suspended over a pot of simmering water, stir 4 ounces semisweet chocolate over simmering water until melted. Using a small brush, paint a thick layer over the backs of the leaves. Do not paint over the edges. Set painted leaves on a flat pan and chill or freeze until chocolate is firm. Starting at the stem end, gently pull leaves away from the chocolate leaf. Keep refrigerated until ready to use or wrap airtight and freeze for up to 1 month.

Shavings or Curls. Line a baking sheet with waxed paper. Place a 1-ounce square of semisweet chocolate on a piece of waxed paper. Microwave on MEDIUM (50 percent) power for 15-second intervals, until the chocolate starts to soften.

Using a folded paper towel so that the body warmth of your fingers does not melt the chocolate further, grip the chunk of chocolate and using a vegetable peeler, scrape the long edge of the chocolate chunk in a down motion, forming flat shavings or curls. As you form the shavings or curls, let them drop onto the prepared baking sheet. If more shavings or curls are needed, repeat the procedure, using a second 1-ounce square of chocolate.

Refrigerate the shavings and curls until ready to use. If made in advance, refrigerate in an airtight container for up to two weeks. One square makes about ½ cup shavings or curls.

Gratings. Grate blocks or squares of chocolate to a finer texture than shavings, using a piece of paper towel to hold the chocolate so your hand doesn't warm the chocolate. A rotary grater (such as a Mouli) works quite well. If you have lots to grate, cut the chocolate into small chunks and pulse them in a food processor. The food processor method works best with semisweet or bittersweet chocolate. Unsweetened chocolate needs to be grated by hand.

Silhouettes. Fill a pastry bag fitted with the writing tip with melted chocolate. Draw squiggles, butterflies, hearts, arrows, etc.—whatever decoration you wish.

....

Chesley's Black Bottom Pie

This recipe comes from Chesley Sanders, a born-and-bred Texan who combines gourmet cooking, lecturing on Texas wines, and fire fighting. Whenever he's on duty at the fire hall, he's the designated "chef of the day," preparing food from down-home Texan to gourmet international specialties. His pie is a favorite of everyone.

3   *cups whole milk*
1   *cup sugar*
½   *cup unbleached all-purpose flour*
½   *teaspoon salt*
2   *ounces semisweet chocolate, chopped*
2   *large egg yolks*
1   *teaspoon pure vanilla extract*
3   *tablespoons dark rum*
1   *cup heavy cream*
    chocolate curls (page 28)
1   *9-inch pie shell (page 173), baked and cooled*

Makes 6 to 8 servings

Into each of two 2-quart saucepans, place 1½ cups milk, 6 tablespoons sugar, ¼ cup flour, and ¼ teaspoon salt. To one saucepan, add the chocolate and place over medium heat, stirring constantly until chocolate has melted and mixture thickens. In a small bowl, beat 1 egg yolk with a fork. Add a couple of spoonfuls of the hot chocolate mixture into the bowl, then put the egg yolk mixture into the saucepan. Stirring constantly, boil for another 3 minutes, remove from heat and stir in vanilla. Set aside to cool for 15 to 20 minutes.

Cook the second saucepan over medium heat, stirring constantly, until mixture thickens. In a small bowl, beat the remaining egg yolk with a fork. Beat a couple of spoonfuls of the hot pudding into the egg yolk, then beat the egg yolk mixture into the saucepan. Stirring constantly, boil for another 3 minutes. Remove from heat and stir in rum. Set aside to cool for 15 to 20 minutes.

TO ASSEMBLE PIE

Pour the chocolate mixture into the bottom of the baked pie shell, spreading evenly with the back of a spoon. Chill for 5 minutes. Carefully spoon the rum mixture on top, smoothing evenly with the back of a spoon. Refrigerate for at least 1 hour.

In a large bowl, whip cream until it forms soft peaks. Gradually add remaining ¼ cup sugar and beat until mixture forms stiff peaks. Carefully spread the whipped cream over the top of the pie. Garnish with chocolate curls. Chill until ready to serve.

Chocolate Chimichangas with Pecans

Arizona claims to be the birthplace of the chimichanga (a fried burrito, usually filled with beef, chicken, cheese, or beans). In recent years, innovative chefs throughout the state have turned this main dish into a dessert. These are easy to make and so meltingly delicious.

Makes 8 servings

6 ounces semisweet chocolate

½ cup coarsely chopped pecans

¼ cup Triple Sec or other orange-flavored liqueur

½ cup granulated sugar

8 8-inch flour tortillas

2 tablespoons unsalted butter, melted

canola oil for deep frying

powdered sugar

Garnish

Whipped cream (optional)

Break up 4 ounces of the chocolate into small pieces. Add pecans and Triple Sec. Set aside.

In a food processor, combine granulated sugar and remaining 2 ounces of chocolate. Pulse until chocolate is finely ground.

Warm the tortillas for a few seconds on a griddle or in a heavy skillet, until pliable. Put them in a plastic bag to stay soft. Lay one tortilla on a work surface. Brush top of tortilla with some of the butter. Sprinkle evenly with 2 tablespoons of the sugar-chocolate mixture. In the center of the tortilla, pile 2 tablespoons of the chocolate-pecan mixture. Fold the sides in and then roll up into a tight package, securing the chimichanga with a toothpick. Repeat with the remaining tortillas and chocolate filling. Refrigerate for at least 30 minutes.

When ready to cook, pour at least 3 inches of oil in a heavy, deep skillet. Heat the oil to 365° on a candy thermometer. Fry the chimichangas, one or two at a time, until light golden, 4 to 5 minutes total, turning once. Drain on paper towels. Repeat until all chimichangas are fried. Dust with powdered sugar shaken through a sifter.

Serve warm with a drift of whipped cream, if desired.

Chocolate Pie with Hazelnut Meringue

My sister-in-law Ruth first made this delicious pie for me when I was 5 years old. Over the years, she's made thousands of pies, never once measuring the ingredients until I asked her for her recipe. A food processor quickens the tedious chore of finely chopping the nuts—in this case, hazelnuts because she grows bushels of them at her Bellevue, Washington, home, where the nuts are also called filberts.

¾   cup granulated sugar

⅓   cup unbleached all-purpose flour

3   tablespoons unsweetened cocoa

2   cups whole milk

3   large eggs yolks, beaten

1   9-inch pie shell (page 173), baked and cooled

Makes 8 to 10 servings

Meringue

⅓   cup hazelnuts

½   cup plus 2 tablespoons powdered sugar

¾   teaspoon unbleached all-purpose flour

3   large egg whites, at room temperature

¼   cup granulated sugar

TO MAKE FILLING

In a heavy saucepan, mix together sugar, flour, and cocoa. Whisk in milk and beaten egg yolks. Place over medium heat and cook, whisking constantly, until the mixture is thick and coats a wooden spoon. Remove from heat and let cool to room temperature, stirring occasionally. When cool, pour into prepared pie shell.

TO MAKE MERINGUE

Preheat oven to 400°. Spread hazelnuts on a baking sheet and place it on the uppermost level in the oven. If they have already been skinned, toast for 7 to 8 minutes. If they still have their bitter-tasting skins, roast for 18 to 20 minutes, turning twice. Place the hot nuts in a clean kitchen towel and chafe away most of the skin by rubbing the nuts with the towel. Place nuts, powdered sugar, and flour in the workbowl of a food processor fitted with a metal blade. Process to a fine powder.

Using an electric mixer on high speed, whip the egg whites until soft peaks form. While the machine is running, add the granulated sugar in a steady stream. Continue to whip on high speed until the whites are very stiff and shiny.

Fold pecan mixture into the whites. Spoon a large amount of meringue on top of the center of the filled pie shell. Put small spoonfuls of meringue around the edge of the pie shell. Spread from the center out to meet the edge, making sure that the entire top if covered and edges are sealed. If desired, using the back of a small spoon, make small peaks in the meringue. Bake for 10 minutes or until golden brown.

Whipped Cream

Whipped cream is one of the simplest garnishes for many desserts. I usually add 1 tablespoon granulated sugar and 1 teaspoon of vanilla for each cup of cream. Before whipping, chill the bowl and the electric mixer beaters for 10 minutes. Shake the carton of cream before pouring it over the sugar and vanilla in the chilled bowl.

Begin whipping with the mixer on medium speed, increasing the speed to high as soon as the mixture thickens. The cream is done when it holds soft peaks. If adding other flavors in place of the vanilla to the whipped cream, do so by hand, whipping with a whisk.

If you wish to flavor the whipped cream with bourbon, rum, liqueurs, or fruit brandies, such as calvados, decrease the sugar to 1 teaspoon per cup and omit the vanilla. When the cream is whipped, stir in 2 tablespoons of the desired liquor or liqueur.

One cup of heavy whipping cream will yield two cups of whipped cream.

Frozen Peanut Butter Pie with Warm Chocolate Sauce

Peanut Butter Pie is a popular dessert in Texas, where farmers have turned to growing peanuts as an alternative cash crop in the Texas Southern Plains. I usually make the pie with a graham cracker crust, but you could also use thin chocolate wafers that have been ground to fine crumbs in the food processor.

Crust

1   cup graham cracker crumbs
¼   cup sugar
¼   cup (½ stick) butter, cut into pieces, at room temperature

Makes 8 to 10 servings

Peanut Butter Filling

8   ounces cream cheese, at room temperature
1   cup creamy peanut butter (do not use old-fashioned style or freshly ground)
1   cup plus 2 tablespoons powdered sugar
2   tablespoons (¼ stick) unsalted butter, at room temperature
½   cup chilled heavy cream
½   teaspoon pure vanilla extract
½   cup roasted peanuts, finely chopped

Warm Chocolate Sauce

6   ounces semisweet chocolate, coarsely chopped
⅓   cup light corn syrup
¼   cup heavy cream
1   teaspoon unsalted butter
2   teaspoons pure vanilla extract

TO MAKE CRUST

Generously butter a 9-inch pie plate. In a medium bowl, mix together the graham cracker crumbs, sugar, and butter. Press mixture evenly in prepared pan. Chill for 1 hour.

TO MAKE FILLING

In a large bowl and using an electric mixer on medium speed, beat together cream cheese and peanut butter until smooth. Add 1 cup powdered sugar and butter; beat until fluffy. In a clean small bowl, beat cream until soft peaks form. Slowly add remaining 2 tablespoons sugar and vanilla. Continue to beat until mixture forms stiff peaks. Fold the whipped cream and chopped peanuts into the cream cheese mixture.

Transfer mixture into prepared shell, smoothing the top with the back of a spoon. Freeze until firm, at least 5 hours.

TO MAKE SAUCE

Meanwhile, put chocolate pieces, corn syrup, heavy cream, and butter in a microwave-safe 1-quart measuring cup. Stir to combine. Cover cup with a piece of waxed paper. Microwave on HIGH for 2½ to 4 minutes, until the mixture comes to a boil. Remove from microwave and whisk until smooth. Stir in vanilla extract.

When ready to serve, let pie stand in refrigerator 30 minutes before serving. Cut into wedges and spoon some of the warm chocolate sauce on top and alongside the pie.

Jack Daniel's Pie

Several Texas restaurants offer a dense chocolate pie made with Jack Daniel's Whiskey. This version is similar to the one served at the Salt Grass Steakhouse, a nearby roadhouse that my husband and I frequent when we're hungry for a great steak.

1½ cups sugar

½ cup flour

2 large eggs, lightly beaten

½ cup (1 stick) butter, melted and cooled to room temperature

⅓ cup Jack Daniel's Whiskey

8 ounces semisweet chocolate, coarsely chopped

1½ cups coarsely chopped pecans

1 9-inch pie shell (page 173), unbaked

Makes 8 to 10 servings

Garnish

Vanilla Ice Cream (page 252) or softly whipped cream (optional)

Preheat oven to 300°.

In a large bowl, combine sugar and flour. In another bowl, whisk together the eggs, butter, and Jack Daniel's. Gradually whisk in sugar-flour mixture. Stir in chocolate and pecans.

Pour mixture into unbaked pie shell. Bake for 45 to 50 minutes, until filling is set. Remove from oven and cool in pan on a rack for at least 30 minutes before serving. Serve warm, topped with a scoop of ice cream or a drift of whipped cream, if desired.

Chocolate Bread Pudding

Because I always keep baking chocolate on hand and usually have heavy cream in the refrigerator and pecans in the freezer, this recipe has been a lifesaver more than once when my husband brought unannounced guests home for dinner, and I had no dessert planned. It goes together quickly and can be baking while you're eating the rest of the meal. Everyone will think you've fussed over the dessert, but you haven't.

Makes 8 servings

½ of a 1-pound loaf of unsliced French bread

1½ cups heavy cream

1 cup whole milk

4 ounces bittersweet chocolate, finely chopped

4 ounces semisweet chocolate, finely chopped

3 large eggs

½ cup plus 2 tablespoons granulated sugar

½ tablespoon pure vanilla extract

½ cup coarsely chopped pecans

pinch salt

Garnish

powdered sugar

Preheat oven to 325°. Lightly butter a shallow 2-quart casserole.

Trim crusts from bread and cut bread into 1-inch cubes. Put the bread cubes in a large bowl.

In a heavy saucepan, heat cream and milk just to a boil over medium-high heat. Reduce heat and gradually add chocolate, stirring until melted and mixture is smooth. Pour mixture over bread and stir gently to combine.

In a medium bowl, whisk eggs until frothy. Whisk in sugar and vanilla extract. Stir in pecans and salt. Pour over bread and stir gently to combine.

Transfer mixture to prepared casserole, smoothing top evenly with the back of a spoon. Cover with aluminum foil and bake for 30 to 40 minutes, until edges are firm but center is still moist. Serve warm with a light dusting of powdered sugar.

Chocolate Crème Brûlée
with Kahlua

I first sampled an incredible dark chocolate brûlée at Susan Feinger and Mary Sue Millikan's popular Border Grill in Los Angeles. Since then, the dessert has been offered on several restaurants menus throughout the West. My version goes together quickly and contains the added kick of Kahlua. Bake the custards the day before so they are well-chilled before you caramelize the sugar topping.

2	cups heavy cream
1¾	cups half-and-half
¼	cup Kahlua
8	ounces semisweet chocolate, finely chopped
8	large egg yolks
¾	cup sugar

Makes 8 servings

Preheat oven to 300°. Place eight ¾-cup custard cups in a large baking pan.

In a large heavy saucepan, bring cream and half-and-half to a boil. Reduce heat to simmer and stir in Kahlua and chocolate. Stir until chocolate melts and mixture is smooth. Remove from heat.

In a medium bowl, whisk egg yolks and ¼ cup sugar. While whisking, add ½ cup of the hot chocolate mixture to the egg yolk mixture. Whisk this mixture into the remaining chocolate mixture. Divide between prepared custard cups.

Fill baking pan with hot water to reach halfway up the sides of the custard cups. Bake about 50 minutes, until custards are set. Remove custard cups from the water and cool on a rack. Cover with plastic wrap and refrigerate overnight or for at least 6 hours.

Just before serving, preheat broiler. Sprinkle each custard with 1 tablespoon sugar. Broil until sugar caramelizes and turns golden brown, being careful to not burn the sugar, about 3 minutes. Remove from oven and cool for at least 15 minutes before serving.

Note: Many restaurants use a small handheld propane torch, found in gourmet cookware shops and some hardware stores, to caramelize the sugar.

Chocolate Frango-Mint Dessert Cups

This is a favorite recipe of Seattle cooks, fashioned after the fabulous Frango Mints sold at the Bon Marché in the Seattle area. Because it does contain uncooked eggs, I am obliged to tell you that the United States Department of Agriculture has found raw eggs to be a possible potential carrier of food-borne illness and recommends not eating raw eggs.

I've been eating this dessert most of my life without a problem, but should you have concerns, you can substitute pasteurized liquid egg substitute for the raw eggs.

Makes
12
servings

2 *cups sifted powdered sugar*
1 *cup (2 sticks) unsalted butter, at room temperature*
4 *large eggs or 1 cup liquid egg substitute*
4 *ounces semisweet chocolate, melted*
4 *teaspoons pure vanilla extract*
1 *teaspoon peppermint flavoring*
  paper or foil 2-inch candy cups
1 *cup vanilla wafer crumbs*

In a large bowl, and using an electric mixer, cream together sugar and butter. Add eggs, one at a time, beating well after each addition. (If using egg substitute, divide in quarters.) Beat in melted chocolate, vanilla extract, and peppermint flavoring.

Using a small spoon, fill candy cups, mounding slightly in the center. Sprinkle each with some of the vanilla wafer crumbs. Freeze until firm.

Let stand at room temperature for 10 minutes before serving. Serve in the cups to eat with a small spoon.

Chocolate Mousse Tostadas

Because dessert tacos are showing up at fast-food Mexican chains, in this recipe I opted for a more sophisticated dessert, topping a crisp cocoa-laced tostada with a rich, creamy chocolate mousse. Assemble these just before serving, as once the mousse and the caramelized tostada connect, the tostada will start to slowly soften.

Tostadas

Makes 8 servings

½ cup packed light brown sugar

3 tablespoons unsweetened cocoa powder

6 tablespoons (¾ stick) unsalted butter

¼ cup light corn syrup

1¼ cup unbleached all-purpose flour

Chocolate Mousse

10 ounces bittersweet chocolate, chopped

1 tablespoon unsalted butter

½ cup plus 2 tablespoons sugar

½ cup water

5 large egg yolks
   dash salt

3 cups heavy cream

1 teaspoon vanilla extract

Garnishes

1 cup raspberries

2 ounces white chocolate, coarsely shaved (see page 28)

8 fresh mint sprigs

Preheat oven to 375°. Line two baking sheets with parchment paper.

In a medium heavy-bottom saucepan, combine sugar, cocoa, butter, and corn syrup. Bring to a boil over medium heat, stirring until sugar and cocoa are dissolved and butter melts. Whisk in flour, mixing well.

Working quickly, drop by heaping tablespoonful onto the parchment paper, at least 3 inches apart (you will get four on each baking sheet). Using the back of a spoon dipped in cold water, smooth each mound of batter to form a 5-inch circle. Bake 5 to 6 minutes, until batter bubbles and darkens. Remove from oven and let cool on the pan until hard and cooled. Carefully transfer tostadas to an airtight container until ready to serve.

TO MAKE MOUSSE

Melt the chocolate and butter in a stainless-steel bowl suspended over simmering water (do not let water touch the bottom of the bowl). Whisk until smooth.

In a small saucepan, combine sugar and water. Bring to a boil over high heat. Stir and boil for 1 minute to form a clear syrup. Remove from heat and cool. In a second stainless-steel bowl, whisk together cool sugar syrup, egg yolks, and salt. Place bowl over the pot of simmering water and cook, whisking constantly until mixture thickens, about 3 minutes. Remove from heat and fold in cooled chocolate mixture, a third at a time. Stir chocolate mixture until it reaches room temperature.

Whip cream and vanilla extract until soft peaks form. Fold into chocolate mixture, a third at a time. Refrigerate until ready to assemble.

TO ASSEMBLE TOSTADAS

Place a tostada on each of eight large dessert plates. Spoon chocolate mousse onto each tostada. Scatter raspberries around each serving and sprinkle each serving with some of the shaved white chocolate. Garnish with mint sprig and serve.

Separating Eggs

I find it easiest to separate eggs when they are cold. Crack the egg at the middle and gently pull apart with your thumbs and fingertips. Tip one half of the shell to catch the yolk, letting the white drop into a bowl. Then place the yolk into a separate bowl. If the egg whites are to be beaten, don't let any of the yolk mix with the whites. Should a drop or two of yolk accidentally slip into the whites, you can usually scoop it out with a piece of shell. If more than a drop or two gets into the whites, I combine the egg parts, refrigerating them for scrambled eggs the next morning, and start over.

Chocolate Paté with Amaretto Whipped Cream

Dense chocolate paté, similar to a large truffle, is quite popular in restaurants throughout the West. I've sampled several over the years, made with dried fruits and nuts, one even flavored with candied chile peppers. One of the simplest and best flavored paté was one made by Donna Nordin, chef and owner of Café Terra Cotta, an excellent Southwestern restaurant with branches in Tucson and Scottsdale, Arizona. There the slices are decorated with a small saguaro cactus made from almond paste that has been colored a bright green.

The paté is really easy to make—just allow adequate time for chilling. I made some changes in the recipe and added dried apricots to the bottom layer. I serve the paté with Amaretto Whipped Cream and don't bother with the almond paste (marzipan) cactus.

Paté

2½ cups heavy cream

1½ pounds bittersweet chocolate, chopped

¼ cup amaretto liqueur

2 teaspoons pure vanilla extract

¾ cup (1½ sticks) unsalted butter

1 cup sliced almonds, toasted

½ cup diced dried apricots

Makes 12 to 16 servings

Amaretto Whipped Cream

1 cup cold heavy cream

1 teaspoon sugar

2 tablespoons amaretto liqueur

chocolate shavings (page 28) for optional garnish

Line an 8½-inch by 4¼-inch by 2½-inch loaf pan with strips of parchment paper to completely cover the bottom, inside sides, and ends of the pan.

TO MAKE PATÉ

In a large saucepan, bring cream to a boil. Remove from heat and stir in chocolate, whisking until chocolate is completely melted. Add the amaretto, vanilla extract, and butter. Whisk until smooth.

Transfer about a third of the chocolate mixture to a bowl. Stir in almonds and apricots. Spread this mixture in the bottom of the prepared loaf pan. Chill until firm, about 30 minutes, keeping remaining chocolate mixture at room temperature. Pour remaining chocolate mixture into the pan. (If necessary, gently stir the chocolate over a pan of hot water to soften.) Chill paté in its pan overnight.

TO MAKE AMARETTO WHIPPED CREAM

Using an electric mixer, whip the heavy cream and sugar until it forms soft peaks. Whisk in amaretto.

TO SERVE

Unmold the paté and with a hot knife, cut into slices about ½-inch thick. Lay the slices on individual dessert plates and add a dollop of the whipped cream to one side. If desired, sprinkle whipped cream with chocolate shavings.

Eggnog and White Chocolate Mousse

Years ago, Knudsen Dairy hosted a Christmas dinner party for Los Angeles home economists. Dessert was a creamy eggnog mousse laced with rum. I've added white chocolate to their recipe and substituted brandy for the rum. This is a festive dessert, perfect for Holiday parties.

2	teaspoons unflavored gelatin
½	teaspoon ground cinnamon
¼	teaspoon ground nutmeg
4	cups purchased eggnog
6	ounces white chocolate, finely chopped
⅓	cup brandy
2	teaspoons pure vanilla extract
	whipped cream
½	cup toasted sliced almonds

Makes 12 servings

In a heavy saucepan, sprinkle gelatin, cinnamon, and nutmeg over eggnog. Let stand for 5 minutes. Place over medium heat and cook, stirring, until mixture comes to a simmer, 7 to 8 minutes.

Remove from heat and stir in chocolate, brandy, and vanilla extract, stirring until chocolate is thoroughly melted and mixture is smooth. Pour into ½-cup dessert cups or china coffee cups. Cover with plastic wrap, taking care to not let the plastic wrap touch the mousse. Chill for at least 4 hours or overnight. Serve, topped with a dollop of whipped cream and a sprinkling of almonds.

Cakes

Coconut Fresh Pineapple Layer Cake, see page 55.

Almond Shortcake with Tipsy Prunes

The California Prune Advisory Board was always a favorite client when I worked for Western Research Kitchens. When I demonstrated this recipe years ago on a Los Angeles TV show, the station received several mail bags of recipe requests. When you're looking for "comfort food," nothing could be better than the humble prune. Another time, serve the prunes over Vanilla Ice Cream (page 252).

Almond Shortcake

Makes 6 to 8 servings

- ¾ cup slivered blanched almonds, toasted
- ⅓ cup plus 1 teaspoon sugar
- 2 cups unbleached all-purpose flour
- ½ teaspoon salt
- 1 tablespoon baking powder
- ½ cup (1 stick) unsalted butter
- ½ cup plus 2 tablespoons heavy cream

Tipsy Prunes

- ½ pound pitted dried prunes
- 2 cups dry red wine such as Merlot, Zinfandel, or Cabernet Sauvignon
- ½ cup sugar
- 2- to 3-inch strips of rind from 1 lemon
- 2 tablespoons lemon juice
- 1 3-inch cinnamon stick

Garnish

softly whipped cream

Preheat oven to 350°. Lightly grease a 8-inch round cake pan.

In a food processor, coarsely grind the almonds and ⅓ cup sugar.

In a medium bowl, combine the almond mixture, flour, salt, baking powder, and butter. Using a pastry blender, mix until mixture forms fine crumbs. Slowly pour in ½ cup plus 1 tablespoon cream; mix just until dough comes together. Do not overmix. Spread mixture in prepared pan. Brush with remaining 1 table-spoon cream and sprinkle top with remaining teaspoon sugar. Bake 35 minutes, until golden brown and a toothpick inserted in the center comes out clean.

Meanwhile, combine prunes, wine, sugar, lemon zest, lemon juice, and cinnamon stock in a large saucepan. Bring to a boil, cover, and reduce heat to simmer. Cook about 30 minutes, until prunes are plump. Remove from stove, cover, and cool to room temperature.

When shortcake is done, cool in pan on a rack for about 10 minutes, then invert out of the pan onto a rack. Continue to cool for 5 minutes. Set shortcake, sugar-crusted side up, on a serving plate.

To serve, cut the shortcake into 6 to 8 wedges. Transfer wedges to individual dessert plates. Top each piece with some of the whipped cream and spoon on some of the prunes and their syrup.

Banana-Pecan Upside-Down Cake

Texans love upside-down cakes, particularly when made with lots of plump pecans from the massive native official Texas state tree. This version teams the pecans with bananas over a cinnamon-scented cake for a year-round dessert. I'd use Steens Ribbon-Cane Syrup to coat the bananas and pecans (see Mail-Order Sources, pages 270–271), but you can use pure maple syrup with good results. Served warm and topped with whipped cream, you've got a dessert "made in heaven."

Topping

Makes 8 to 10 servings

1	cup packed light brown sugar
¼	cup (½ stick) unsalted butter
¼	cup ribbon-cane syrup or pure maple syrup
½	cup coarsely chopped pecans, toasted
4	large firm-ripe bananas

Cake

1	cup unbleached all-purpose flour
2	teaspoons baking powder
1	teaspoon ground cinnamon
¼	teaspoon salt
¾	cup granulated sugar
6	tablespoons (¾ stick) unsalted butter, at room temperature
2	large eggs
½	teaspoon pure vanilla extract
¼	cup whole milk

Garnish

whipped cream sweetened with 2 teaspoons ribbon-cane syrup or maple syrup (optional)

Preheat oven to 325°.

TO MAKE TOPPING

In a heavy saucepan over low heat, combine brown sugar and butter. Cook, stirring constantly, until butter melts and mixture is smooth. Pour into a 9-inch metal cake pan, spreading to coat bottom evenly. Drizzle evenly with ribbon-cane syrup. Sprinkle with pecans.

Peel bananas and slice diagonally into ¼-inch slices. Arrange in slightly overlapping concentric circles on top of the pecans, covering the bottom of the pan. Set aside.

TO MAKE THE CAKE

Onto waxed paper, sift together the flour, baking powder, cinnamon, and salt. In a medium bowl and using an electric mixer, cream granulated sugar and butter. Add eggs, one at a time, beating well after each addition. Beat in vanilla extract. Beat in flour mixture in three parts, alternating with milk, beginning and ending with flour mixture. Spoon cake batter into the prepared pan. Bake for 50 to 55 minutes, until a tester inserted in the center comes out clean.

Remove cake from oven and place pan on a rack. Immediately run a sharp knife around the pan sides. Let cool in pan for 30 minutes, then invert cake onto a cake plate. Let stand for 5 minutes, then carefully lift off the pan. If any pecans or bananas stick to the pan, carefully remove and replace on top of the cake.

Serve warm. If desired, offer a bowl of whipped cream flavored with the ribbon-cane syrup, using about 2 teaspoons syrup per 1 cup heavy cream.

Bourbon Pecan Fruitcake

Texas is the fruitcake capital of the Western World. Several renowned East Texas bakeries bake and ship their fruitcakes worldwide, and many Texas cooks have a family recipe that they make at Christmas time. My personal favorite is a recipe given to me by Selma Andrews, food editor of the now defunct *Los Angeles Herald-Examiner*. Selma got the recipe from a Texas relative who lived in Palestine, Texas—right in the middle of Texas fruitcake country. The cake is heavier on pecans than candied fruit—just the way I like fruitcake!

Makes 16 to 20 servings

1   cup whole red candied cherries
1   cup golden raisins
1   cup bourbon
1   cup (2 sticks) butter, softened
1   cup granulated sugar
1   cup firmly packed dark brown sugar
4   large eggs, separated
2½ cups sifted unbleached all-purpose flour
3   cups pecan halves, toasted
1   teaspoon baking powder
1   teaspoon ground nutmeg
½   teaspoon salt
    additional bourbon, for soaking

In a medium mixing bowl, combine candied cherries, raisins, and bourbon. Cover and refrigerate overnight.

Preheat oven to 275°. Grease a 10-inch loaf pan. Line with parchment paper; grease and flour the parchment paper.

Drain fruits and reserve bourbon. In a large bowl and using an electric mixer on medium speed, cream butter until light and fluffy. Add sugars gradually, beating until well blended. Add egg yolks, beating until well blended.

Combine ½ cup of the flour with the pecans. Sift the remaining flour with the baking powder, nutmeg, and salt. Add 1 cup of the sifted flour to the creamed mixture, stirring until well mixed. Add the reserved bourbon and the remaining flour mixture, mixing well after each addition.

Beat egg whites until they form stiff peaks. Stir one-third of beaten egg whites into cake batter to lighten it. Carefully fold in remaining beaten egg whites, drained fruit, and the flour-coated pecans. Mix well. Spoon batter into prepared pan and bake for 2 hours, until a tester inserted in the center comes out clean. Cool in pan on a rack for 2 hours. Turn out and peel off parchment paper. Turn cake right side up and wrap in cheesecloth which has been saturated with bourbon. Place the fruitcake in a tightly covered metal food container. Refrigerate for at least 2 weeks before cutting into thin slices to serve.

Boysenberry Jam Cake

Every Christmas I receive several gift packs from Knott's Berry Farm, the Buena Park, California, berry farm that made boysenberries famous. Boysenberries are a curious cross between the red raspberry, blackberry, and loganberry. Last year I had no less than three huge jars of boysenberry jam, a cup and a half of which ended up on top of a simple yellow cake made with sour cream. The dessert delighted the children at that night's dinner and has since become a family favorite. Culinary historians claim that jam cake was often made by the early settlers of the West, eliminating the need for making a frosting.

Makes 12 to 16 servings

1¾ cups unbleached all-purpose flour

1 teaspoon baking powder

¼ teaspoon baking soda

½ cup (1 stick) unsalted butter, softened

1¼ cups sugar

3 large eggs, separated

⅔ cup sour cream

1 teaspoon pure vanilla extract

1½ cups boysenberry jam

Preheat oven to 325°. Grease and lightly flour two 8-inch round cake pans.

Onto a piece of waxed paper, sift together flour, baking powder, and baking soda. In a medium bowl, cream the butter and sugar until light and fluffy, about 3 minutes. Add egg yolks, one at a time, beating well after each addition.

Add the dry ingredients to the butter mixture, alternating with the sour cream, beginning and ending with the flour. Stir in vanilla. In clean bowl, beat egg whites until they form stiff peaks. Stir one-third of the beaten egg whites into the cake mixture to lighten it. Carefully fold in remaining egg whites.

Transfer mixture to prepared cake pans, smoothing the top with the back of a spoon. Bake until golden and tester comes out clear, about 40 to 50 minutes. Let cakes cool in the pan on a rack for 10 minutes before turning out onto racks to cool completely.

When ready to serve, heat boysenberry jam in a saucepan over medium-low heat until jam is runny. Brush any crumbs off a cake layer and place on a serving plate. Top with half of the heated jam, spreading to the edges with a knife. Top with second cake layer and spread remaining jam on the top layer. Allow the jam to naturally drip down the sides.

California Orange Cake with Bittersweet Glaze and Candied Orange Peel

One of the orange packing houses in Orange, California, sold baked goods made by the packer's wife and daughter. A particular favorite was an intensely orange flavored cake with a bittersweet chocolate glaze. My Texas friends make candied orange peel every Christmas for gifts. The candied peel makes a tangy sweet-tart garnish for the cake. The orange peel recipe is simple, but it does take some time so plan to make it a day or so ahead.

Candied Orange Peel

2   large navel oranges

    water

2¼ cups sugar

1   tablespoon fresh lemon juice

Makes 10 to 12 servings

Orange Cake

3   cups unbleached all-purpose flour

1   teaspoon baking powder

½   teaspoon salt

1   cup fresh orange juice

1   tablespoon grated orange rind

⅓   cup water

1   cup (1 stick) unsalted butter, at room temperature

1⅔ cups sugar

4   large eggs

1   cup good-quality orange marmalade

2   tablespoons Grand Marnier or other orange liqueur

Bittersweet Chocolate Glaze

4   ounces bittersweet chocolate, finely chopped

5   tablespoons unsalted butter

2   teaspoons light corn syrup

TO MAKE CANDIED ORANGE PEEL

Cut oranges in half and juice. Refrigerate juice to use in the cake. Scrape out the fruit membrane of the oranges with a spoon, leaving the shell intact. Cut each orange half in half, then slice the orange pieces into long strips about 1/4 inch wide.

Fill a medium saucepan with water. Bring to a boil over high heat. Add the orange peels and boil for 5 minutes. Drain the peels, discarding the water. Fill the saucepan with fresh water and again bring to a boil. Add orange peels and boil for 5 minutes. Drain. Repeat this boiling process two more times to remove the bitter flavor from the peels.

In a clean medium saucepan, bring 2 cups sugar, 1½ cups water, and lemon juice to a boil, stirring until sugar is completely dissolved. Reduce heat to medium-low, add orange peels, and cook until the peels are translucent, about 1 to 1½ hours.

Drain the peels and arrange in a single layer on a wire rack to air-dry overnight. Next morning, toss the dried orange peels with remaining ¼ cup sugar. Pack into small jars and seal. Use within a week.

TO MAKE CAKE

Preheat oven to 350°. Grease and flour two 9-inch round cake pans.

Onto a sheet of waxed paper, sift together the flour, baking powder, and salt. In a 2-cup glass measuring cup, stir together the orange juice, orange rind, and water.

In a mixing bowl and using an electric mixer on medium speed, cream the butter and sugar until light and fluffy, 3 to 5 minutes. Add the eggs one at a time, beating well after each addition. Reduce speed to low and alternately add the flour mixture and the orange juice mixture, beginning and ending with flour. Divide the batter between the prepared pans.

Bake for about 30 minutes, until a tester inserted in the middle comes out clean. Cool in pans on a rack for 10 minutes, then invert cakes onto the rack. Turn the cakes right side up and cool completely. Meanwhile, combine orange marmalade and Grand Marnier. Set aside.

TO MAKE BITTERSWEET GLAZE

Melt chocolate, butter, and corn syrup in the top of a double boiler or in a stainless steel bowl set over simmering water (make sure the bottom of the bowl doesn't actually touch the water). Whisk until chocolate melts and glaze is smooth. Remove from stove and let stand 10 minutes to thicken.

TO ASSEMBLE CAKE

Place one cake layer on a cake plate and evenly spread the orange marmalade mixture over the top. Stack second cake layer on top of the first layer. Pour chocolate glaze over the top of the cake, letting it drizzle down the sides. Smooth the glaze on the sides and top. Let set for at least 15 minutes for glaze to harden. Let set for 30 minutes, then decorate top with candied orange peel.

Coconut Fresh Pineapple Layer Cake

I sampled several fresh pineapple desserts on our last visit to Hawaii, but the best by far was the pineapple coconut cake served at David Paul's Lahaina Grill on Maui, a dreamy cake frosted with a Seven-Minute Frosting and covered with toasted coconut. I adapted a family recipe, replacing canned pineapple with fresh, then added the embellishments of David Paul's cake. Most supermarkets now sell fresh pineapple already conveniently peeled and cored. This luscious cake deserves to sit on your prettiest pedestal cake plate.

Cake

Makes 12 to 14 servings

2⅓ cups cake flour (not self-rising)
2½ teaspoons baking powder
½ teaspoon salt
1 cup (2 sticks) unsalted butter, softened
1½ cups sugar
5 large eggs, lightly beaten
1½ teaspoons vanilla extract
1 cup whole milk

Pineapple Filling

1 16-ounce pineapple, peeled, cored, and cut into small chunks
2 tablespoons cornstarch
⅓ cup sugar

Seven-Minute Frosting

2 large egg whites
1½ cups sugar
½ cup water
1 tablespoon light corn syrup
1 teaspoon pure vanilla extract

Garnish

1 7-ounce bag sweetened flaked coconut, toasted

Preheat oven to 350°. Line two 9-inch round metal cake pans with parchment paper. Lightly butter the papers and dust the pans with flour, knocking out excess.

Onto a sheet of waxed paper, sift together the cake flour, baking powder, and salt. In a large mixing bowl, using an electric mixer, cream butter on medium speed for 1 minute. While beating, add the sugar in a slow, steady stream. Continue to beat until light and fluffy, about 4 minutes, occasionally scraping down sides of the bowl. Add the beaten eggs a little at a time, beating well after each addition until pale and fluffy. Stir in vanilla extract.

Stir in flour mixture in four batches, alternating with milk, beginning and ending with flour mixture. Stir well after each addition. Divide batter between prepared cake pans and bake in middle of oven for 25 to 30 minutes, until a tester inserted in the middle comes out clean. Cool cakes in pans on racks for 10 minutes. Remove cakes from the pans, inverting onto cake racks to cool completely.

To Prepare Filling

Put the pineapple and any juice in the workbowl of a food processor or blender. Pulse until the pineapple is finely chopped and releases its juices. Transfer pineapple and juice to a heavy saucepan. Stir in cornstarch until cornstarch dissolves. Stir in sugar and bring mixture to a boil over medium-high heat, stirring constantly. Reduce heat and simmer for 3 minutes. Remove from stove and completely cool filling.

Using a long serrated knife, cut each cake layer in half horizontally. Place a cake layer onto a cake plate and spread top with one third of the pineapple filling. Add a second layer and spread top with one third of the filling. Add the third layer and spread top with remaining filling. Top with remaining layer.

To Prepare Frosting

In a large metal bowl and using a handheld electric mixer, beat together all frosting ingredients except vanilla extract. Place bowl over a saucepan of boiling water and beat on high speed until mixture holds stiff, glossy peaks, about 7 to 8 minutes. Remove bowl from the water and beat in the vanilla extract. Continue to beat until frosting is cool and smooth. Frost sides and top of cake, then cover sides and top with toasted coconut.

Toasting Coconut

To toast coconut, line a large baking sheet with parchment paper. Spread coconut evenly on the paper and toast in a preheated 325° oven until coconut is golden brown, about 8 to 10 minutes, stirring occasionally. Watch carefully because coconut burns easily.

Date Cake with Whipped Cream Frosting

Introduced to the New World by the Spaniards, date palms thrived in the desert areas of both Arizona and California since the early 1900s. Today, few commercial date gardens still remain in Arizona, most giving way to new housing developments. This almost flourless cake is dense, its seductive date flavor perfectly complemented by a simple whipped cream frosting.

4   large eggs, separated
1   cup sugar
1   tablespoon fresh orange juice
1   teaspoon pure vanilla extract
3   tablespoons unbleached all-purpose flour
1   teaspoon baking powder
1½ cups chopped dates
1   cup chopped walnuts
¼   teaspoon cream of tartar

Makes 8 to 12 servings

Whipped Cream Frosting

1   cup heavy cream
¼   cup sugar
1   tablespoon pure vanilla extract

Garnish

whole pitted dates (optional)

Preheat oven to 325°. Lightly butter a 9-inch by 13-inch baking pan.

In a large bowl, whisk eggs yolks and sugar until mixture is thick and pale yellow. Whisk in orange juice and vanilla extract. In a small bowl, combine flour and baking powder. Toss with dates and walnuts. Fold into egg batter.

In a bowl, beat egg whites and cream of tartar until stiff peaks form. Gently fold into the egg-date mixture. Spoon into the prepared pan, smoothing the top with the back of a spoon. Bake for 45 to 50 minutes, until a tester inserted in the center comes out clean. Remove from oven and cool in pan on a rack.

TO MAKE FROSTING

When cake is cool, whip cream until soft peaks form. While beating, gradually add sugar, beating until stiff peaks form. Stir in vanilla extract. Spread over top of cake and, if desired, decorate top with whole dates.

Della Robia Cake

During my later years in Southern California, I ran a small catering business, specializing in posh dinner parties and small, intimate weddings. One bride, who was to be married in an at-home candlelight ceremony just a few days before Christmas, insisted on a Della Robia Cake as her wedding cake. The combination of dried apricots, cranberries, and toasted almonds was absolutely delicious, and the three-tiered cake decorated with fresh lemon leaves and tiny red rosebuds was in keeping with the colors of the season.

I've cut the original three-layer recipe that served 40 to 50 people down to family size to bake in a large bundt pan with a Lemon Cream Cheese Frosting. If you're like most of us and keep at least one bag of cranberries in the freezer, you'll be able to make this stunning cake any time of the year, using other pesticide-free edible flowers such as violets, pansies, or nasturtiums in place of rosebuds. You could also use dried cranberries, plumped first in some warm water and drained.

Cake

6	ounces dried apricots
1½	cups sugar
1⅓	cups fresh orange juice
⅓	cup Cognac or brandy
2½	cups sifted cake flour
1½	teaspoons baking powder
½	teaspoon baking soda
1	teaspoon salt
3	large eggs, lightly beaten
1	teaspoon pure vanilla extract
½	cup (1 stick) butter, melted
1	cup fresh cranberries, picked over
1	cup slivered almonds, toasted

Makes 12 to 16 portions

Glaze

½	cup apricot jam
3	tablespoons Cognac or brandy

Lemon Cream Cheese Frosting

8 ounces cream cheese, at room temperature

6 tablespoons (¾ stick) unsalted butter, at room temperature

½ tablespoon finely grated lemon rind

½ tablespoon fresh lemon juice

1 teaspoon pure vanilla extract

3 to 3½ cups powdered sugar

Garnish

fresh lemon leaves, optional

pesticide-free tiny red rosebuds or other edible flowers, optional

Preheat oven to 350°. Butter and flour a 9½-inch bundt pan.

TO MAKE CAKE

Process apricots and sugar in a food processor until apricots are chopped, stopping twice to scrape down the sides. Transfer mixture to a small saucepan and stir in ⅓ cup of the orange juice and the Cognac. Bring to a boil over medium-high heat. Remove from heat and let stand for 30 minutes.

In a large bowl, combine flour, baking powder, baking soda, and salt. Make a well in the center. In a large glass measuring cup, combine remaining 1 cup orange juice, eggs, vanilla extract, and butter. Add to the dry ingredients, stirring until blended. Stir in apricot mixture, cranberries, and almonds. Pour batter into prepared pan.

Bake for 50 minutes or until a tester inserted in the middle comes out clean. Cool in pan on a rack for 10 minutes, then invert onto a wire rack to cool completely. Turn cake right side up.

TO MAKE GLAZE

Heat the jam and Cognac in a small saucepan, stirring until the jam melts. Using a pastry brush, brush the top and sides of the still-warm cake with the glaze. Cool cake completely.

TO MAKE FROSTING

In a large bowl, beat together the cream cheese and butter until fluffy. Beat in lemon rind, lemon juice, and vanilla extract. Gradually beat in sugar until smooth and spreadable. Spread over sides and top of cake. Refrigerate until 30 minutes before serving. If desired, surround the base of the cake with fresh lemon leaves and decorate the base with tiny rosebuds or other edible flowers.

Dried Fig Cake with Pine Nuts

More than 30 million pounds of dried figs are produced each year in California's Central Valley. Here I've combine dried figs with pine nuts, the highly prized nut that's harvested from a variety of pine trees grown in the Southwest. You can buy the pine nuts in bulk at natural food stores. Since the nuts have such a high fat content, refrigerate them once home until ready to use.

1½ cups unbleached all-purpose flour
1 teaspoon baking powder
½ teaspoon ground allspice
½ teaspoon ground nutmeg
½ teaspoon salt
1 teaspoon anise seed
1½ cups chopped dried figs, about 8 ounces
¾ cup coarsely chopped pine nuts
¾ cup (1½ sticks) unsalted butter, at room temperature
⅔ cup granulated sugar
3 large eggs
2 teaspoons grated orange zest
powdered sugar

Makes 8 to 10 servings

Preheat oven to 350°. Grease and flour a 9-inch cake pan.

Onto a piece of waxed paper, sift together flour, baking powder, allspice, nutmeg, and salt. Add anise seed, figs, and pine nuts. Toss to mix well.

In a large bowl, using an electric mixer on medium speed, cream butter and sugar until light and fluffy. Add eggs, one at a time, beating well after each addition. Stir in orange zest and the dry ingredients. Unlike a typical cake batter, the mixture will be very stiff, resembling a soft cookie dough. Spoon into prepared pan and smooth the top with the back of a spoon.

Bake for 1 to 1¼ hours, until a tester into the center comes out clean. Cool in pan on a rack for 10 minutes. Invert onto the rack, turn cake right-side-up, and cool completely. Just before serving, dust top of the cake with powdered sugar. Cut into thin slices to serve.

Elaine's Lemon Cloud Cake

Elaine Rogers was media director when I worked at Western Research Kitchens in Los Angeles. As an accomplished cook, Elaine's desserts were shining examples of her love of good food prepared with a minimum of effort. Here, she transforms a store-bought angel food cake into a showy dessert, worthy of your most discriminating guests.

Makes 12 to 15 servings

1   *tablespoon unflavored gelatin*

1   *cup fresh lemon juice*

6   *large egg yolks, lightly beaten*

1½ *cups granulated sugar*

1   *tablespoon grated lemon rind*

¼   *cup pasteurized dried egg whites, reconstituted in ¾ cup warm water or 1 cup plus 1 tablespoon pasteurized liquid egg whites*

¾   *cup warm water*

1   *16-ounce homemade or store-bought angel food cake*

1½ *cups heavy cream*

3   *tablespoons powdered sugar*

1½ *teaspoons pure lemon extract*

Garnish

12 to 15 perfect strawberries with green leafy hulls intact, rinsed and drained on paper towels

Sprinkle gelatin over ¼ cup lemon juice to soften. Set aside. In a heavy saucepan, beat egg yolks with ¾ cup granulated sugar until thick and light yellow. Add remaining ¾ cup lemon juice and cook, stirring constantly, over medium heat until mixture thickens to form a soft custard and coats the back of a wooden spoon, about 20 to 25 minutes. Remove from heat and stir in softened gelatin mixture. Chill until cool and thick, but not set. Stir in grated lemon rind.

In a metal bowl, stir dried egg whites into warm water until completely dissolved, about 2 minutes, or pour in liquid egg whites. Beat with an electric mixer on medium-high speed until egg whites form soft peaks. While beating, gradually add remaining ¾ cup sugar until egg whites form stiff peaks. Stir a third of the beaten egg whites into the cooled lemon custard. Gently fold in remaining egg whites.

Break angel food cake into bite-size pieces and layer with custard mixture in a nonstick 10-inch angel food or tube cake pan, beginning and ending with custard mixture. Cover and chill for at least 3 hours.

To unmold cake, run a thin-bladed knife around the edge of the cake to loosen it from the pan. Dip the pan in warm water for a few seconds to just below the rim of the cake pan. Invert onto a large cake plate. Return to refrigerator.

Meanwhile, in a cold metal bowl, whip cream on medium speed until cream begins to thicken. Add powdered sugar and lemon extract and continue to beat until blended and cream folds into soft mounds when beaters are lifted. With a heldheld balloon whisk, whip until the cream thickens, is smooth, and holds its shape. Frost sides and top of chilled cake with whipped cream. Position the strawberries around the outer edge of the top of the cake. Chill until ready to serve.

Fresh Pineapple Upside-Down Cornmeal Cake

Cornmeal has always been a staple in Southwestern kitchens and particularly during the time of flour rationing around World War II, it found its way into many a cake. Here, I've used stone-ground yellow cornmeal for a pineapple upside-down cake for an interesting change in flavor and texture. I like to bake this cake in my well-seasoned cast iron skillet, but a lightly oiled 10-inch cake pan will work just fine.

Pineapple Layer

Makes 8 to 10 servings

2   tablespoons unsalted butter

2   tablespoons dark brown sugar

3   tablespoons dark rum or orange juice

1   small fresh pineapple, peeled, cored, and cut into 8 rings

Cornmeal Cake Layer

2   tablespoons milk

6   tablespoons sugar

½ of a ¼-ounce package active dry yeast

2   large eggs, separated

2   teaspoons pure vanilla extract

⅔   cup stone-ground yellow cornmeal

2   additional egg whites, at room temperature

Preheat oven to 350°.

TO MAKE TOPPING

Place butter, brown sugar, and rum in the bottom of an 11-inch cast-iron skillet or 10-inch cake pan. Place in oven until butter and sugar melt, about 8 minutes. Mix well.

Arrange pineapple slices over bottom of skillet, cutting some in thirds to fill in gaps between whole slices. Set aside.

TO MAKE CAKE

In a small saucepan, warm milk. Remove from stove; add 1 teaspoon sugar and yeast, stirring until yeast is dissolved.

In a large bowl, beat together egg yolks and remaining sugar until mixture is pale yellow. Add vanilla; mix well. Sift cornmeal into the egg mixture, stirring constantly. Add yeast mixture; mix well.

Beat all 4 egg whites until they form stiff peaks. Stir a third of the beaten egg whites into the cornmeal mixture. Carefully fold in remaining egg whites. Pour batter over the pineapple and smooth the top. Bake for 25 to 30 minutes or until a toothpick, inserted in the center, comes out clean. Cool cake on a rack, then turn out onto a large serving plate.

Grapefruit Cake

Grapefruit grow in abundance in the tropical climates of California, Arizona, and Texas. A year-round fruit, its juice also comes fresh to the grocery stores in convenient cartons or glass bottles. Here, I used the juice and grated rind of white grapefruits for a luscious cake, worthy of your prettiest cake plate. You'll need to buy at least one whole grapefruit for the grated rind; the juice can either be freshly squeezed from grapefruits, or you can purchase the juice. Please don't try to substitute canned grapefruit juice or grapefruit juice made from frozen concentrate. The end result will simply not be as magnificent as here.

Cake

*Makes
8 to 10
servings*

½   cup (stick) plus 2 tablespoons unsalted butter, at room temperature

1¾ cup sugar

2   large eggs

3   cups sifted cake flour (not self-rising)

2½ teaspoons baking powder

¼   teaspoon salt

½   cup freshly squeezed grapefruit juice

¾   cup whole milk

1   teaspoon grated grapefruit rind

1½ teaspoons pure vanilla extract

Filling

2   large egg yolks

1   cup water

¾   cup sugar

⅓   cup unbleached all-purpose flour

1   teaspoon grated grapefruit rind

⅓   cup freshly squeezed grapefruit juice

1   tablespoon unsalted butter

Frosting

1½ cups sugar

2 large egg whites

1 tablespoon light corn syrup

⅛ teaspoon salt

⅓ cup freshly squeezed grapefruit juice

Garnish

2 tablespoons grated grapefruit rind

Preheat oven to 350°. Butter and flour two 9-inch layer cake pans.

In a large bowl and using an electric mixer on medium speed, cream butter until fluffy. Gradually beat in sugar. Add eggs, one at a time, beating well after each addition.

Mix together flour, baking powder, and salt. Add to butter mixture, alternating with grapefruit juice, beginning and ending with flour mixture. Gradually beat in milk. Stir in grapefruit rind and vanilla extract. Pour batter evenly into prepared pans. Bake for 25 to 30 minutes, until a tester inserted in the center comes out clean. Cool in pans on a rack for 10 minutes. Remove from pans, turn cakes right side up, and cool on a rack.

TO MAKE FILLING

In a bowl, combine egg yolks and water, whisking until smooth. In a heavy saucepan, combine sugar and flour. Add the egg yolk mixture and grated rind. Cook over medium heat, stirring, until mixture comes to a boil and thickens. Remove from heat; stir in juice and butter. Cover and chill for at least 1 hour.

TO MAKE FROSTING

In the top of a double boiler or stainless-steel bowl suspended over simmering water (do not let bottom of bowl actually touch the water), combine sugar, egg whites, corn syrup, salt, and grapefruit juice. Beat with an electric mixer on low speed for 30 seconds. Increase mixer speed to high and beat for 7 to 8 minutes, until stiff peaks form. Remove from heat and continue to beat another 1 to 2 minutes, until frosting is thick enough to spread.

TO ASSEMBLE CAKE

Place one layer on a cake plate. Spoon chilled filling evenly on cake to within ½-inch of edges. Top with second layer. Spread frosting over the top and sides of the cake. Sprinkle grated grapefruit rind over the top.

Hazelnut Cheesecake

Hazelnuts seem to have an affinity for cream cheese and orange. Here, the three are used in a luscious, crustless cheesecake that tastes like a rich, baked mousse. If made ahead and refrigerated, let stand at room temperature for an hour before serving.

Makes 10 to 12 servings

1   cup hazelnuts

4   8-ounce packages cream cheese, at room temperature

1¾ cup sugar

4   large eggs

2   tablespoons Grand Marnier or Cointreau

1   teaspoon finely grated orange rind

Preheat oven to 350°. Butter a 10-inch springform pan.

Spread hazelnuts on a baking sheet and toast for 10 minutes, stirring once. Rub the skins off. Chop the nuts in a food processor or nut chopper. Maintain oven temperature.

In a large bowl and using an electric mixer, beat the cheese until light and fluffy. While beating, gradually add the sugar. Add the eggs, one at a time, beating well after each addition. Beat in Grand Marnier. Fold in hazelnuts and orange rind.

Transfer mixture to prepared pan. Set the pan into a larger baking pan and fill larger pan with boiling water to come halfway up the sides of the springform pan. Bake for 1½ hours, until a tester comes out clean. Remove from oven and immediately run a thin knife around the edge of the cheesecake. Turn off oven and return cheesecake to oven. With door positioned ajar, let cheesecake slowly cool off in oven for 1 hour. Serve, or cover with plastic wrap and refrigerate for up to 2 days before serving.

Lemon-Ricotta Cheesecake

During one winter we loaned our fully furnished Palm Springs condo to the owner of Precious Ricotta Cheese and his wife. On the day they left, we found this stunning not-too-sweet cheesecake in the refrigerator, along with the recipe. Couldn't ask for a more delicious thank you!

Crust

	canola oil, for brushing
5	tablespoons Grape Nuts cereal
2	tablespoons chopped walnuts
2	tablespoons sugar
¼	teaspoon ground cinnamon

Makes 10 to 12 servings

Cheesecake Filling

⅓	cup golden raisins
⅓	cup diced dried apricots
⅓	cup dark rum or orange juice
2	pounds cream cheese, softened
1	cup ricotta cheese
1¼	cups sugar
2	large eggs
	pinch salt
1½	tablespoons lemon juice
2	teaspoons grated lemon rind

TO MAKE CRUST

Preheat oven to 325°. Coat a 10-inch springform pan without a hole in the center with canola oil.

In a food processor, combine cereal, walnuts, sugar, and cinnamon. Pulse until mixture forms fine crumbs. Place the crumb mixture in prepared pan; tilt and rotate pan to coat the bottom and sides evenly. Set aside.

TO MAKE FILLING

In a small saucepan, combine raisins, apricots, and rum. Heat over low heat until mixture begins to form bubbles. Immediately remove from heat and set aside.

Meanwhile, in a large bowl of an electric mixer, combine cream cheese, ricotta, and sugar. On medium speed, beat until smooth. Add the eggs, salt, lemon juice, lemon rind. Mix until well combined. By hand, stir in raisin-apricot mixture, mixing well. Spoon the filling into the prepared pan.

Set the filled pan in a large baking pan. Place the baking pan on a rack in the middle of the oven, filling the larger pan with hot water to come halfway up the sides of the springform pan. Bake until all but the center of the cheesecake is set, 45 to 55 minutes.

Carefully remove the cheesecake from the baking pan. Run a knife around the edge of the cheesecake. (This prevents the cheesecake from sticking to the pan as it cools, making cracks in the middle of the cheesecake.) Cool to room temperature, then refrigerate for several hours before removing from springform pan and cutting into wedges to serve.

Nectarine-Almond Upside-Down Cake

Although nectarines are only grown commercially in California and the Yakima Valley area of Washington, the tree is popular in home orchards in other western states, particularly in the higher elevations of Southern Arizona.

A nectarine has similar characteristics to a peach, but botanically, it's quite unique with the gene for fuzziness dominant. Nectarines should have an orange-red background color and yield to gentle pressure but not be as soft as peaches. Here, nectarines combine with almonds in a scrumptious cake that's worthy of a flute of your favorite western champagne.

Topping

Makes 10 to 12 servings

¼ cup (½ stick) unsalted butter, melted
¼ cup sugar
1 teaspoon grated lemon rind
2 tablespoons fresh lemon juice
1 teaspoon ground cinnamon
4 cups sliced unpeeled firm ripe nectarines, about 2 pounds total
½ cup whole blanched almonds

Cake

2 cups unbleached all-purpose flour
1 teaspoon baking powder
1 teaspoon baking soda
½ teaspoon salt
½ cup (1 stick) unsalted butter, at room temperature
1½ cups sugar
4 large eggs plus 2 large egg yolks, at room temperature
1 teaspoon pure vanilla extract
½ teaspoon almond extract
1 cup buttermilk
whipped cream (optional)

Preheat oven to 350°. Butter and flour a 13-inch by 9-inch metal baking pan.

TO PREPARE TOPPING

Spread melted butter over the bottom of the prepared pan. Sprinkle with sugar, lemon rind, lemon juice, and cinnamon. Arrange nectarine slices on top of sugar mixture. Arrange whole almonds between the nectarine slices. Set aside.

TO MAKE CAKE

Onto waxed paper, sift together flour, baking powder, baking soda, and salt. Set aside.

In a large bowl and using an electric mixer on medium-high speed, cream the butter until light and fluffy. Gradually add the sugar, beating well. Add the eggs and egg yolks, one at a time, beating well after each addition. Beat in vanilla and almond extracts.

Reduce mixer speed to low and add flour mixture in three parts, alternating with buttermilk, beginning and ending with flour mixture. Once all flour is added, continue to beat for another minute. Transfer batter to the prepared pan, smoothing the top with the back of a spoon.

Bake until cake is a deep golden brown and a tester inserted in the center comes out clean, about 45 to 40 minutes. Transfer to a rack to cool for 5 minutes. Run a thin-bladed knife around the edge and invert the cake onto a large serving platter. Carefully lift off pan. If any nectarines or almonds remain in pan, remove and patch into the cake while still hot. Serve warm with whipped cream, if desired.

Oatmeal Cake

Diane Joy lives on the outskirts of Las Vegas, Nevada. An excellent cook with lots of fine family recipes, she sent me this old-fashioned recipe for Oatmeal Cake that was popular among the early settlers of the West. Made by her family for several generations, it's a cake that pleases everyone each time it's made. Packaged shredded coconut didn't come on the western culinary scene until 1927, at which time it was added to the recipe.

1¼ cups boiling water

1 cup rolled oats

½ cup applesauce

1 cup packed light brown sugar

1 cup granulated sugar

3 large eggs

1 teaspoon ground cinnamon

1 teaspoon pure vanilla extract

1½ cups unbleached all-purpose flour

1 teaspoon baking soda

¼ teaspoon salt

Makes 9 servings

Topping

¼ cup (½ stick) unsalted butter, at room temperature

¾ cup granulated sugar

3 tablespoons whole milk

1 cup shredded coconut

1 cup chopped walnuts or pecans

Preheat oven to 350°. Grease and flour a 9-inch square cake pan.

In a medium bowl, pour boiling water over the oats. Let stand for 10 minutes. In a large bowl, combine applesauce, brown sugar, granulated sugar, 1 whole egg, 2 egg whites (reserve yolks for topping), cinnamon, and vanilla. Mix well. Stir in oat mixture and mix thoroughly.

Gradually stir in flour, baking soda, and salt. Mix well. Pour batter into prepared pan. Bake for 30 minutes.

TO MAKE TOPPING

Meanwhile, in a medium bowl, cream together the butter and granulated sugar. Stir in milk, 2 reserved egg yolks, coconut, and walnuts. Mix well. Spread evenly over the hot cake and continue to bake for another 15 minutes. Cool in pan on a rack before cutting into squares.

Orange Almond Cake
with Orange Glaze

Iexperimented with several varieties of oranges in my Southern California back-yard grove, thick-skinned navel and Temple for eating out of hand and thin-skinned Valencia for juicing. Every Saturday during the growing season, November to June, we'd harvest that week's crop, producing plenty of oranges for eating and several quarts of juice of drinking. Invariably a few oranges each week would end up in a delectable cake.

If blood oranges are in season, you could use them for an even more pro-nounced orange flavor. These red-fleshed beauties are now being grown com-mercially in California and Texas.

Makes 10 to 12 servings

6 ounces blanched almonds

1 cup unbleached all-purpose flour

1 tablespoon baking powder

4 large eggs

1½ cups sugar

½ cup canola oil

½ cup fresh orange juice

1 tablespoon grated orange zest

Orange Glaze

1 cup good-quality orange marmalade

1½ tablespoons orange liqueur or fresh orange juice

2 oranges, thinly sliced and cut in half, for garnish

Preheat oven to 350° and position rack in lower third of oven. Butter and flour a 9½ inch bundt pan.

Using a food processor fitted with a metal blade, process almonds until finely ground with the texture of fine bread crumbs. In a medium bowl, combine ground almonds, flour, and baking powder.

In a large bowl and using an electric mixer on medium speed, beat eggs until light and frothy. Beat in sugar and canola oil until mixture is thick and lemon col-ored. Slowly add the flour mixture, alternating with the orange juice, beginning and ending with flour. Stir in orange zest.

Transfer the mixture to the prepared pan. Bake for 50 to 60 minutes, until a tester inserted in the center comes out clean. Cool in pan on a rack for 10 minutes, then invert onto a cake plate that has been lined at the edge with pieces of waxed paper.

TO MAKE GLAZE

In a small saucepan, bring the marmalade and orange liqueur to a boil. Strain through a fine strainer. Pour the hot glaze over the warm cake, allowing it to naturally drip down the sides of the cake. Cool to room temperature, then carefully remove the waxed paper liners. Arrange orange slices on the top or around the sides of the cake and serve.

Orange Meringue Cake

Californians have the feeling that their ubiquitous and enormous orange groves were always there. In fact, in July of 1769, the Spanish Franciscan missionary Junipero Serra planted the first orange tree to grow in California at the Mission of San Diego de Alcala. It wasn't until 1805 that the first California orange grove of any size was planted at San Gabriel Mission near Los Angeles.

Here, I've baked slices of navel oranges, introduced as a commercial variety in 1875, inside a meringue cake that has been fortified with ground almonds. The dessert could also be made with blood oranges or tangelos.

1¾	cup blanched whole almonds
3	large eggs, separated
1	cup sugar
	grated rind of 1 large navel orange
2	tablespoons Grand Marnier or other orange-flavored liqueur
1	tablespoon unbleached all-purpose flour
2	navel oranges, peeled and thinly sliced crosswise
2	large egg whites

Makes 8 to 10 servings

Preheat oven to 350°. Butter a 9-inch pie pan.

In a food processor fitted with the metal blade, process almonds until they form a fine powder. Set aside.

In a large bowl and using an electric mixer, beat egg yolks and ¾ cup of the sugar until yolks are very pale and thick. Stir in orange rind, Grand Marnier, 1 cup of the ground almonds, and the flour. Mix well.

In another bowl, beat the 3 egg whites until they form stiff peaks. Stir a third of the beaten egg whites into the yolk mixture to lighten the mixture, then fold in remaining whites. Transfer mixture to the prepared pan and bake 30 minutes, until lightly browned.

Remove from oven and arrange orange slices on top of cake in overlapping concentric circles. Beat the 2 egg whites until they form soft peaks. Gradually add remaining ¼ cup sugar and beat until stiff peaks form. Gently fold in remaining ground almonds. Spread meringue over the orange slices, covering oranges completely. Return cake to oven and continue to bake until meringue is golden, about 15 minutes.

Pear Fluden

One of my many Jewish friends from Palm Springs, California, Elaine Gold-man, was determined that I learn two fine points of Jewish cooking: how to make proper chopped chicken liver and how to make fluden, a deep-dish pie of layers of flaky pastry alternating with finely chopped fruit, nuts, and spices that her family made for religious holidays. You can vary the fruits, nuts, and spices—you're limited by only your own imagination. Here it's made with pears and almonds. In the summer, make it with peaches and walnuts. Another time, use apples and hazelnuts or apricots and pecans.

Makes 9 servings

¾ cup (1½ sticks) butter, at room temperature

1¾ cups sugar

2 large eggs

1 teaspoon pure vanilla extract

3¼ cups unbleached all-purpose flour

1 teaspoon baking powder

½ teaspoon salt

3 tablespoons fresh lemon juice

4 cups finely chopped peeled and cored firm-ripe Bartlett pears

1½ cups golden raisins

½ cup coarsely chopped sliced almonds

1 teaspoon ground cinnamon

¼ teaspoon ground allspice

pinch ground nutmeg

3 tablespoons butter, for dotting

Lemon Glaze

1 cup sifted powdered sugar

3 to 4 tablespoons fresh lemon juice

1 teaspoon grated lemon rind

dash pure vanilla extract

In a large bowl, cream together the butter and ¾ cup sugar. Beat until light and fluffy. Add eggs, one at a time, beating after each addition. Beat in vanilla extract.

Onto a piece of waxed paper, sift together 3 cups of the flour with baking pow-der, and salt. Add half of the flour mixture to the butter mixture. Blend in lemon juice, then stir in remaining flour mixture. Mix well to form a dough. Wrap in plastic wrap and chill for at least 4 hours or overnight.

Preheat oven to 350°. Butter a 9-inch square baking pan.

Divide the dough into four equal portions. On a lightly floured work surface, roll out each portion to form a 9-inch square, trimming the dough as necessary to fit into the prepared pan. Place three of the dough squares on a piece of waxed paper. Place the fourth square in the pan. Cover evenly with a third of the pears, a third of the raisins, and a third of the almonds.

In a small bowl, combine remaining 1 cup sugar, the remaining ¼ cup flour, and the cinnamon, allspice, and nutmeg. Sprinkle a third of this mixture over the fruits and nuts. Cut 1 tablespoon of the butter into small pieces and dot over the fruit mixture. Top with a second pastry layer by inverting the waxed paper over the first layer and peeling away the waxed paper (this helps to prevent the dough from tearing). Top with another third of the pears, raisins, almonds, flour mixture, and another tablespoon of butter. Repeat with another pastry layer and remaining pears, raisins, almonds, flour mixture, and butter. Top with the fourth layer of pastry which has been pricked with the tines of a fork. Bake until crust is nicely browned and pastry cooked through, about 60 to 70 minutes. Remove from oven and cool in pan on a rack.

TO MAKE LEMON GLAZE

While fluden is still hot, in a small bowl, combine glaze ingredients, beating until smooth. Spread evenly over the top. Serve warm, cut into squares.

Pistachio Pound Cake

Driving through central California's pistachio country when the trees are in full bloom is a glorious experience. All too often one thinks of walnuts or pecans when baking a cake, but pistachios add a subtle, delicate flavor to this pound cake made with powdered sugar. When buying unshelled pistachios, look for shells that are partially open—it's easier to get the nutmeat out. A totally closed pistachio means that the nutmeat has not matured.

Makes 10 to 12 servings

3¾ cups powdered sugar

1½ cups (3 sticks) butter, at room temperature

6   large eggs

1   teaspoon vanilla extract

2¾ cups sifted cake flour

1   cup coarsely chopped pistachios

Preheat oven to 300°. Generously butter a 12-cup bundt pan. Sprinkle 2 table-spoons of the powdered sugar on the bottom and sides of the pan, tilting pan to evenly coat.

In a large bowl with an electric mixer, beat 1½ cups (3 sticks) butter on medium speed until creamy. Gradually add the remaining powdered sugar, beating until lightly and fluffy. Beat in eggs, one at a time, beating well after each addition. Beat in vanilla extract. Gradually beat in flour. Stir in pistachios. Transfer mixture to prepared pan and smooth the top with the back of a spoon.

Bake for 1¼ to 1½ hours, until a tester inserted in the center comes out clean. Cool in pan on a rack for 10 minutes. Turn out onto a rack, upright cake, and cool. Serve warm or at room temperature, cut into thin slices. Will keep when wrapped airtight for up to 2 days.

Plum Pound Cake

I developed this recipe years ago for a Los Angeles television show in celebration of the new harvest of California plums. The cake can also be made with fresh peaches or nectarines.

1	pound fresh red plums, pitted and quartered
1	cup water
2	tablespoons fresh lemon juice
2	cups sugar
1¾	cups cake flour (not self-rising)
¼	teaspoon ground cinnamon
¼	teaspoon salt
½	cup (1 stick) unsalted butter, at room temperature
3	large eggs plus 1 large egg yolk
½	cup heavy cream
1	teaspoon pure vanilla extract
	sugar

Makes 9 servings

In a heavy saucepan, bring plums, water, lemon juice, and ½ cup of the sugar to a boil. Reduce heat and simmer mixture, stirring occasionally, for 30 minutes. Drain plums well. Set aside.

Meanwhile, preheat oven to 350°. Butter and flour a 9-inch square cake pan. Set aside.

In a bowl, sift together the cake flour, cinnamon, and salt. In another bowl and using an electric mixer, beat together remaining 1½ cups sugar and butter. Add eggs and egg yolk, one at a time, beating well after each addition. Beat in half of the flour mixture, then the cream. Stir in remaining flour mixture and vanilla. Fold in drained plums.

Transfer mixture to prepared pan and bake for 50 to 60 minutes, until a tester inserted in the center comes out clean. Cool in pan on a rack . While still warm, sprinkle top of cake with sugar, cut cake into squares, and serve.

Prickly Pear and Dried Cranberry Torte

In 1995, the State Legislature of Texas designated the prickly pear cactus as the official state plant. Prickly pear is prevalent in Texas, growing wild in most parts and easily cultivated anywhere in the state. Prickly pears are also used in cooking in Arizona and other parts of the Southwest where the cactus thrives on the arid desert. State laws protect the plants from destruction on public lands, but the fruit may be gathered with discretion. You can also buy prickly cactus pads (nopalitos) in many supermarkets. Look for them near the chiles and exotic fruits.

From a culinary standpoint, prickly pear cactus can be pickled, stir-fried, stewed, or baked in casseroles. The dethorned nopalitos (pads) can be made into a salsa or candy that has a flavor similar to watermelon. Here I've used the nopalitos with dried cranberries for a buttery torte. Cooked this way, the cactus has a flavor similar to apples.

Dough

Makes 8 to 10 servings

3 large eggs
¾ cup plus 2 tablespoons light brown sugar
¾ cup (1½ sticks) butter, melted and cooled
2 cups all-purpose flour
½ teaspoon baking powder
2 tablespoons whole milk
½ teaspoon pure vanilla extract

Filling

6 nopalitos with thorns and "eyes" removed, diced
½ cup dried cranberries
2 teaspoons fresh lemon juice
¾ cup sugar
1 teaspoon ground cinnamon
1 tablespoon butter

In a large bowl and using an electric mixer, lightly beat together the eggs and brown sugar. Combine the melted butter, flour, and baking powder. Add to the egg-sugar mixture in 3 parts, mixing well after each addition. Mix in the milk and vanilla extract. Let batter rest for 15 minutes.

TO MAKE FILLING

Cook cactus, covered, for 3 minutes in boiling, lightly salted, water to cover. Add dried cranberries and let stand, covered, for 2 minutes. Drain well. Rinse under running cold water and drain again. Combine cactus mixture, lemon juice, sugar, and cinnamon.

Preheat oven to 400°. Line a 10-inch round cake pan with parchment paper. Pour batter into the pan. Spoon cactus mixture on top, pressing down lightly. Dot with butter. Bake for about 40 minutes, until the cake is golden and the fruit is tender. Let cool in the pan on a rack for 1 hour before removing. Run a knife around the edges and turn out onto a serving plate. Turn torte right side up and cut into wedges to serve.

Prune Spice Cake

One of the many food stalls at Farmer's Market on Melrose Avenue in Los Angeles sells slices of a fabulous spice cake that is extra moist with the addition of prunes that had been soaked in apple juice. For a more grown-up version, I've soaked the prunes in brandy, adding them to a basic spice cake recipe that's been in my family since the popularity of bundt cakes in the 1950s.

Makes 10 to 12 servings

2 cups pitted dried prunes, packaged (about 12 ounces)
2 cups water
⅓ cup brandy or apple juice
3 cups unbleached all-purpose flour
1 tablespoon baking soda
2 teaspoons ground cinnamon
1 teaspoon ground allspice
1 teaspoon ground nutmeg
½ teaspoon ground cardamon
½ teaspoon ground cloves
1 teaspoon grated lemon rind
1 teaspoon salt
1½ cups canola oil
2¼ cups sugar
5 large eggs
2 tablespoons pure vanilla extract
1½ cups buttermilk

Brown Sugar Glaze

¼ cup (½ stick) butter
¼ cup packed light brown sugar
¼ cup heavy cream
1 cup sifted powdered sugar
½ teaspoon pure vanilla extract

Preheat oven to 350°. Grease and flour a 12-cup bundt pan.

In a heavy saucepan, combine prunes, water, and brandy. Simmer until prunes are tender, about 15 minutes. Remove from stove and let stand.

On a piece of waxed paper, sift together flour, baking soda, spices, lemon rind, and salt. In a large bowl and using an electric mixer, beat oil, sugar, eggs, and vanilla on medium speed until well blended. Gradually beat in flour mixture, alternately with buttermilk, beginning and ending with flour mixture. Mix well until batter is smooth.

Drain and coarsely chop prunes. Add chopped prunes to cake batter and transfer mixture to the prepared pan. Bake until a tester inserted near the center comes out clean, about 65 minutes. Cool in pan on a rack for 15 minutes, then turn out onto a cake plate.

TO MAKE BROWN SUGAR GLAZE

While cake is cooling, melt the butter and sugar together in a small saucepan over low heat. Stir in heavy cream and cool slowly, stirring constantly, until the mixture comes to a gently boil. Simmer 1 to 2 minutes.

Remove from heat and gradually add powdered sugar in thirds, whisking until smooth after each addition. Stir in vanilla. Glaze should be pourable. If it's too thick, thin with drops of extra cream. Spoon glaze over top, allowing the glaze to naturally drip down the sides. Serve cake warm.

Spiced Carrot Cake with Macadamia Nuts

Recipes for carrot cake abounded during the '60s. One of the very best was given to me by the late actor Robert Young, of the popular *Father Knows Best* and *Marcus Welby, M.D.* television series. His off-screen hobby was cooking, and because I worked with a close relative of his, I was often the grateful recipient of his culinary experiments. He used walnuts in his cake, but substituting macadamia nuts gives this classic a new exciting flavor.

Makes 12 to 16 servings

- 2 cups sugar
- 1½ cups canola oil
- 3 large eggs
- 2 teaspoons pure vanilla extract
- 2 cups unbleached all-purpose flour
- 2 teaspoons baking soda
- 1 teaspoon ground cinnamon
- 1 teaspoon ground allspice
- ½ teaspoon salt
- ¾ cup canned juice-packed crushed pineapple, well drained
- 3 cups grated carrots
- 1 cup shredded coconut
- 1 cup chopped macadamia nuts
- Lemon Cream Cheese Frosting (page 60)

Preheat oven to 350°. Butter and flour a 12-cup bundt pan.

In a large bowl and using an electric mixer, beat sugar, oil, eggs, and vanilla extract. Onto waxed paper, sift together the flour, baking soda, cinnamon, allspice, and salt. Gradually add to sugar mixture, beating well.

Stir in well-drained pineapple, carrots, coconut, and nuts. Transfer batter to prepared pan, smoothing the top with the back of a spoon. Bake for 50 to 60 minutes, until a tester inserted in the center comes out clean. Cool in pan on a rack for 10 minutes, then turn out onto a rack. Turn cake right side up and cool completely before frosting with Lemon Cream Cheese Frosting.

Sunshine Cake
with Mango Sauce

My California friend and former neighbor Pat Pierringer gave me the recipe for this light and luscious cake, which she frosted with whipped cream. I like to serve the cake, unfrosted, with a fresh mango sauce spooned alongside. The cake is also delicious for breakfast, toasted in a toaster oven, with a spoonful of orange marmalade.

Cake

12 large eggs, separated
2   teaspoons cream of tartar
1¼ cups sugar
1   cup cake flour
1   tablespoon fresh lemon juice
1   tablespoon finely grated lemon rind

Makes 10 to 12 servings

Mango Sauce

5   tablespoons sugar
⅓ cup water
3   ripe mangoes
½ teaspoon fresh lemon juice

Preheat oven to 325°. Lightly butter and flour a 9½-inch bundt pan.

In a large bowl and using an electric mixer, beat egg whites until frothy. Add cream of tartar and beat until soft peaks form. While beating, gradually add ¾ cup sugar and beat until whites form stiff peaks. Set aside.

Onto a sheet of waxed paper, sift together the flour and remaining ½ cup sugar. In another large bowl, beat egg yolks and lemon juice until thick and light yellow in color. Stir in lemon rind. While beating, gradually add flour mixture. Mix well. Stir in a third of the beaten egg whites, then gently fold in remaining egg whites.

Gently spoon batter into prepared pan, smoothing the top with the back of a spoon. Bake for 60 to 70 minutes, until a tester inserted in the center comes out clean. Remove from oven and cool in pan on a rack for 10 minutes. Invert out onto a rack, turn cake right side up, and cool.

TO MAKE MANGO SAUCE

Meanwhile, in a small saucepan, bring sugar and water to a boil, stirring until sugar dissolves. Remove from stove and cool.

Peel mangoes and cut pulp away from the seed. Discard the seeds. Place the mango pulp in a food processor fitted with the metal blade. Add the sugar mixture and lemon juice. Process to a smooth puree. Transfer to a serving bowl; cover and refrigerate until ready to serve. (Makes about 3 cups.)

To serve, thinly slice the cake. Pass the Mango Sauce to spoon over each serving.

Vanilla Wafer Crumb Cake with Brown Sugar Frosting

This recipe comes from my longtime friend Ann Hite, of Laguna Niguel, California. I love to take this cake on family picnics and beach outings. It holds up well when the temperature's soaring.

Makes 12 to 16 servings

½   cup solid shortening
1   cup granulated sugar
3   large eggs
½   cup evaporated milk
1   teaspoon baking powder
2   cups finely crushed vanilla wafer crumbs
1   3½-ounce can angel coconut
1   cup chopped pecans

Brown Sugar Frosting

¼   cup evaporated milk
¼   cup (½ stick) butter
½   cup packed brown sugar
1½ cups powdered sugar

Preheat oven to 350°. Grease and flour a 9-inch x 13-inch baking pan.

TO MAKE THE CAKE

In a large bowl, cream shortening, granulated sugar, and eggs. Stir in evaporated milk, baking powder, vanilla wafer crumbs, coconut, and pecans, mixing only until blended. Transfer mixture to prepared pan, smoothing the top with the back of a spoon. Bake until top is dry, about 30 minutes. Do not overbake. Cool in pan on a rack.

TO MAKE FROSTING

When cake is cool, heat evaporated milk, butter, and brown sugar in a saucepan over medium heat. Stir until butter is melted and brown sugar dissolved. Remove from heat and beat in powdered sugar until smooth. Spread over cake. Serve at room temperature.

Cobblers & Such

Apple Blackberry Crisp, see page 92.

Apple Blackberry Crisp

If you live in the Pacific Northwest, cultivated fresh blackberries are inexpensive or wild berries are free if you'll willing to tackle the thorny bushes growing alongside the road or arid vacant lots. Over the years, I've tried growing a thorn-free variety of blackberries with moderate success. Whenever I have a good crop or run across a special promotion at the produce market, I freeze the berries for off-season use in cobblers, tarts, and crisps like this.

Makes 6 to 8 servings

3 pounds Golden Delicious apples, peeled, cored, and thinly sliced
2 cups fresh blackberries, rinsed and drained, or frozen, rinsed, and drained
¼ cup sugar
2 tablespoons unbleached all-purpose flour

Topping

1 cup unbleached all-purpose flour
¾ cup sugar
½ teaspoon ground cinnamon
¼ teaspoon salt
½ cup (1 stick) unsalted butter, chilled and cut into small pieces

Garnish

whipped cream flavored with vanilla extract or vanilla ice cream

Preheat oven to 350°. Lightly grease a 7-inch x 11-inch baking dish.

In a large bowl, gently toss apples, blackberries, sugar, and flour. Spread evenly in prepared baking dish.

In a food processor or bowl, combine flour, sugar, cinnamon, and salt. Add butter and process, using pulse, on/off turns, or cut butter into flour mixture using a pastry blender or two knives, until mixture resembles coarse crumbs. Sprinkle mixture evenly over the fruits. Bake for 30 to 35 minutes, until topping browns and fruits bubble. Cool for 15 minutes before serving with vanilla-flavored whipped cream or ice cream.

To Freeze Berries

To freeze whole berries, arrange unwashed berries on paper-towel-lined baking sheets. Freeze until firm. Pack the frozen berries lightly in freezer containers (not self-sealing plastic bags). Label and date the container. Use within 6 months, rinsing and draining while still frozen before using in cooked dishes.

Apple Dumplings with Cinnamon Sauce

My sister-in-law Ruth makes these delicious dumplings frequently, using Washington apples grown in my niece's small orchard.

Makes 6 servings

2¼ cups unbleached all-purpose flour

1 teaspoon salt

¾ cup quick rolled oats

1 cup (2 sticks) butter

8 tablespoons cold water

6 medium Golden Delicious or Granny Smith apples, peeled and cored

2 tablespoons dark raisins

2 tablespoons chopped walnuts

2 tablespoons packed light brown sugar

2 tablespoons butter, melted

Cinnamon Sauce

½ cup sugar

2 tablespoons cornstarch

¼ teaspoon salt

3 tablespoons red cinnamon candies

½ teaspoon ground cinnamon

1 cup hot water

few drops red food coloring (optional)

Into a large bowl, sift together flour and salt. Stir in oats. Using a pastry blender or two knives, cut in butter until mixture resembles coarse crumbs. Gradually add water, tossing mixture with a fork until dry ingredients are evenly moistened. Divide into six parts. On a lightly floured work surface, roll out each portion to form an 8-inch square.

Preheat oven to 415°. Line a baking sheet with parchment paper.

Place a peeled and cored apple in the center of each square. In a small bowl, combine raisins, walnuts, brown sugar, and butter. Stuff centers of the apples with a rounded tablespoon of the raisin mixture. Bring pastry up over apples, pinching edges together. Prick the surface of the dough with the tines of a fork. Place on prepared baking sheet and bake for 30 minutes, until pastry is golden brown, and apples, tender. Cool on a rack slightly before serving.

TO MAKE CINNAMON SAUCE

Meanwhile, when apples are almost done, combine sugar, cornstarch, salt, cinnamon candies, and ground cinnamon in a small saucepan. Add water and bring to a boil over medium-high heat, stirring constantly, until thickened. If desired, add a few drops of red food coloring to intensify the color.

To serve, place each dumpling on a dessert plate. Spoon sauce over warm dumplings and serve.

Apple Kuchen

There's a definite German influence in Texas, particularly around New Braunfels and Fredericksburg in the Texas Hill Country. There German bakeries abound. On our last visit we stopped for coffee about 4 o'clock, served with thin slices of a delicious apple-filled kuchen, which was probably yeast raised, but I find using baking powder works as well.

Here, I've combined apples with dried sour cherries for an easy-to-make cake that's equally welcome year round with afternoon coffee or for breakfast.

1	cup dried sour cherries
¼	cup apple juice
½	teaspoon ground cinnamon
1½	cups unbleached all-purpose flour
2	teaspoons baking powder
½	teaspoon salt
¼	teaspoon ground allspice
½	cup (1 stick) unsalted butter, at room temperature
¾	cup sugar
1	large egg
½	cup half-and-half
4	large apples—Granny Smith, Golden Delicious, Jonathan, or Gravenstein

Makes 8 to 10 servings

Preheat oven to 350°. Lightly butter a 10-inch round cake pan.

In a small saucepan, combine cherries, apple juice, and cinnamon. Bring to a boil over medium-heat, stirring constantly. Remove from heat and set aside to cool.

Onto waxed paper, sift together the flour, baking powder, salt, and allspice.

In a large bowl and using an electric mixer, cream butter until light and fluffy. Gradually beat in sugar and the egg. In batches, add the flour mixture, alternating with the half-and-half, beginning and ending with flour mixture. Mix until a stiff batter forms. Transfer batter to prepared pan and smooth the top with the back of a spoon.

Peel, core, and slice apples. Press apple slices, core side down, side by side into the batter like the spokes of a wheel following the shape of the pan. (The apples will reach to almost halfway into the center of the cake). Spoon cherry mixture onto the center not covered by apples, gently pressing cherries into the batter and filling in any cracks between the apple slices. Bake for 45 to 50 minutes, until a tester inserted in the center comes out clean. Serve warm, cut into thin wedges.

Brewing a Perfect Pot of Coffee

Coffee with dessert or a cup of the perfect brew with a little sweet is the best pick-me-up for those of us who run out of steam in the late afternoon. Like most of the rest of the world, westerners are particular when it comes to their coffee. When the West was settled, the coffeepot was the first thing put on the cook fire in the morning and the last thing to be emptied at night. It was in 1865 that San Francisco's coffee-roaster James A. Folger began to sell roasted, ground, and packaged coffee. From that time on, coffee from Central America was available to everyone. Prior to that time, people purchased green beans that had to be roasted and ground at home. In the '70s the gourmet revolution with interest in specialty coffees—freshly roasted, high-quality varieties or blends specifically selected by the consumer or whole-roasted beans to be ground at home—swept the nation. In 1980, entrepreneur Howard Schultz bought Starbucks, originally a Seattle coffee bean business, and started the explosion of coffeehouses in Seattle and throughout the West.

There are so many kinds of coffee to choose from; do a little testing if you haven't already done so. Visit a coffeehouse or shop in your area and experiment with their different blends or try blending two or more coffees on your own for your own special blend. Invest in a coffee grinder or purchase pre-ground coffee in small batches, storing them in airtight containers in the freezer. Because many of your guests may be cutting down on caffeine, offer them one of the excellent decaffeinated types now available.

The key ingredient beyond the coffee is the water. The quality of the water will be reflected in the final cup of coffee. If you have water that is heavily chlorinated or tastes of chemicals, always use filtered or bottled spring water for making coffee. For regular-strength coffee, use 1 coffee measure or 2 tablespoons freshly ground coffee for each 6-ounce cup. For extra-strength coffee, use 1 coffee measure or 2 tablespoons coffee for each 4 ounces of water. Double-strength coffee takes 2 coffee measures or 4 tablespoons coffee to each 6 ounces of water. Offer cream or milk and sugar to add to the taste. When serving espresso, serve with a twist of lemon and a sugar cube and a tiny spoon.

Basically there are three ways to brew coffee inexpensively at home without a special machine—using a drip-filter coffeemaker, using a plunger pot, or using a stove-top espresso pot. For full flavor drip-filter coffee, use fine grind for cone-shaped filters and a slightly coarser grind for flat-bottomed filters. Pour boiling water through the filter. Stir the coffee before serving.

I personally favor the French method of brewing coffee in a plunger pot. This brews a rich, full-bodied coffee with a fine sediment. For best results, rinse the glass pot with hot water and add coarsely ground coffee. Fill to the marked level with boiling water. Replace top, leaving the plunger in the top position. Let coffee steep for 4 minutes, then slowly push down the plunger, trapping the grounds on the bottom. The coffee is ready to pour.

Although I love espresso and always order it when dining in a restaurant, I don't have the cabinet space or money for a restaurant-size espresso machine so I've opted for an at-home stovetop espresso pot. With this, I get a thick, strong brew with little effort or expense. Put water in the bottom of the pot reservoir. Fill the filter with finely ground coffee, tamping it down lightly. Screw on the top and place on the stove. Bring to a boil, forcing the water up through the coffee into the top of the pot, from where the coffee is poured.

Coffee variations are quite popular in the West—Italian *caffe latte* or French *café au lait* are made with equal amounts of hot, freshly brewed, strong brewed coffee and hot milk, which are poured into a coffee cup simultaneously. Also popular is Italian cappuccino, which can be easily made at home without a cappuccino machine by whipping hot milk in a blender for 1 minute to produce a bit of foam. Combine equal portions of very strong, fresh brewed Italian-roast coffee with the frothy milk, dust with chocolate shavings and ground cinnamon. Serve with sugar. In towns on or close to the Mexican border, coffee is frequently blended with orange rind, brown sugar, cinnamon sticks, and whole cloves for *café de olla*.

After dinner coffee should be special—this is not the time for a quick cup of instant coffee. It's easy to brew a great cup of coffee. You and your guests will notice and appreciate the difference.

Apricot Kuchen

Apricots came to Arizona by way of California, the state that produces most of the fresh apricots found in the supermarket. In areas where nighttime temperatures don't dip too low, backyard apricot trees provide excellent shade, clusters of pretty pink flowers each spring, and delicious fruit for eating. My sister Eileen Ryberg, who lives in Phoenix, makes this often during the apricot season.

Makes 8 to 10 servings

½ cup (1 stick) unsalted butter, at room temperature

2 cups sugar

8 large eggs

2 cups unbleached all-purpose flour

2½ pounds fresh apricots, pitted and quartered

1 teaspoon ground cinnamon

2 tablespoons fresh lemon juice

1 teaspoon finely grated lemon rind

1¼ cups sour cream

1 teaspoon pure almond extract

4 sugar cubes, crushed, or 4 teaspoons granulated sugar

Preheat oven to 350°. Lightly butter a 9-inch by 13-inch glass baking pan.

In a large bowl and using an electric mixer, beat butter and ½ cup sugar until mixture is light and fluffy. Add 4 eggs, one at a time, beating well after each addition. Stir in 1½ cups of the flour. Spread batter evenly in prepared pan.

In a large bowl, mix apricots with remaining ½ cup sugar, cinnamon, lemon juice, and lemon rind. Spoon mixture evenly over the batter.

In a large bowl, combine remaining 1 cup sugar with the remaining ½ cup flour. Stir in sour cream, remaining eggs, and almond extract. Beat until thoroughly mixed. Pour batter over the apricots, smoothing the top with the back of a spoon. Sprinkle crushed sugar cubes over the top. Bake about 70 to 80 minutes, until a tester inserted into the center comes out clean. Remove from oven and cool in pan on a rack for at least 30 minutes before cutting into squares to serve.

Blackberry Cobbler

Now in retirement, my brother Laile Towner has taken up cooking as a hobby. When blackberries begin to ripen, he's already scouted out the biggest and best growing on the vacant land near his Washington home. Armed with his berry picking buckets, which hang by a rope around the neck, leaving both hands free to pick the berries, he sets out most every morning for a race against the birds. A lot of the berries end up frozen for later in the year, but he's sure to make a cobbler or two before the season ends.

Dough

1½ cups unbleached all-purpose flour

¼ cup sugar

1½ teaspoons baking powder

1 teaspoon baking soda

¼ teaspoon salt

3 tablespoons solid vegetable shortening, frozen

2 tablespoons cold unsalted butter, cut into bits

½ cup buttermilk

Makes 8 servings

Filling

6 cups fresh blackberries, washed and drained

¾ cup sugar

4 sugar cubes, crushed (for texture), or 4 teaspoons granulated sugar

Garnish

whipped cream or ice cream (optional)

Preheat oven to 400°. Lightly butter a 9-inch round casserole dish that is at least 2 inches deep.

In a large bowl, combine flour, sugar, baking powder, baking soda, and salt. Using a pastry blender or two knives, cut in shortening and butter until mixture forms coarse crumbs. Make a well in the center and pour in the buttermilk. With a fork, stir until just combined. Turn dough out onto a lightly flour board and roll or pat dough to form a rough 8-inch circle.

TO MAKE FILLING

In a bowl, toss blackberries and sugar. Pile into prepared dish. Gently lift the circle of dough and place over the berries, pinching together any breaks or tears in the dough. (The dough should look rustic and "cobbled.") Sprinkle the top with the crushed sugar cubes or granulated sugar.

Bake until fruit bubbles and top is golden brown, about 25 to 30 minutes. Cool in pan on a rack for at least 20 minutes before serving warm with whipped cream or ice cream, if desired.

California Peach and Golden Raisin Clafouti

This recipe comes from my sister-in-law Helen Giedt who makes the clafouti with whatever fruit she has ripening in her yard—peaches, nectarines, apricots, pears, plums, or apples along with golden raisins which she always has in her pantry. It's truly a multitude of different desserts, wrapped up in one recipe.

1	*pound fresh peaches, nectarines, apricots, pears, plums, or apples*
2	*large eggs*
1¾	*cup heavy cream*
¼	*cup unbleached all-purpose flour*
¼	*cup granulated sugar*
⅛	*teaspoon ground allspice*
	pinch salt
¼	*cup golden raisins*
1½	*tablespoons packed light brown sugar, plus more for garnish*

Makes 6 servings

Preheat oven to 400°. Lightly butter a 12-inch round shallow casserole or gratin dish.

Peel, pit or core, and thinly slice fruit. Arrange in bottom of prepared dish. Set aside.

In a food processor fitted with the metal blade, combine eggs, 1 cup of the cream, flour, granulated sugar, allspice, and salt. Process until smooth batter is formed. Pour batter around the fruit and sprinkle with the raisins.

Bake for 12 minutes, until top begins to set. Sprinkle with 1½ tablespoons brown sugar. Continue to bake until clafouti is set and golden brown on top, about 8 minutes. Remove from oven and cool in pan on a rack.

Whip remaining ¾ cup cream until soft peaks form. Serve the warm clafouti, cut into wedges, with the whipped cream, sprinkled with a little brown sugar.

Cherry Cobbler

Orchard-grown cherries are not usually associated with the Southwest, but at cooler elevations above 3,500 feet, sweet Bing, Rainier, and Lambert cherry trees grow in random areas. However, if you're wanting a variety of you-pick cherries, you need to be in the Northwest where on both sides of the Cascades cherry trees thrive.

Dough

Makes 8 servings

1½ cups unbleached all-purpose flour
2 tablespoons packed light brown sugar
¼ teaspoon salt
5 tablespoons solid vegetable shortening, frozen
¼ cup (½ stick) cold unsalted butter
4 to 5 tablespoons ice water

Cherry Filling

1 cup water
3 tablespoons cornstarch
6 cups pitted fresh cherries
1 tablespoon grated lemon rind
½ cup granulated sugar
1 teaspoon almond extract
1 tablespoon unsalted butter, cut into bits
4 sugar cubes, crushed (for texture), or 4 teaspoons granulated sugar
¼ cup sliced almonds

In a large bowl, combine flour, brown sugar, and salt. Using a pastry blender or two knives, cut in shortening and butter until mixture forms coarse crumbs. Add water, 1 tablespoon at a time, tossing mixture with a fork until dough begins to cling together. Gather into a ball and place between two sheets of waxed paper to flatten to a round disk. Refrigerate for 30 minutes.

Preheat oven to 375°. Lightly butter a 9-inch ovenproof dish that is at least 2 inches deep.

On a lightly floured work surface, roll out dough to a rugged circle about 15 inches in diameter. Transfer pastry circle to the prepared casserole, lining the bottom and sides of the dish and letting the excess dough drape over the sides. Set aside.

TO MAKE FILLING

In a heavy saucepan, whisk together water and cornstarch. Add cherries, lemon rind, and granulated sugar. Cook over medium heat, stirring, until thickened, about 5 minutes. Remove from heat and stir in almond extract.

Spoon mixture into prepared pan. Dot with butter. Bring the pastry crust up over cherries mixture (it will not quite cover the fruit—use any scraps that fall off to patch). Sprinkle with crushed sugar cubes or granulated sugar.

Bake 35 to 45 minutes, until crust is golden brown and cherry mixture bubbling. Remove from oven and sprinkle with sliced almonds. Serve warm.

Cranberry-Apple Brown Betty

Some recipes for brown betty call for finely ground toasted bread crumbs, but I prefer to use fresh bread crumbs that I've made in my food processor.

Cranberries have been commercially grown on Long Beach Peninsula in Southwestern Washington for more than 100 years. Because fresh cranberries are only available during the Thanksgiving to New Year's season, freeze a few bags to make this and other desserts during the rest of the year. If fresh or frozen cranberries are not available, substitute dried cranberries, plumping them first in a little warm water.

Makes 8 servings

- 5 *large baking apples, such as Granny Smith, McIntosh, or Gravenstein*
- 1 *cup packed light brown sugar*
- ¾ *teaspoon ground nutmeg*
- ½ *teaspoon ground cinnamon*
- 1 *teaspoon grated lemon rind*
- 2 *cups fresh bread crumbs made from sourdough bread*
- ⅓ *cup unsalted butter, melted*
- 1½ *tablespoons fresh lemon juice*
- 2 *cups fresh cranberries, picked over*

Garnish

whipped cream or ice cream (optional)

Preheat oven to 350°. Lightly butter a 9-inch square baking dish.

Peel, core, and thinly slice apples. Arrange half of the apple slices over the bottom of the prepared pan. In a small bowl, combine brown sugar, nutmeg, cinnamon, and lemon rind. Sprinkle half of the sugar mixture over the apples. Spread half of the bread crumbs over the top and drizzle with half of the butter and lemon juice. Top with the cranberries.

Layer with remaining apple slices, remaining brown sugar mixture, remaining bread crumbs, remaining butter, and remaining lemon juice. Cover dish with aluminum foil and bake for 40 minutes. Uncover and, using the back of a spoon, gently press down on the topping to allow it to absorb some of the fruit juices below. Continue baking for an additional 15 to 20 minutes, until topping is golden brown and fruit is bubbling.

If desired, serve warm with whipped cream or ice cream.

Dewberry Cobbler

Dewberries are a trailing-vine variety of blackberries that grow rampant along the sandy banks of the Brazos River in South Texas. Where I live in the Dallas area, I can occasionally buy them at my local farmer's market; other times I use commercially grown blackberries. During the berry season, I always buy extra to freeze and use later. This particular cobbler has no secrets, except its simplicity.

Filling

6   cups fresh dewberries or blackberries

¾   cup sugar

1½ tablespoons unbleached all-purpose flour

Makes 8 to 10 servings

Topping

1½ cups sugar

1½ cups unbleached all-purpose flour

½   cup (1 stick) butter, cut into 8 pieces

Preheat oven to 350°. Lightly butter a 10-inch round ovenproof dish that is at least 2 inches deep.

In large bowl, toss the berries with sugar and flour. Place in prepared dish.

TO PREPARE THE TOPPING

In a large bowl, combine sugar and flour. Using a pastry blender, cut in butter until mixture forms fine crumbs. Sprinkle evenly over the berries.

Place the dish on a large baking sheet and bake for 35 minutes. Let cool for 10 to 15 minutes before serving.

Note: If using frozen berries, rinse and drain well before using.

Old-Fashioned Peach Cobbler

The peaches grown in California and the Texas Hill Country are some of the sweetest, juiciest peaches on earth. Select tree-ripened peaches for best flavor. The addition of lemon juice and grated lemon rind updates this old-time recipe to good effect. Another time, substitute your favorite berry or California nectarines for the peaches.

Crust

Makes 10 to 12 servings

1½ cups unbleached all-purpose flour
1 tablespoon sugar
¼ teaspoon salt
⅓ cup solid vegetable shortening, frozen
¼ cup (½ stick) unsalted butter, frozen
   grated rind and juice of ½ lemon
3 tablespoons ice water

Filling

8 cups sliced peeled peaches (about 7 large peaches)
   grated rind and juice of ½ lemon
¾ cup plus 2 tablespoons sugar
¼ cup (½ stick) butter, cut into small bits
1 egg, beaten with 1 tablespoon water

Garnish

whipped cream or Cinnamon Ice Cream (page 252)

Preheat oven to 400°. Lightly butter a deep 11-inch × 7–inch ovenproof dish. Set aside.

Place the flour, sugar, and salt in the workbowl of a food processor fitted with a metal blade. Add the frozen shortening and butter. Pulse until mixture is the size of small peas. Add the lemon rind, lemon juice, and ice water. Process until mixture begins to form a ball. Remove and shape with your fingers into a small round disk about 2 inches thick. Wrap and chill for at least 30 minutes.

Place the peach slices in the prepared pan and sprinkle with lemon rind and lemon juice. Top with ¾ cup sugar and dot with the bits of butter. Roll the dough out on a floured work surface to form a rectangle, roughly 7 × 9 inches. Place the rolled dough over the peaches, tucking the edges in. Cut a steam hole in the center and brush the dough with the egg mixture. Sprinkle on the remaining 2 tablespoons sugar.

Bake, uncovered, for about 45 minutes, until the crust is golden brown and the filling is bubbling. Remove from the oven and let cool for 15 minutes before serving with whipped cream or Cinnamon Ice Cream.

Papaya Cobbler

Baking a papaya intensifies its flavor, making it a perfect candidate for an extraordinary tangy-sweet cobbler with a little heat from an unexpected jalapeño chile pepper. For this, use the yellow-fleshed papaya, not the pink-fleshed variety. Choose fruit with firm, unblemished skin and no soft patches. A ripe papaya will give slightly when pressed.

Cobbler Dough

Makes 6 to 8 servings

2	cups unbleached all-purpose flour
1	tablespoon baking powder
1	tablespoons granulated sugar
½	teaspoon salt
¼	cup (½ stick) cold unsalted butter, cut into small pieces
1	cup heavy cream

Papaya Filling

3	large ripe papayas, about 1½ pounds each
1	fresh jalapeño chile pepper, seeded and finely minced
½	cup packed light brown sugar
¼	teaspoon ground cinnamon
¼	teaspoon ground nutmeg
	juice and grated rind of 2 fresh limes
3	tablespoons unsalted butter
4	sugar cubes, crushed (for texture), or 4 teaspoons granulated sugar

Preheat oven to 375°.

In a large bowl, combine flour, baking powder, granulated sugar, and salt. Using a pastry blender or two knives, cut in butter until mixture forms coarse crumbs. Gradually add cream, tossing with a fork, to form a thick dough. Gather dough into a ball, wrap in plastic wrap, and chill for at least 30 minutes.

On a lightly floured work surface, roll out dough to a shape slightly smaller than a 10- or 12-cup shallow oven-to-table baking dish. Trim the edges.

Peel, seed, and slice papayas. Place in a bowl and toss with jalapeño, brown sugar, cinnamon, nutmeg, lime juice, and lime rind. Transfer mixture to the baking dish and dot with butter. Top with prepared pastry dough (the dough will not quite touch sides of dish). Using a sharp knife, cut steam vents in dough, at least 1/4-inch wide and deep enough to expose fruit. Sprinkle dough with crushed sugar cubes or granulated sugar.

Bake until crust is golden brown and papaya is tender when pierced with a sharp knife, about 35 to 45 minutes. Allow to cool at least 15 minutes before serving.

Pat's Sunday Supper Cobbler

This recipe came to me from my good friend Pat Eby, of Incline Village, Nevada. Typical of Pat's recipes, it's easy to make, mixed and baked in the same pan, and the flavor may be varied by whim or what you happen to have on hand—in this case, canned fruit and spices. A favorite on a cold, snowy day, the baking cobbler fills the house with sweet fragrances and the kitchen is warmed by the oven.

¼ cup (½ stick) unsalted butter

1 cup sugar

1 cup unbleached all-purpose flour

2 teaspoons baking powder

¾ cup whole milk

1 16-ounce can fruit with juice—apples, apricots, pitted cherries, or peaches

*Makes
6 to 8
servings*

CHANGES DEPENDING ON THE FRUIT USED:

apples: sprinkle with 1 tablespoon light brown sugar and 1 teaspoon ground cinnamon

apricots: add ⅓ cup sliced almonds to the dry ingredients

cherries: add 1 teaspoon almond extract to the milk

peaches: add ½ teaspoon ground nutmeg to the dry ingredients

Garnish

whipped cream or ice cream

Preheat oven to 325°. Put the butter in a 2-quart casserole and place in oven until butter melts, about 5 minutes. Add the sugar, flour, and baking powder. (If making apricot cobbler, add ⅓ cup sliced almonds; if making peach cobbler, add ½ teaspoon ground nutmeg.) Blend. Pour milk over all (if making cherry cobbler, add 1 teaspoon almond extract to milk) and blend until just mixed. Spoon the fruit and juice from the can of fruit over the top, but do not stir. (If making apple cobbler, sprinkle top with 1 tablespoon light brown sugar and 1 teaspoon ground cinnamon).

Bake for 45 to 50 minutes, until top is browned and the fruit is bubbling. Serve warm with whipped cream or a scoop of ice cream, if desired.

Peach and Mixed Berry Cobbler

Wolfgang Puck, chef and owner of Spago and Chinois, and I go way back to earlier days when he became the chef at the famed Ma Maison and guest chef at an International Wine & Food Show I was coproducing at the Anaheim Convention Center. One of the many dishes he demonstrated to thousands of fans was a simple peach and mixed berry cobbler, topped with rich, buttery shortcakes instead of the usual cobbler dough or streusel topping.

Shortcakes

Makes 8 servings

2 cups plus 3 tablespoons sifted cake flour

5 tablespoons sugar

1 tablespoon finely grated orange rind

1 tablespoon baking powder

½ teaspoon salt

½ cup (1 stick) cold unsalted butter, cut into bits

¾ cup plus 1 tablespoon heavy cream

Peach and Berry Filling

8 or 9 large peaches, about 3 pounds total

1 cup fresh blackberries

1 cup fresh blueberries

1 cup fresh raspberries

3 tablespoons sugar

3 tablespoons unbleached all-purpose flour

3 tablespoons fresh orange juice

2 tablespoons Grand Marnier or other orange liqueur

½ teaspoon ground cinnamon

⅛ teaspoon ground nutmeg

In a food processor fitted with the metal blade, combine flour, 3 tablespoons of the sugar, orange rind, baking power, and salt. Scatter the butter over the flour mixture and process until coarse crumbs form. With motor running, add the cream through the feed tube. Process until dough comes together.

On a floured work surface, pat dough out to ¾-inch thickness. Using a 3-inch cookie or biscuit cutter, cut out 8 rounds, reworking scraps as necessary. Set biscuit rounds aside.

Preheat oven to 375°. Lightly butter a 12- or 13-inch shallow casserole.

TO MAKE FILLING

Peel and pit peaches. Cut into slices and put in a large bowl. Add remaining filling ingredients, tossing lightly to mix. Transfer mixture to the prepared casserole.

Evenly place biscuits over the fruit filling. Sprinkle tops of biscuits with the remaining 2 tablespoons sugar. Bake until biscuits are nicely browned and fruit filling is bubbling, about 35 to 45 minutes. Let cool for at least 15 minutes before serving.

Pear Dumplings with Red Currant Sauce

Brenda Owens of Salem, Oregon, sent me this recipe for pastry-wrapped pears. Since the pears take a long time to cook, she gently poaches and chills the pears before they are wrapped. You could omit the red currant sauce and serve these sweet dumplings with a scoop of ice cream alongside. You can also make these homey dumplings using good baking apples such as Cortlands or Ida Reds.

Makes 6 servings

	juice and grated rind of 1 lemon
1	*cinnamon stick*
1	*star anise*
3	*whole cloves*
1	*cup dry white wine*
½	*cup water*
6	*small firm but ripe Bartlett or Bosc pears, with stems left on, peeled*
⅓	*cup sugar*
3	*tablespoons unsalted butter, cut into small pieces*
2	*teaspoons ground cinnamon*
1	*17¼-ounce package frozen puff pastry sheets, thawed*
1	*large egg, beaten with 2 teaspoons water*

Red Currant Sauce

1	*tablespoon unsalted butter*
¼	*cup crème de Cassis (a black currant-flavored liqueur)*
½	*cup red currant jelly*

In a large saucepan, combine the lemon juice and rind, cinnamon stick, star anise, whole cloves, wine, and water. Bring the mixture to a boil and cook for 5 minutes. Add the pears, lower the heat, and gently cook for 20 to 30 minutes. Transfer the pears to a plate. Chill.

Using a melon baller or sharp knife, carefully core the cooled pears to within ½ inch of the top, being careful to leave the stems intact. Combine sugar, butter, and cinnamon. Stuff the center of the pears with the sugar mixture.

Preheat oven to 400°. Line a large baking sheet with parchment paper.

Roll out the pastry to a thickness of no more than ⅛ inch. Using a sharp knife, cut into six 8-inch squares. Cut as many leaf shapes as possible from remaining pastry scraps, using the back of the knife to make the leaf vein markings. To wrap pears, place a filled pear upright in the center of each square. Bring the four corners of the dough together, molding and shaping the dough to the contours of the pear. Moisten the dough edges with water and pinch or press to seal. Paste on leaves as desired, using a little water to seal the leaves. Place finished dumpling on the prepared pan. Repeat until all pears are wrapped.

Brush the dumplings with the beaten egg and bake for 10 to 13 minutes, until pastry is puffed and nicely browned.

TO MAKE SAUCE

While pears are baking, melt butter in a small saucepan over medium heat. Add remaining ingredients and cook, stirring occasionally, until jelly melts and sauce is syrupy.

To serve, spoon a "puddle" of the sauce onto each of six dessert plates. Transfer warm dumplings, standing upright, in the sauce. Serve at once.

Plum-Blueberry Crisp

Plums fill the produce markets with a rainbow of colors—crimson, yellow, orange, green, purple, and black. Each variety has its own shape and distinctive taste, but all have a pleasing balance of sweet and tart.

When plums are at their height of their season, Texas blueberries are also in season. One of the newest crops to be grown in the Lone Star State, blueberries have a short season in Texas, so I always buy extra to pack, unwashed, into plastic freezer bags. That way, I have plenty for later in the year.

Makes 8 servings

- 3 *fresh plums, pitted and cut into eighths*
- 2 *cups fresh blueberries*
- ½ *cup sugar*
- 2 *tablespoons quick-cooking tapioca*
- 1 *tablespoon fresh orange juice*
- 1 *teaspoon finely grated orange rind*
  butter

Topping

- 1 *cup unbleached all-purpose flour*
- ½ *cup sugar*
- ½ *teaspoon ground cinnamon*
- ¼ *teaspoon salt*
- ½ *cup (1 stick) chilled unsalted butter, cut into 8 pieces*
- 1 *tablespoon finely grated orange rind*

Garnish

Vanilla Ice Cream (page 252)

In a large bowl, toss together the plums, blueberries, sugar, tapioca, orange juice, and orange rind. Let stand at room temperature for 30 minutes.

Preheat oven to 350°. Lightly butter a shallow 2-quart casserole. Pile fruit mixture into casserole, mounding slightly at the center.

In a medium bowl, combine flour, sugar, cinnamon, and salt. Using a pastry blender or two knives, cut in butter until mixture forms coarse crumbs. Stir in orange rind. Evenly sprinkle crumbs over the top of the fruit. Bake until fruit is tender and topping light brown and crisp, about 45 minutes.

Spoon warm crisp into deep dessert bowls. Top with scoops of Vanilla Ice Cream and serve.

Strawberry Cobbler

Our first California home was built near the massive commercial strawberries farms in Orange County. Strawberries used to have an April-to-July peak growing season. Nowadays, everbearing varieties are cultivated to have an extended year round harvest with other western states joining in strawberry production.

This cobbler takes a long time to bake, but it goes together quickly. Start it before tackling the rest of the meal so it has time to bake and cool slightly by dessert time. Another time, try the cobbler made with fresh blueberries, blackberries, or raspberries.

2	quarts fresh strawberries, rinsed and hulled
1½	cups plus 1 tablespoon sugar
2¼	cups unbleached all-purpose flour
1	tablespoon fresh lemon juice
1	tablespoon baking powder
1	teaspoon salt
1¼	cups whole milk
½	cup (1 stick) unsalted butter, melted
¼	teaspoon ground nutmeg

*Makes
8 to 10
servings*

Garnish

whipped cream

Preheat oven to 350°. Lightly grease a 13-inch oval deep baking dish or 2-quart casserole.

In a large bowl, combine strawberries, ½ cup of the sugar, and ¼ cup of the flour. Arrange berry mixture in prepared baking dish. Sprinkle with lemon juice.

In a food processor or blender, combine 1 cup sugar, 2 cups flour, baking powder, and salt. Process to combine. Add the milk and butter; process until smooth. Pour batter over strawberries, making sure the batter reaches the edges of the baking dish to help prevent juice spillovers during baking. Sprinkle top with remaining 1 tablespoon sugar and nutmeg.

Bake for 50 to 60 minutes, until crust is brown and cooked through and the berries are bubbling. Cool for 10 minutes before serving with whipped cream.

Cookies & Candy

Cowboy Cookies, see page 124.

Aniseed Cookies

These cookies, called *bizcochitos*, have been designated the "state cookie" by the New Mexico state legislature. Traditional for Christmas in New Mexico, they are usually cut into fancy shapes, a fleur-de-lis is the favorite, but sometimes they're formed into stars or plain circles. Usually the cookies are made with lard, whipped until it's as light as cream. I much prefer the flavor when the cookies are made with unsalted butter, but if you wish to use lard, use ½ pound (1 cup).

Makes about 2½ dozen

3   cups unbleached all-purpose flour
1½ teaspoons baking powder
¼   teaspoon salt
1   cup (2 sticks) unsalted butter, at room temperature
¾   cup sugar
1   teaspoon aniseed
2   large egg yolks
¼   cup fresh orange juice
1   tablespoon ground cinnamon

Preheat oven to 350°. Line a large baking sheet with parchment paper.

Onto waxed paper, sift together the flour, baking powder, and salt. Set aside.

In a large bowl and using an electric mixer, cream butter and ½ cup of the sugar until very light and fluffy. Beat in aniseed and egg yolks, one at a time, beating well after each addition. Beat in orange juice. Slowly beat in flour mixture until just incorporated. Gather the dough and divide into two balls. Wrap in plastic wrap and chill for 15 minutes.

On a lightly floured work surface, roll out each ball of dough to ¼-inch thickness. Using a cookie cutter roughly 3 inches in diameter, cut out dough to desired shapes. Place the cutouts on the prepared baking sheet about 2 inches apart.

In a small bowl, combine remaining ¼ cup sugar and cinnamon. Sprinkle tops of cookies with the cinnamon sugar and bake until lightly browned, 8 to 10 minutes. Transfer cookies to racks to cool.

Caneberry Bars

From June through September, the Willamette Valley of Oregon grows the largest variety of caneberries (berries that grow on a cane) in the world, accounting for more than 95 percent of the black raspberries, 50 percent of the red raspberries, 95 percent of the loganberries, 86 percent of the blackberries, and 50 percent of the boysenberries that are commercially grown. Once just a summer item, the berries are now picked at their peak of flavor and individually quick frozen (IQF) at large packing plants in the area. They are usable in place of fresh in most recipes.

All of these caneberries have an affinity for the rich flavor of almonds. Here, the two combine to produce a luscious bar cookie. You'll need a food processor fitted with the metal blade to grind the almonds.

½	cup (1 stick) plus 1 tablespoon unsalted butter, cut into bits
3	tablespoons granulated sugar
2	large egg yolks
1½	cup unbleached all-purpose flour
	pinch salt

Makes about 24 bars

Filling

1	cup plus 2 tablespoons granulated sugar
¾	cup (1½ sticks) unsalted butter
5	large eggs
½	cup unbleached all-purpose flour
1½	teaspoons pure almond extract
8	ounces blanched almonds, finely ground
3	cups caneberries—blackberries, boysenberries, loganberries, or raspberries
	powdered sugar

Preheat oven to 375°. Lightly butter a 13-inch by 9-inch baking pan.

In a large bowl and using an electric mixer, cream together the butter and sugar. Add the egg yolks and mix well. Stir in flour and salt to form a soft dough. Press the dough evenly in prepared pan. Prick with the tines of a fork and bake for 12 to 15 minutes, until dough is firm, but not browned. Remove from oven and set aside. Reduce oven temperature to 350°.

TO MAKE FILLING

In a large bowl and using an electric mixer, cream together sugar and butter. Add the eggs, one at a time, mixing well after each addition. Stir in the flour and almond extract, mixing until just blended. Stir in ground almonds.

Arrange the berries on top of the partially cooked dough. Spread the filling batter evenly over the berries and bake for 40 to 50 minutes, until firm and lightly browned. Cool in pan on a rack for 30 minutes, before cutting into bars. Just before serving, dust each bar with powdered sugar.

Christmas Fruit Cookies

For over 75 years, this has been a favorite of the Sanders family of Burleson, Texas, a family who has produced four generations of fire fighters for the city of Forth Worth. Although the cookies are called a Christmas cookie, they're made and sent in huge boxes to the fire station year round.

1   cup (2 sticks) unsalted butter, at room temperature
2   cups packed light brown sugar
2   large eggs
1   teaspoon pure vanilla extract
4   cups unbleached all-purpose flour
1   teaspoon salt
1   teaspoon baking soda
1   teaspoon cream of tartar
¾   cup chopped pitted dates
¾   cup chopped candied cherries
½   cup chopped pecans

Makes
3 dozen

Preheat oven to 400°. Line a large baking sheet with parchment paper.

In a large bowl and using an electric mixer, cream together butter and brown sugar. Add eggs, one at a time, beating well after each addition. Stir in vanilla.

Combine flour, salt, baking soda, and cream of tartar. In another bowl, combine dates, cherries, and pecans. Add ½ cup of the flour mixture and toss. Gradually stir remaining flour mixture into the egg-sugar mixture, mixing well. Stir in date-pecan mixture until well blended.

Drop by teaspoonfuls onto prepared baking sheet and bake 9 to 10 minutes until golden and firm to the touch. Do not overbake. Transfer cookies to racks to cool.

Citrus and Pepita Sugar Cookies

I first tasted this delightful cookie served alongside a bowl of Mexican Vanilla Ice Cream at Mark Miller's Coyote Café in Santa Fe. The play of the tang of the citrus and the crunch of the toasted pepitas made them an intriguing accompaniment to the ice cream heavily perfumed with vanilla. I tested several versions before settling on this one. Make the cookies small; they're quite rich. Pepitas, hulled pumpkin seeds, are sold in Mexican markets, some gourmet shops, and by mail-order (see Mail-Order Sources, pages 270–271).

Makes about 4 dozen

2⅓ cups sugar

½ cup (1 stick) unsalted butter

1½ teaspoons finely grated lemon rind

1½ teaspoons finely grated orange rind

2 large eggs

2 tablespoons fresh lemon juice

2 tablespoons fresh orange juice

3½ cups unbleached all-purpose flour

1 teaspoon baking soda

½ teaspoon salt

½ cup pepitas, toasted and chopped

Preheat oven to 350°. Line a large baking sheet with parchment paper.

In a large bowl, cream 2 cups sugar and butter until light and fluffy. Stir in ½ teaspoon grated lemon rind and ½ teaspoon grated orange rind. Add eggs, one at a time, beating well after each addition. Stir in lemon juice and orange juice.

Onto waxed paper, sift together the flour, baking soda, and salt. Gradually add to the creamed mixture, mixing well. Stir in pepitas. Cover and chill for at least 30 minutes.

In a small bowl, combine remaining ⅓ cup sugar, the remaining 1 teaspoon grated lemon rind, and remaining 1 teaspoon grated orange rind. Set aside.

Remove cookie dough from refrigerator and form into round balls about 1 inch in diameter. Roll each ball in the citrus zest-sugar mixture, then place on prepared baking pan, about 2 inches apart. Bake 9 to 10 minutes, until golden brown around the edges and slightly firm to the touch. Transfer cookies to racks to cool.

Toasting Pepitas

To toast pepitas, heat the pepitas, stirring constantly, in a dry heavy skillet over medium heat until pepitas become fragrant and crunchy, about 4 to 5 minutes. Cool and chop before adding to dough.

Coconut Jam Bars

You can vary this delicious cookie by using different kinds of jam—apricot, raspberry, strawberry, blackberry, or blueberry. It's an excellent basic recipe I used for holiday baking classes that I taught for the Los Angeles Department of Water and Power.

1	cup sugar
¾	cup (1½ sticks) butter
2	cups plus 1 tablespoon sifted unbleached all-purpose flour
1	large egg, lightly beaten
½	cup chopped walnuts
1¼	cups grated coconut
1	teaspoon pure vanilla extract
1	12-ounce jar fruit jam—apricot, raspberry, or your choice

Makes about 2½ dozen

Preheat oven to 350°.

In a large mixing bowl and using a pastry blender, combine sugar and butter. Add flour and lightly mix. Stir in egg; mix lightly. Add walnuts, coconut, and vanilla. Remove one-third of the mixture and set aside.

With your fingers, pat remaining two-thirds of the mixture on the bottom of a 9-inch nonstick square cake pan. Bake for 20 minutes. Remove from oven and cool slightly. Spread jam on top of baked cookie mixture to within ⅛-inch of the edges. Pat remaining reserved dough over the jam. Continue baking for 30 minutes.

While still warm, cut into bars. When cool, remove from pan.

Cowboy Cookies

Having learned to cook at my mother's knee as she made meals for hungry farmhands, I always make my cookies quite large. These delicious cookies are chockfull of oats, raisins, and nuts. Tuck a couple into your "cowboy's" lunch bag.

Makes about 1½ dozen

2¼ cups unbleached all-purpose flour
1 teaspoon baking soda
½ teaspoon ground cinnamon
¼ teaspoon salt
1 cup (2 sticks) unsalted butter, at room temperature
1½ cups packed light brown sugar
⅓ cup granulated sugar
2 large eggs
¼ cup whole milk
1 teaspoon pure vanilla extract
2¾ cups rolled oats
1 cup dark raisins
1 cup finely chopped walnuts

Preheat oven to 350°. Lightly grease a large cookie sheet.

Onto a piece of waxed paper, sift together flour, baking soda, cinnamon, and salt. Set aside.

Using an electric mixer at medium speed, cream the butter and both sugars in a large bowl until light and fluffy. Add the eggs, milk, and vanilla. Beat well. Gradually add the flour mixture, beating well after each addition.

By hand, stir in oats, raisins, and walnuts. Mix well. Drop the dough by heaping double tablespoons onto the prepared baking sheet, 3 inches apart. Bake until golden brown, about 10 minutes. Using a metal spatula, transfer cookies to a rack to cool. Repeat, using the rest of the dough until all cookies are baked. Store in an airtight container for up to 1 week.

Date-Orange Balls

The Coachella Valley of Southern California is the only area in the Western Hemisphere where dates are grown commercially. The large Medjhools, soft and sensuous, are the most popular and are available nationally in natural food stores.

This delicious cookie was handed out to the press at one of the annual date festivals by date growers from the Hadley Date Gardens who were dressed as Arabian princesses and desert merchants. The recipe was printed on a post card that pictured the date palms with clusters of dates wrapped for slow ripening.

½ cup (1 stick) butter, softened
¾ cup granulated sugar
2 large eggs, slightly beaten
2 cups unbleached all-purpose flour
1 teaspoon baking powder
1 teaspoon cinnamon
¼ teaspoon salt
1 cup chopped dates
1 tablespoon grated orange rind
  powdered sugar

Makes about 4 dozen

In a large bowl, cream butter and sugar. Beat in egg. Onto a sheet of waxed paper, sift together flour, baking powder, cinnamon, and salt. Gradually add to butter-egg mixture, stirring until well blended. Stir in dates and orange zest. Chill for 1 hour.

Preheat oven to 375°. Lightly grease a baking sheet.

Using your hands, form the dough into balls about 1½ inches in diameter. Place on prepared baking sheet. Bake for 10 to 15 minutes until done when lightly touched in the center. Cool on pan on a rack, then transfer cookies to a rack to cool completely. When cool, dust tops with sifted powdered sugar.

Glazed Fresh Apple Cookies

Martha Kimball, director of the Los Angeles test kitchen that I worked for when I was just out of college, gave me this recipe. I find that at least a half dozen or so cookies disappear as soon as they come out of the oven—even before I can get them frosted.

Makes about 3 dozen

½ cup (1 stick) unsalted butter, at room temperature

1⅓ cups packed light brown sugar

½ teaspoon salt

1 teaspoon ground cloves

1 teaspoon ground cinnamon

½ teaspoon ground nutmeg

1 large egg

2 cups sifted unbleached all-purpose flour

1 teaspoon baking soda

1 cup finely chopped unpared apple

1 cup golden raisins

1 cup chopped walnuts

¼ cup whole milk

Frosting

2 to 2½ tablespoons whole milk

1½ cups sifted confectioners' sugar

1 tablespoon soft unsalted butter

¼ teaspoon pure vanilla extract

⅛ teaspoon salt

Preheat oven to 375°. If not using a nonstick cookie sheet, lightly grease.

In a large bowl, combine butter, brown sugar, salt, cloves, cinnamon, nutmeg, and egg. Beat until smooth. Combine flour and baking soda. Add half to the butter mixture, mixing well. Stir in chopped apple, raisins, walnuts, and milk. Add remaining flour mixture, stirring until well combined. Drop by rounded teaspoonfuls onto a nonstick, or lightly greased cookie sheet, leaving enough space between cookies for them to expand.

Bake 11 to 15 minutes, until golden and done when touched in the center. Transfer cookies to racks to cool.

TO MAKE FROSTING

In a small bowl, combine frosting ingredients, starting with 2 tablespoons of the milk. Beat until smooth and creamy. If necessary, thin with remaining ½ tablespoon milk. Using a small metal spatula, spread some of the frosting over the top of each cookie. Continue to cool until frosting sets.

Howdy Doody Sugar Cookies

In the early days of my career, I was frequently a guest on several different Los Angeles-based children's syndicated cartoon shows with a short segment called *Cooking with Fran*. On one such appearance, Howdy Doody, Buffalo Bob, Clarabell, and I baked these sugar cookies. The making of the cookies was quite hilarious with Clarabell dancing around, knocking flour and sugar onto the floor; Howdy Doody reading (and misreading) the recipe from the cue card; and peals of laughter from the live audience of children. The show was deluged with mail bags of letters from moms requesting the recipe. Buffalo Bob said, "Hey kids, these are great." With that endorsement, the recipe bears including here!

Makes about 4 dozen

1   cup (2 sticks) butter, at room temperature
1   cup granulated sugar
1   cup powdered sugar
1   cup canola oil
2   large eggs
1   teaspoon pure vanilla extract
½   teaspoon almond extract
4½ cups unbleached all-purpose flour
1   teaspoon cream of tartar
1   teaspoon baking soda
    granulated sugar for sprinkling

Preheat oven to 350°.

In a large bowl, cream together butter and sugars. Gradually beat in oil and eggs, one at a time, vanilla extract, and almond extract.

Onto a piece of waxed paper, sift together flour, cream of tartar, and soda. Gradually add to butter mixture, mixing well. Drop by teaspoonfuls onto a cookie sheet and bake for 9 to 12 minutes, until golden brown. Transfer cookies to a rack and immediately sprinkle tops with granulated sugar. Cool.

Jeweled Candy Cookies

A delightful addition to any cookie tray, these luscious cookies are the invention of Elsie Everett, a fellow fundraiser for the Free Outpatient Clinics at Children's Hospital of Orange County, California.

1	cup (2 sticks) butter
1	cup sifted powdered sugar
1	large egg, lightly beaten
1	teaspoon pure vanilla extract
2¼	cups unbleached all-purpose flour
1	cup coarsely chopped pecans
1	cup candied red cherries, halved
1	cup candied green cherries, halved

Makes about 9 dozen

In a large bowl, cream together butter and powdered sugar. Blend in egg and vanilla. Toss flour with pecans. Stir into butter mixture. Blend in candied cherries. Chill mixture for 1 hour. Shape into 3 logs, 10 inches long. Wrap in plastic wrap and chill for 3 hours.

Preheat oven to 325°. Cut logs into ⅛-inch slices and place on a nonstick cookie sheet. Bake for 12 to 15 minutes, until lightly browned on the edges.

Note: The logs of unbaked dough can be wrapped in plastic wrap and frozen for up to 1 month. Defrost for 30 minutes before slicing and baking.

Lemon Biscotti

The first time I tasted these was at a coffeehouse in Laguna Beach, California. Because I've always grown lemons when living in Southern California, I went home and quickly made up a batch. They've been part of my cookie repertoire ever since.

Makes
about
2 dozen

1½ cups unbleached all-purpose flour

½ cup sugar

1 teaspoon baking powder

¼ cup (½ stick) cold unsalted butter, cut into small bits

1 large egg

2 tablespoons finely grated lemon rind

¼ cup fresh lemon juice

Preheat oven to 325°. Line a large baking sheet with parchment paper.

In a food processor, combine flour, sugar, and baking powder. Scatter the butter on the flour mixture; pulse until mixture forms fine crumbs. Add egg, lemon rind, and lemon juice. Pulse until mixture forms a dough around the blade.

Turn dough out onto a lightly floured work surface. Knead two or three times, adding additional flour if needed (dough should be slightly sticky). Form dough into a log about 2 inches in diameter. Transfer log to the prepared baking sheet. Bake for 25 minutes.

Remove from oven and let cool on the baking sheet on a rack for 15 minutes. Reduce oven temperature to 275°.

With a sharp knife, cut the log diagonally into ½-inch slices. Arrange slices, cut side down, on prepared baking sheet. Bake for 10 minutes, turn over, and continue to bake for another 5 minutes, until firm and dry. Turn off the oven and let biscotti cool completely in oven with the door slightly ajar.

Store in an airtight container at room temperature for up to 1 week.

Lemon Madeleines

Years ago, a colleague and I gave a baby shower for Barbara Robinson, then newly appointed vice president of Sunkist Growers and a fellow board member of the Los Angeles chapter of Home Economists in Business. We served these Lemon Madeleines at the shower. You'll love their fresh lemony flavor.

The Madeleine pan, usually with 12 shallow scallop-shaped cups, is sold in cookware shops or the housewares section of a large department store. You'll only need one pan as the batter will hold up fine while you're baking the remaining madeleines.

Madeleines

1	cup (2 sticks) unsalted butter, at room temperature
2½	cups sifted powdered sugar
4	large eggs
2	cups unbleached all-purpose flour
1	tablespoon finely grated lemon rind

Makes about 3 dozen

Glaze

¼	cup powdered sugar
2	large egg yolks
2	tablespoons fresh lemon juice
2	teaspoons finely grated lemon rind

Preheat oven to 350°. Generously butter the scallop-shaped cups in a Madeleine pan. Lightly dust with flour.

In a large bowl and using an electric mixer, cream butter on medium speed until fluffy. Gradually add the powdered sugar; beat until well blended. Add eggs, one at a time, beating at high speed after each addition. Thoroughly mix in flour and grated lemon peel. Fill each cup with 1½ tablespoons of the batter.

TO MAKE GLAZE

In a small bowl, combine powdered sugar, egg yolks, lemon juice, and lemon rind. Mix until smooth. Lightly brush each Madeleine with glaze. Bake until lightly browned, about 15 to 20 minutes. Remove from pan and cool on a rack, glaze side up.

Note: If you're using one pan, you'll need to wash, dry, butter, and flour the pan before reusing.

Lemon Squares

Lemon bars have long been a favorite of the West. My personal favorite version came to me from my Aunt Miriam Sherwood, whose handwritten kitchen journal portrays a culinary history of that branch of our family. They're scrumptious.

Makes about 2 dozen

1 cup (2 sticks) butter, softened

2¼ cups unbleached all-purpose flour

½ cup powdered sugar

½ cup sweetened shredded coconut

4 large eggs, at room temperature

2 cups granulated sugar

grated rind of 1 large lemon

½ cup fresh lemon juice

1 teaspoon baking powder

sifted powdered sugar for sprinkling

Preheat oven to 350°. Butter a 9-inch by 13-inch baking pan.

In a large bowl and using an electric mixer on medium speed, cream the butter. Gradually beat in 2 cups flour and powdered sugar. Stir in coconut. Press mixture into bottom of prepared pan and bake until golden, about 15 to 20 minutes.

In another bowl, whisk together eggs, remaining ¼ cup flour, granulated sugar, lemon rind, lemon juice, and baking powder. Pour mixture over crust and continue to bake until topping is set and light brown, about 25 minutes.

Remove from oven and cool in pan on a rack. When cool, cut into squares. Dust tops with sifted powdered sugar and serve.

Macadamia Nut-Filled Cookies

These rich nuts are actually an import from Australia, introduced to the Hawaiian Islands as a backyard nut tree in 1881, not planted commercially until 1921, and then later in California in 1950. Here, surrounded in a sweet, buttery pastry, macadamia nuts are even more addictive than just eating the nuts plain.

3	cups unbleached all-purpose flour
2	teaspoons baking powder
¼	teaspoon salt
½	cup (1 stick) butter, at room temperature
⅔	cup sugar
1	large egg
½	cup whole milk
1	teaspoon pure vanilla extract
36	whole, shelled, and roasted macadamia nuts
	powdered sugar

*Makes
3 dozen*

Preheat oven to 385°. Line a large baking sheet with parchment paper.

Onto a sheet of waxed paper, sift together the flour, baking powder, and salt.

In a large bowl, beat together the butter and sugar until light and fluffy. In a separate bowl, whisk together the egg, milk, and vanilla. Add to the butter mixture, alternating with the flour mixture, beating well after each addition.

Using your hands, divide the dough into pieces about the size of a walnut. Form each dough piece into a round ball with a macadamia nut in the center. Place on prepared baking dish, pushing dough down to slightly flatten the bottom. Repeat, using remaining dough and nuts. Bake for about 15 minutes, until cookies are lightly browned and baked through. Transfer cookies to a wire rack to cool. Once cool, dust tops with powdered sugar.

New Mexican Pine Nut Cookies

Driving through New Mexico, one frequently sees people alongside the road, harvesting pine cones, inside which are delicious pine nuts. Getting the little nuts is labor-intensive, but well worth the effort. Fortunately, the nuts are sold in jars at the grocery store, albeit quite expensive.

Here I've used the pine nuts in a crumbly cornmeal cookie that goes well with Blackberry Sorbet (page 260).

Makes about 3 dozen

1   cup (2 sticks) unsalted butter, at room temperature
1   cup powdered sugar
½   tablespoon pure vanilla extract
½   tablespoon grated orange rind
¼   teaspoon salt
2   large whole eggs
2   cups unbleached all-purpose flour
1½ cups stone-ground cornmeal
½   cup pine nuts, lightly toasted and coarsely chopped

Preheat oven to 350°. Line a large baking sheet with parchment paper.

In a large bowl and using an electric mixer, cream butter until light and fluffy. While beating, gradually add powdered sugar. At low speed, beat in vanilla extract, orange rind, salt, and eggs.

Stir in flour and 1 cup cornmeal. Blend well. Stir in pine nuts. Put remaining ½ cup cornmeal in a shallow bowl. Form dough into small balls about 1 inch in diameter. Roll each ball in the cornmeal and place on prepared baking sheet about 2 inches apart. Flatten each ball slightly with a smooth-bottomed drinking glass that has been dipped in cornmeal. Bake until browned around the edges, 20 to 22 minutes. Transfer cookies to wire racks to cool.

No-Fail Pecan Pralines

My friend Debra Sanders, a fifth generation Texan, swears by this family recipe—it can't fail! At Christmas, she makes extra batches for her husband to take to the fire station when he's on duty as the driver of a state-of-the-art fire truck.

2½ cups packed dark brown sugar

1   5-ounce can evaporated milk

2½ tablespoons unsalted butter, melted

1¼ cup coarsely chopped pecans

2   teaspoons pure vanilla extract

Makes about 1½ dozen

In a large saucepan, combine sugar, milk, and butter. Cook, stirring constantly, over medium heat until mixture comes to a boil. When mixture reaches a full boil, add pecans and continue to cook at a full boil for 6 minutes. Remove from stove and stir for 1½ minutes. Stir in vanilla.

Spoon out 2-inch circle on waxed paper and let cool. Mixture will be runny, but sets up fast. Store in an airtight container.

Pecan Pie Squares

Texas vies with Georgia as the country's largest producer of pecans. Each fall my neighbor's trees produce bushels of these delicious nuts, which she so generously shares. I spend the better part of a day cracking the nuts and freezing them in 1-quart self-sealing freezer bags for use throughout the year.

These delicious cookies are easy to make and make a lovely hostess gift when packed in decorative tins for any season of the year—not just the Thanksgiving to Christmas holidays. In Texas, we'd use ribbon cane syrup in place of the dark corn syrup. The result would be a darker filling with a light molasses flavor.

Makes 16 squares

1 cup unbleached all-purpose flour

¼ cup confectioner's sugar

½ cup (1 stick) plus 2 tablespoons unsalted butter, cut into 10 pieces

¾ cup firmly packed light brown sugar

3 large eggs, lightly beaten

½ cup ribbon cane syrup or dark corn syrup

1 teaspoon pure vanilla extract

¼ teaspoon salt

1¾ cups pecan halves, coarsely chopped

Preheat oven to 350°.

Put the flour, confectioner's sugar, and 1 stick of the butter in the workbowl of a food processor fitted with the metal blade. Process, using the pulse feature, or on/off switch, until mixture first resembles fine crumbs, then begins to clump together, about 15 seconds. Firmly press mixture into an ungreased 8-inch square nonstick baking pan. Bake for 20 minutes, until firm and golden brown.

Meanwhile, add the remaining 2 tablespoons butter, brown sugar, eggs, ribbon cane syrup or dark corn syrup, vanilla, and salt to the workbowl. Process until smooth, about 15 seconds, scraping the sides of the workbowl twice. Using a wooden spoon, stir in the pecans.

Spread the mixture over the baked crust. Bake until set, about 40 minutes. Cool and cut into 2-inch squares.

Penuche

I used to buy this delicious candy from a stall at Farmer's Market in Los Angeles. In Texas, I can sometimes find it at Mexican grocery stores, but it's easy to make. The Mexicans use a special brown sugar called *piloncillo;* regular cane brown sugar works with good results.

3	cups packed light brown sugar
1	cup granulated sugar
1	cup (2 sticks) butter
2	tablespoons light corn syrup
1	cup half-and-half
½	teaspoon salt
1	teaspoon maple extract
1	cup coarsely chopped pecans

Makes about 1½ pounds

Butter a 15¼-inch by 10¼-inch by ¾-inch baking pan.

In a 4-quart saucepan, combine brown sugar, granulated sugar, butter, corn syrup, half-and-half, and salt. Cook on medium-low heat until a candy thermometer reaches 236°, soft ball stage. Remove from heat and stir in maple extract.

Add pecans and spread to ¼-inch thickness in prepared pan. Allow to cool and cut into small squares.

Brewing a Proper Pot of Tea

After dinner tea with dessert is becoming increasingly popular in the West. Offer your guests a choice of robust black tea, more delicate *oolong*, pale green teas, and/or caffeine-free herbal mixtures.

The best tea is brewed in a pot with loose tea leaves, not tea bags. Brewed tea will remain hot longer if the pot is first heated by pouring a little hot water from the kettle or the tap into the tea pot, swirling it around, then pouring it out.

Add the loose tea leaves directly into the pot or use a stainless-steel infusion ball, allowing 1 heaping teaspoon per cup plus 1 extra for the pot. Pour in boiling water, cover the pot, and let steep for at least 3 minutes for small-leaf teas and longer for large-leaf teas. Timing will also be determined by the tea variety. Experiment to determine the strength you like. With practice you will find the ideal steeping time. If you've used loose tea without an infusion ball, hold a small tea strainer over each individual tea cup to catch the leaves as the tea is poured. Offer milk, lemon slices, and sugar or honey for guests to add as they like.

Two Kinds of Persimmons

Although there are two types of persimmons grown in California and available throughout the country, I have only used the Hachiya persimmon in my recipes in this book—simply because it is the type I love with a passion and is the best for baking. While the Hachiya persimmon is quite unpleasant to eat when not fully ripened, once ripe it has a soft and sweet jellylike flesh. The second type of persimmon, the Fuyu, is a smaller, more squat-looking sphere and is still firm when ripe. Its tangy, almost spicy, flavor adds an interesting accent to winter fresh fruit salads or sliced fresh over baby greens with a lemon-poppy seed dressing. Often your produce person will let you sample a Fuyu persimmon before you buy.

Persimmon Cookies

My California neighbor, Betty Barnes, and I shared a large persimmon tree that was quite prolific. The tree was actually planted on her side of the fence, but most of the crop was on my side. We continually passed the fruit and our kitchen experiments back and forth. One day she came over with a plate of these cookies, still warm from the oven. An hour and two pots of spiced tea later, most of them were gone.

1   teaspoon baking soda

1   cup Hachiya persimmon pulp

2   cups unbleached all-purpose flour

½   teaspoon ground cinnamon

½   teaspoon ground cloves

¼   teaspoon ground ginger

½   teaspoon salt

½   cup (1 stick) butter, at room temperature

1   cup plus ⅓ cup sugar

1   large egg, lightly beaten

1   cup coarsely chopped pecans

1   cup golden raisins

Makes about 6 dozen

Preheat oven to 350°.

Stir baking soda into persimmon pulp. Set aside. Onto waxed paper, sift together flour, cinnamon, cloves, ginger, and salt.

In a large bowl, cream together butter and 1 cup sugar until light and fluffy. Beat in egg. Stir flour mixture and persimmon pulp into creamed mixture. Stir in pecans and raisins. Drop by teaspoonfuls onto nonstick cookie sheets. Bake for 10 to 12 minutes, being careful to not scorch the bottoms. Transfer cookies to wire racks and immediately sprinkle hot cookies with some of the remaining ⅓ cup sugar. Cool.

Pineapple Melt-Aways

Similar to the Mexican Wedding Cookies that are so popular throughout the Southwest, these powdered sugar-coated cookies practically dissolve on the tongue. They're lovely for a cookie tray or perfect with a bowl of fresh berries at any time.

Makes about 3½ dozen

1   cup (2 sticks) unsalted butter, at room temperature
½   tablespoon pineapple extract
⅓   cup plus 1½ cups powdered sugar
2   cups unbleached all-purpose flour
1   cup natural juice-packed crushed pineapple, very well drained

Preheat oven to 300°. Line a baking sheet with parchment paper.

In a food processor or with an electric mixer, blend butter, pineapple extract, ⅓ cup powdered sugar, and flour until a stiff dough forms. Stir in crushed pineapple that has been drained of as much of its liquid as possible.

Using your hands, shape dough into 1¼-inch balls. Place on prepared baking sheet about 1 inch apart. Bake for 25 to 30 minutes, until cookies are pale golden brown. Cool on pans for 5 minutes.

Sift remaining 1½ cups confectioners' sugar into a shallow bowl. Place a few of the warm cookies in the sugar, gently turning each cookie to coat all sides. Transfer coated cookies to a rack to cool. Repeat with remaining cookies. When cool, coat each cookie again with sugar. Serve or store in an airtight container for up to 1 week. Freeze for longer storage.

Pistachio Lemon Verde Cookies

This is a fabulous cookie. I first became intrigued with it when I stumbled across the Internet Website for Bite-Size Bakery of Moriarity, New Mexico. Up to that time, I wasn't aware that pistachios were grown commercially in New Mexico. When I asked the bakery owner, Lucia Deichmann, for the recipe for her lemon pistachio cookies, one of six cookies and crackers that she sells (see Sources), she graciously sent me this scaled-down version. Her bakery formula makes 45 pounds of one-bite cookies.

The southern desert of New Mexico is one of the few places in the United States with long, hot, dry summers necessary to produce a delicious pistachio, a native of the Middle East.

2   cups unbleached all-purpose flour
¼   cup cornstarch
⅓   cup granulated sugar
1½ teaspoons lemon extract
      grated rind of 1 lemon
1   cup (2 sticks) butter, chilled
1   cup chopped pistachio nuts, unsalted
      powdered sugar, sifted (optional)

Makes about 4 dozen

Into a large bowl, sift together flour, cornstarch, and sugar. Add lemon extract and lemon rind. Mix well. Using a pastry blender or two knives, cut in butter until mixture resembles crumbs. Add the pistachio nuts and mix well.

Transfer dough to a work surface and form a ball. Cut the dough into four pieces and form each portion into a ¾-inch thick log. Place the logs on a cookie sheet and freeze for 30 minutes.

Preheat oven to 350°. Butter three large cookie sheets.

Remove the dough from the freezer and slice the logs ½-inch thick. Place each piece, cut side down and 1 inch apart, on the prepared cookie sheets. Using a fork, gently press down on each cookie.

Bake for 12 to 15 minutes, until the bottoms of the cookies are lightly golden. Remove from oven and allow to cool 2 to 3 minutes. Transfer to a wire rack to cool completely.

If desired, lightly dust the cookies with powdered sugar by tapping the sugar from a strainer over the cookies.

Sugarplums

In 1903, George Dorris had 50 hazelnut saplings shipped by boat from a French nurseryman in California to his ranch along the McKenzie River in Oregon. The trees thrived on the mild climate and the ranch eventually became the first commercial grower of hazelnuts in the United States.

Here, hazelnuts are baked in a rich cookie dough. During the Christmas season, sprinkle the tops of the glazed cookies with green or red decorator sugar.

Makes about 3 dozen

1   *cup (2 sticks) unsalted butter*

1   *large egg*

½   *cup chopped hazelnuts*

2½ *cups unbleached all-purpose flour*

½   *teaspoon baking powder*

⅛   *teaspoon salt*

1   *teaspoon pure vanilla extract*

2 to 3 *tablespoons whole milk, as needed*

Glaze

2   *cups sifted powdered sugar*

3   *tablespoons whole milk*

green or red decorator's sugar (optional)

Preheat oven to 375°. Lightly butter a 9-inch square baking pan.

In a large bowl and using an electric mixer on medium speed, cream together the butter and egg. Toss hazelnuts with 2 tablespoons of the flour. Set aside.

Gradually beat remaining flour, baking powder, salt, and vanilla into the butter-egg mixture. If dough seems too stiff to press together, beat in the milk, a little at a time. Stir in floured hazelnuts. Using your fingers, firmly press dough into prepared pan. Bake 25 to 30 minutes. Cool on a rack before cutting into 1½-inch squares.

TO MAKE GLAZE

In a small bowl, combine powdered sugar and milk, beating until smooth. Using a small spatula or knife, frost the top of each cookie with a little of the glaze. If desired, sprinkle with colored decorator's sugar.

Texas Pecan Lace Cookies

No one in Texas seems to really know the origin of these delicate cookies—the old timers just tell of their mamas making them. Similar to *tuiles,* French for "tiles," these can be formed into a cigar-shaped cookie or draped over a tin can to make a cookie basket. If any break, don't worry. The crumbled cookie's great as a topping for ice cream.

⅔   cup packed light brown sugar

½   cup light corn syrup

½   cup (1 stick) unsalted butter

1   cup finely chopped pecans

⅔   cup cake flour

Makes 8 cookies

Preheat oven to 325°. Position oven rack in the middle of the oven.

In a medium saucepan, bring brown sugar, corn syrup, and butter to a boil over medium heat. Remove from heat and stir in pecans and flour.

Drop 2 tablespoons of batter on a nonstick baking sheet and smooth with the back of a spoon to form a 5-inch circle. Repeat, adding a second cookie to the baking sheet. Bake for 12 minutes, until golden. Remove from oven and let cool for 30 seconds. Using a wide metal spatula, carefully remove a cookie and immediately roll it around a chopstick for cigar-shaped cookies or drape the cookie over the end of a 15½-ounce can, loosely molding the cookie to the can. Repeat until you have 8 cookie cigars or 8 cookie cups. Cool on a rack until dried. Store in an airtight container until ready to use.

Texas Spiced Pecans

Several Texas companies sell bags and tins of pecans at airport gift shops and trendy boutiques, which are at once sweet and spicy. This recipe's easy and sure to please. To ensure proper drying of the pecans, make this recipe on a day when the humidity is low. You can easily double or triple the recipe by using extra baking pans.

Makes about 2 cups

2   cups pecan halves

3   tablespoons unsalted butter, melted

¼   cup sugar

2   teaspoons ground cumin

2   teaspoons good-quality chili powder

½   teaspoon cayenne pepper

⅛   teaspoon salt

Preheat oven to 325°. Line a large baking sheet with parchment paper.

Toss pecans with butter. In a bowl, combine sugar and remaining ingredients. Sprinkle sugar mixture over pecans, stir, and spread in a single layer on prepared baking sheet. Bake for 12 minutes, stirring occasionally. Cool and store in airtight containers.

Walnut Divinity

I've been making this delicious holiday candy for years—sometimes using chopped pecans or black walnuts, but usually English walnuts, named in honor to the English merchant marines whose ships once transported the nuts for trade to ports around the world. Culinary historians claim English walnuts are one of the oldest tree foods known to man and prefer the name "Persian" walnut because the birthplace of these nuts was Persia. Today about two-thirds of the world's English walnut crop comes from the southern areas of California.

At other times of the year, use the hot divinity mixture as a frosting for a baked and cooled chocolate or white layer or sheet cake. Although you can test the cooked syrup mixture using the cold water method, using a candy thermometer is easier and more accurate. As with most candies, the recipe is best made on a dry, low-humidity day.

Makes about 3 dozen

2½ cups sugar
½ cup water
½ cup light corn syrup
2 large egg whites, at room temperature
    pinch salt
1 cup English walnuts, coarsely chopped
1 teaspoon pure vanilla extract

In a small saucepan, combine 2 cups sugar, water, and corn syrup. Bring to a boil and continue to boil until mixture reaches 248° on a candy thermometer or forms a firm ball when a little of the mixture is dropped into a dish of cold water.

While syrup is cooking, using an electric mixer, beat the egg whites and salt until foamy. While beating, gradually add remaining ½ cup sugar until they form stiff peaks. When the syrup reaches 248°, pour about half of the syrup into the beaten egg whites, beating well.

Return the remaining syrup to the stove and continue to cook until mixture reaches the hard-ball stage, 260° on a candy thermometer. Pour the boiled mixture in a steady stream into the egg white mixture, beating all the while. Continue to beat on high speed for another 2 or 3 minutes. Fold in walnuts and vanilla.

Working quickly, drop by heaping teaspoonfuls onto waxed paper and cool. Store in an airtight container.

Fruits—

Fresh

&

Cooked

Almond Zabaglione with Mixed Berries, see page 148.

Almond Zabaglione with Mixed Berries

At a recent dinner party with friends in Texas, our host and chef for the evening found he didn't have sufficient heavy cream to whip for a topping for a bowl of mixed berries he'd planned for dessert. Taking stock of what he did have, Chesley set about making zabaglione, a last-minute dessert that never fails to please everyone. He used amaretto (almond) liqueur instead of the traditional Marsala.

Makes 6 servings

6   *egg yolks*

3   *tablespoons sugar*

3   *tablespoons amaretto*

3   *tablespoons heavy cream*

6   *cups mixed berries—raspberries, blackberries, and blueberries, rinsed and drained*

3 *tablespoons sliced almonds*

In the top of a double boiler or a metal bowl set over a pot of water (don't let the water touch the bottom of the bowl), combine egg yolks, sugar, and amaretto. Place over medium heat and whisk vigorously until mixture becomes foamy and begins to thicken.

Remove from heat and whisk in cream, beating until cream is thoroughly incorporated and mixture has the consistency of a thick custard sauce.

Divide berries between six dessert bowls or stemmed goblets. Top each with some of the almond zabaglione and sprinkle with almonds.

Baked Apples with Cajeta

Apples from Washington have an affinity for caramel—so it only makes sense to bake the beauties stuffed with nuts from the region and serve them with luscious Cajeta (goat's milk caramel sauce).

6 very large Granny Smith or other tart baking apples

½ cup packed dark brown sugar

½ cup chopped hazelnuts

3 tablespoons unsalted butter

1 tablespoon unbleached all-purpose flour

ground cinnamon

1½ cup apple cider

Cajeta Sauce (recipe follows)

Makes 6 servings

Preheat oven to 375°. Position a rack in the center of the oven.

Core each apple to within ¾ inch of the bottom, being careful to not pierce the bottom of the apple. Remove a ring of peel 1 inch wide from around the stem area. Trim a thin slice off the bottom, if necessary, so that apples will sit upright.

In a small bowl, combine brown sugar, hazelnuts, butter, and flour. Using a small spoon, fill the apple centers with the mixture. Place the filled apples, standing upright, in a shallow baking dish. Sprinkle the top of each apple with cinnamon. Pour apple cider around the apples. Cover with aluminum foil and bake for 30 minutes. Uncover and continue to bake for another 10 minutes, until apples are tender at the bottom when pierced with the tip of a sharp knife.

Transfer apples to individual dessert dishes, topping each with some of the apple cider and a generous portion of Cajeta. Serve warm.

Cajeta

2 cups sugar

½ teaspoon salt

1 tablespoon fresh lemon juice

1 tablespoon water

½ cup goat's milk or heavy cream

Makes about 4 cups

In a wide heavy saucepan, combine sugar, salt, lemon juice, and water. Place over medium-low heat, cover saucepan and cook, stirring occasionally, until sugar melts and turns amber colored, about 10 to 12 minutes. Watch carefully to not let sugar burn.

Remove from heat and whisk in goat's milk. Let cool completely. Drizzle over baked apples. Refrigerate any remaining Cajeta to serve over ice cream.

Baked Bosc Pears with Hazelnuts

Fruit growing is prolific in each of the Pacific states, but in the Oregon Rogue Valley near Medford, the crop is pears. Here I've baked Bosc pears with hazelnuts for a simple dessert that is so elegant in taste you'll want to serve it to company.

6   tablespoons (¾ stick) unsalted butter

6   tablespoons sugar

⅓   cup hazelnuts, roasted and skinned

6   firm-ripe unpeeled Bosc pears (about 2½ pounds total), stems intact

3   tablespoons Frangelico (hazelnut liqueur)

¾   cup heavy cream

Makes 4 servings

Preheat oven to 400°. Spread 2 tablespoons butter on the bottom of a baking pan just large enough to comfortably hold the pears upright. Set aside.

In a food processor fitted with the metal blade, combine 3 tablespoons sugar and the hazelnuts. Process to a fine powder. Set aside.

With a sharp knife trim a very thin slice from bottom of each pear to enable pears to stand upright. Using a pastry brush, paint top half of each pear with some of the Frangelico and immediately roll pears in sugar-nut mixture. Stand pears in the prepared dish. Sprinkle bottom of dish with remaining 3 tablespoons sugar and dot with remaining 4 tablespoons butter.

Bake pears for 10 minutes. Pour the cream over the pears and continue to bake until undersides are tender when pierced with a knife, about 20 to 25 minutes. To serve, transfer each pear, standing upright, to a dessert plate or dish. Spoon sauce around the pear and serve warm.

Baked Peaches with Cream

Gillespie County in the middle of the Texas Hill Country is known for its luscious fresh peaches sold at roadside stands from spring to the end of summer. Sometimes the simplest of recipes taste like you've fussed, but you didn't. If you don't have access to these sweet Texas peaches, any freestone peach will work with good results.

Makes 4 servings

2 *very large fresh peaches*

6 *purchased amaretti cookies (almond macaroons), crumbled into fine crumbs*

2 *teaspoons honey*

2 *tablespoons butter, melted*

2 *tablespoons fresh lemon juice*

heavy cream

Preheat oven to 375°. Lightly butter a shallow baking dish.

Peel and halve peaches; pit. Place in prepared dish, cut side up.

In a small bowl, combine crushed cookies, honey, and melted butter. Divide equally between the peaches, filling the peach centers. Bake 15 minutes. Sprinkle with lemon juice and continue to bake for another 10 to 15 minutes, until peaches are tender, but still hold their shape. Remove from oven and cool slightly.

To serve, place each peach half in a dessert bowl and top with a bit of heavy cream. Serve warm.

Baked Winter Western Fruits

Poached fruit has been popular in the West since the area was territories, not states. Here I've oven-poached a mixture of winter fruit in a pale golden Chardonnay from any of the many fine wineries in California, Washington, Oregon, Texas, or New Mexico. Ask for a Chardonnay with rich fruit overtones. For superior flavor, purchase your dried fruits from a natural food or organic market. If you prefer to not use the wine, increase the orange juice by another 2 cups.

2   large navel oranges

1   large ruby grapefruit

3   cups mixed dried fruits—combination of apples, apricots, peaches, pears, figs, and pitted prunes (the more variety, the better)

2   cups Chardonnay wine

1   cup fresh orange juice

2   cinnamon sticks

6   whole cloves

    heavy cream (optional)

Makes 6 to 8 servings

Working over a large bowl to catch any juice and using a small sharp knife, remove the peel and white pith from an orange and discard. Cut in half vertically and remove any white membrane and tiny strings on the cut surfaces. Cut the orange halves crosswise into slices ¼-inch thick and place in the bowl. Repeat, slicing the second orange and the ruby grapefruit.

Add the dried fruits, the Chardonnay, and orange juice. Gently stir to mix well. Cover and refrigerate for at least 6 hours or overnight.

Preheat the oven to 350°.

Transfer fruits and liquid to a shallow 2-quart casserole. Add cinnamon sticks and whole cloves, gently pushing them down into the liquid. Cover with aluminum foil and bake until fruits are very soft, about 40 to 45 minutes.

Remove from oven and let cool for at least 15 minutes. Remove and discard cinnamon sticks and whole cloves before spooning into individual dessert bowls. If desired, pass a small pitcher of heavy cream to pour over each serving.

Berries and Honeydew with Balsamic Vinegar and Grand Marnier

Like cooks in the rest of the country, western cooks have adopted balsamic vinegar, the exquisite Italian vinegar made from white Trebbiano grape juice and aged in barrels of various woods and graduating sizes over a period of years. The vinegar's pungent sweetness combines delightfully with Grand Marnier and fresh fruit to serve alone or over bowls of vanilla ice cream or slices of angel food cake.

Makes 6 servings

3   *cups fresh strawberries, hulled and quartered*
1   *cup fresh raspberries, rinsed and drained*
1   *cup fresh blueberries, rinsed and drained*
1½ *cups diced honeydew melon*
¼   *cup balsamic vinegar*
⅓   *cup Grand Marnier liquer*
⅓   *cup granulated sugar*

Place strawberries, raspberries, blueberries, and honeydew melon in a large glass bowl. In a small bowl, whisk together balsamic vinegar, Grand Marnier, and sugar. Pour over fruit and gently mix to evenly coat.

Cover and chill for at least 4 hours. Serve in small bowls or spoon over ice cream or angel food cake.

Black Figs Stuffed with Goat Cheese and Pistachios

Black Mission figs, named for the mission fathers who planted the fruit as they traveled north along the California coast, have a short growing season, with harvests in July and again in September. At other times, use a golden-skinned or creamy amber colored variety, or whatever's available at your local farmer's market.

6   large black figs

3   ounces fresh goat cheese

3   tablespoons heavy cream

1   teaspoon honey

1   teaspoon grated orange rind

¼   cup chopped pistachios

Makes 6 servings

Preheat broiler.

Using a sharp knife, cut each fig into sixths, cutting from the top to within 1 inch of the bottom. Spread the segments open like a flower, making sure not to break them. Place in an oven-to-table baking dish.

In a bowl, beat together goat cheese, heavy cream, honey, and orange rind until mixture is smooth. Divide the cheese mixture evenly, placing it in the center of each fig. Broil until cheese is lightly browned and bubbling, about 4 minutes. Sprinkle with pistachios and serve immediately.

Brandied Grapes

Fruit has been brandied for hundreds of years in the West as a means of preserving. Here I've combined the familiar green seedless grape with the newcomer to the grape industry—the ruby red seedless grape, developed by the University of California at Davis in the early '80s. Wonderful served without further embellishment, the grapes are also terrific with a spoonful of Crème Fraîche or softly whipped cream.

Makes 8 servings

9 *tablespoons honey*
¼ *cup Cognac or brandy*
1 *tablespoon fresh lemon juice*
1 *pound green seedless grapes, washed and dried, stems removed*
1 *pound ruby red seedless grapes, washed and dried, stems removed*
Créme Fraîche (recipe follows) or softly whipped cream

In a large bowl, whisk together honey, Cognac, and lemon juice. Add the grapes and gently stir to evenly coat grapes. Cover and refrigerate for at least 6 hours or overnight, stirring occasionally.

To serve, spoon into individual dessert goblets or dishes. Top each serving with Crème Fraîche or whipped cream.

Crème Fraîche

The tang of Crème Fraîche pairs very well with all kinds of fresh and cooked fruit. Now available in many grocery stores, it's a snap to make at home, and a staple in my refrigerator.

Makes 2 cups

1 cup heavy cream
1 cup sour cream

In a bowl, whisk together the heavy cream and sour cream. Cover loosely with plastic wrap and let sit at room temperature for 8 hours, until thickened. (In cold weather, this may take up to 24 hours.) Refrigerate for at least 4 hours before serving. Use within one week.

Cherimoya Custard Sauce

If you haven't yet discovered cherimoyas, you're in for a treat. Until recently grown only in the Caribbean and South and Central America, cherimoyas, sometimes called custard apples, are one of the newest commercial crops in California, finding the soil and temperate climate to their liking. With an elusive combination of flavors—overtly a blend of mango and pineapple, more subtly, banana and strawberry—they make a delicious sauce to serve over ice cream, cake (particularly chocolate), and other fresh fruits such as sections of navel oranges and ruby red grapefruit as I sampled at Boudro's on the Riverwalk in San Antonio, Texas.

When selecting a cherimoya, choose one that is heavy for its size, dark green in color, and slightly soft. Once cut open, it's easy to scoop out the rich flesh, discarding the large black watermelon-like seeds.

3 large ripe cherimoyas
1 cup whole half-and-half
½ vanilla bean
⅓ cup superfine sugar
3 large egg yolks
⅓ cup heavy cream

Makes about 3 cups

Cut cherimoyas in half and scoop out the pulp, discarding the seeds. Place the pulp in a food processor or blender and puree. Set aside.

In a heavy saucepan, bring half-and-half and vanilla bean to a boil. Remove from heat, cover, and let stand for 5 minutes. Meanwhile, in a bowl, whisk sugar and egg yolks until a ribbon forms when the whisk is lifted. Discard vanilla bean, adding any scrapings to the hot liquid. Gradually whisk hot mixture into the egg mixture. Return mixture to the saucepan and cook, stirring constantly, over medium heat until thickened. Whisk in heavy cream, cover, and chill for 2 hours, stirring occasionally.

Once chilled, whisk in reserved cherimoya puree.

Citrus Marinated Pomegranates

For the home orchard in the mild climates of the West, pomegranates are hard to beat with their lovely scarlet flowers in the spring and their reddish gold fruit from late summer through Christmas. Although I've grown pomegranates and cooked with pomegranate seeds and the ruby red juice for many years, my favorite way of serving them is simple—marinated overnight in citrus and brandy, then spooned over rich vanilla ice cream.

Makes 6 servings

3   *medium pomegranates*
    juice and finely grated rind of 1 lemon
    juice and finely grated rind of 1 lime
    juice and finely grated rind of ½ navel orange
6   *tablespoons sugar*
6   *tablespoons orange liqueur or brandy*
    Vanilla Ice Cream (page 252)

Remove the skin from the pomegranates and free the seeds (see below). Put the seeds in a crockery or glass bowl. Add citrus juices and grated rind. Sprinkle with sugar and the orange liqueur. Gently stir to mix well.

Cover and refrigerate for at least 3 hours before serving. To serve, spoon the seeds and some of the juice over individual bowls of Vanilla Ice Cream.

Seeding a Pomegranate

If you work under water when freeing the seeds of a pomegranate, you won't get the bright crimson juice all over you and the kitchen. Cut the pomegranate into quarters. Place in a deep bowl of cool water. While working under water, gently remove the connecting pulp to free the seeds. Discard shell and pulp. Drain seeds on paper towels.

Fresh Raspberry Gratin with Fresh Basil

This used to be just a summertime dish when raspberries were in season and fresh basil was growing rampant in my herb garden. Nowadays, fresh raspberries are available year-round and bunches of fresh basil from California are shipped everywhere, allowing one to enjoy this exhilarating dessert any time.

Because the gratin must be served immediately, it cannot be prepared in advance, but it does go together quickly. Serve it with fluted glasses of champagne; raspberries seem to have an affinity for champagne.

3	cups fresh raspberries
10	large fresh basil leaves, torn into pieces
4	large egg yolks, at room temperature
2	tablespoons water
2	tablespoons Framboise (raspberry-flavored) liqueur
¾	cup Crème Fraîche (page 156) or heavy cream, whipped to soft peaks
1	tablespoon sugar

Makes 6 servings

Preheat the broiler.

In a food processor or blender, puree 1 cup raspberries and basil leaves. Divide mixture evenly between six ½-cup soufflé dishes or ramekins. Divide remaining whole berries between the dishes.

In the top of a double boiler or in a stainless-steel bowl suspended over simmering water (do not let the water touch the bottom of the bowl), whisk egg yolks until foamy. Whisk in water and cook, whisking constantly, until mixture is pale yellow. Whisk in Framboise and continue cooking, whisking constantly, until mixture is very fluffy and mounds slightly.

Remove from heat and whisk until cool. Combine Crème Fraîche and sugar. Fold into egg yolk mixture. Spoon over raspberries and place under the broiler until lightly browned around the edges, about 2 to 3 minutes. Watch carefully and do not let the topping get too brown. Serve at once.

Gooseberry Fool

Gooseberries are small round fruits with a thin translucent skin and soft, tiny-seeded insides. Primarily a European fruit, gooseberries are now being grown in the cool, damp climate of Oregon. A "fool" is of old-fashioned English origin—cooked fruit that is then pureed and swirled into whipped cream. Usually made with gooseberries, it can also be made with raspberries, blackberries, strawberries, cherries, or mangoes. The combinations are endless. Adjust the amount of sugar to the sweetness of the fruit. Serve with Texas Pecan Lace Cookies (page 143) on the side.

Makes 6 servings

2 *cups fresh gooseberries, topped and tailed*
¾ *cup sugar*
1 *tablespoon water*
2 *cups heavy whipping cream*

Set aside ¼ cup gooseberries for garnish. In a heavy saucepan, combine remaining gooseberries, ½ cup of the sugar, and water. Simmer over medium heat until berries are very soft, about 8 to 10 minutes. Remove from stove and puree in a food processor or blender until smooth. Force through a coarse sieve, leaving the small seeds. Chill puree for at least 30 minutes.

In a bowl, whip cream with remaining ¼ cup sugar until soft peaks form. Partially fold chilled puree into cream, leaving some swirls of the puree visible. Spoon into individual dessert goblets or dishes. Chill until ready to serve.

Grilled Peaches with Goat Cheese and Raspberry Sauce

Production of western goat cheese in significant quantities is relatively new on the food scene—first in California in the early 1970s, then spreading to New Mexico and Texas where goats seem to thrive on the semi-arid plains and higher elevation grasslands. Several of my Texas friends make goat cheese with milk from their own herds, but I can always get excellent quality fresh goat cheese at the supermarket.

This is a wonderful dessert to serve after a spicy Southwestern meal.

1½ cups fresh raspberries

¼ cup water

2 teaspoons cornstarch

2 firm, ripe fresh peaches

2 tablespoons sugar

3 tablespoons balsamic vinegar

1 tablespoon fresh lemon juice
  freshly ground pepper

4 ounces fresh goat cheese, at room temperature, cut into 4 rounds
  sprigs of fresh mint for garnish (optional)

Makes 4 servings

In a small saucepan, bring 1 cup of the raspberries and water to a boil over medium-high heat. Remove from heat and strain through dampened cheesecloth, squeezing out as much juice as possible. Discard the solids. Return the juice to the saucepan and whisk in cornstarch. Cook over medium heat until mixture boils, whisking constantly. Transfer to a bowl and set aside to cool.

Cut peaches in half vertically and remove the pits. In a shallow dish, whisk together the brown sugar, balsamic vinegar, and lemon juice. Place peaches, cut side down, in the mixture and let stand at room temperature for at least 30 minutes.

Preheat a gas or charcoal grill. Place peach halves flesh side down over medium-hot coals until grill marks form on the peaches, about 2 minutes. Turn peaches over and sprinkle with black pepper. Place a goat cheese round in the center of each peach and continue to grill until peaches are tender, about 5 minutes.

Spoon a "puddle" of the raspberry mixture onto each of four dessert plates. Top with a grilled peach half. Scatter remaining fresh raspberries over each serving and drizzle with any remaining sauce. If desired, garnish the plate with mint sprigs. Serve warm.

Hot Peach Crepe Soufflé

Each summer, I'm filled with eager anticipation for the season's first freestone peaches from California (local native peaches don't arrive until much later). Here the lovely ancient fruit fills light crepes that crisp and puff up for a stunning dessert, inspired by a cherry crepe soufflé dessert served by my chef friend Carole Peck.

Crepes take a little practice, but once you learn to make them, you'll want to keep some in the freezer, ready for spontaneous use. Make the crepe batter at least 30 minutes ahead to let it rest.

Crepe Batter

Makes 8 servings

1 cup unbleached all-purpose flour

3 tablespoons powdered sugar

pinch salt

2 large eggs, lightly beaten

¼ cup (½ stick) unsalted butter, melted

1 cup minus 2 tablespoons whole milk

melted unsalted butter, for cooking crepes

Peach Soufflé Filling

2 cups diced, peeled fresh peaches , about 3 medium

1 cup peach liqueur

1 cup whole milk

¼ vanilla bean, split lengthwise

3 large egg yolks

¼ cup granulated sugar

1½ tablespoons unbleached all-purpose flour

5 large egg whites

powdered sugar

TO MAKE CREPES

In a large bowl, combine flour, powdered sugar, and salt. Add eggs, melted butter, and milk. Beat until smooth. Let rest 30 minutes before using.

Using a heavy 7-inch nonstick skillet, brush a little melted butter into the pan. Place 3 tablespoons of the crepe batter into pan. Turn and tilt pan so that the batter covers the bottom. Place over high heat. As soon as the crepe begins to bubble and brown around the edges, about 30 to 45 seconds, turn crepe over to lightly cook the other side, about 15 seconds. Remove crepe and set aside on a plate. Repeat the procedure, making 8 small crepes. (The crepes can be made ahead of time and stacked between sheets of waxed paper. Wrap in plastic wrap and refrigerate or freeze until ready to use.)

Preheat oven to 350°. Line two large baking sheets with parchment paper.

TO MAKE FILLING

In a small bowl, combine peaches and peach liqueur. Set aside to marinate for 10 minutes.

Meanwhile, in a medium saucepan scald the milk with the vanilla bean and its scrapings. While the milk is being scalded, in a medium bowl and using an electric mixer, beat egg yolks, granulated sugar, and flour on high speed until mixture is pale yellow and forms a ribbon when beaters are lifted from the bowl.

Turn mixer speed to low and beat in about half of the hot milk mixture. Transfer egg-milk mixture back to the saucepan and cook over medium-high heat, stirring constantly with a wooden spoon, until mixture forms a thick custard and bubbles begin to appear on the surface. Strain into a clean stainless-steel bowl. Discard vanilla bean, scraping any remaining seeds into the custard. Place in the freezer for 6 minutes to chill, stirring after 3 minutes.

Drain peaches, reserving peach liqueur. Mix peaches with the prepared custard. Beat egg whites until they form stiff peaks. Fold into peach mixture.

Working very quickly, spoon peach mixture onto a crepe, covering half of the crepe. Fold the top of crepe over the peach mixture. Place on prepared baking sheet. Repeat, filling remaining crepes. Sprinkle each crepe lightly with powdered sugar. Bake for 12 minutes, until puffed and lightly browned.

Place a baked crepe on each of eight dessert plates. Spoon a little of the reserved peach liqueur onto each crepe and serve immediately.

Lemon Soufflés

Whenever I want something light and refreshing for dessert, I think of this recipe for Lemon Soufflés. The original recipe came from the Tea Room of Bullock's Wilshire in Los Angeles, a grand department store that, alas, no longer exists, but the memory of their delicacy lingers on.

Makes 8 servings

	powdered sugar
1	cup whole milk
⅓	cup plus 1 tablespoon granulated sugar
1	tablespoon grated lemon peel
3	large egg yolks
¼	cup fresh lemon juice
3	tablespoons unbleached all-purpose flour
6	large egg whites, at room temperature
	pinch salt
2	tablespoons brandy

Preheat oven to 400°. Generously butter eight ⅔-cup soufflé dishes or custard cups. Dust with powdered sugar and set on a large baking sheet.

In a heavy medium saucepan, bring milk, ⅓ cup granulated sugar, and lemon peel to a boil, stirring occasionally. Remove from heat and let stand 15 to 20 minutes to cool.

In a medium bowl, whisk egg yolks and lemon juice. Gradually add flour, whisking until smooth. Whisk in milk mixture. Return egg-milk mixture to saucepan and bring to a boil over medium heat, stirring constantly. Remove from heat, cover surface with plastic wrap and chill in the freezer for 10 minutes.

Meanwhile, beat egg whites and salt until soft peaks form. Gradually add remaining 1 tablespoon sugar, beating until stiff peaks form. Stir brandy into chilled egg mixture. Stir in half of the beaten egg whites. Gently fold in remaining whites and divide evenly between the prepared soufflé dishes. Bake until puffed and browned, about 10 to 12 minutes. Sift powdered sugar over each soufflé and serve immediately.

Pears in Zinfandel

Few desserts are simpler than a pear poached in wine. I love the flavor combination of pear and raspberries, so I usually scatter a few berries on top of each serving, along with a dollop of Crème Fraîche (page 156) or softly whipped cream. It's an easy dessert for ending dinner with finesse.

The source of the Zinfandel wine for poaching is your choice—California, Oregon, Washington, or one of the new Texas vintners who are starting to capture gold, silver, and bronze medals in national and international wine competitions.

Makes 4 servings

1   *750 ml bottle Zinfandel*
1   *vanilla bean, split in half*
½   *teaspoon black peppercorns*
½   *cinnamon stick*
⅓   *cup sugar*
1   *cup fresh orange juice*
4   *firm ripe pears with stems*
1   *lemon*
1   *cup fresh raspberries*
    Crème Fraîche (page 156) or softly whipped cream (optional)

In a medium saucepan, combine Zinfandel, vanilla bean, peppercorns, cinnamon stick, sugar, and orange juice. Bring to a boil and stir until sugar dissolves.

Peel the pears, leaving the stems intact. From the bottom of each pear, core with a small spoon or melon baller, taking care to not break the pears. Place stem side up in the wine mixture. Cover and poach over medium heat until pears are tender, about 20 minutes. Using a slotted spoon, lift pears from poaching liquid. Set aside.

Return poaching liquid to the stove over medium-high heat and reduce by one-third to form a thin syrup. Strain the mixture, discarding the peppercorns and cinnamon stick. Arrange a poached pear on each of four dessert plates. Briefly dip the raspberries in the wine syrup until warmed, but not cooked. Drain and scatter around the pears. Drizzle some of the syrup over all and place a dollop of Crème Fraîche alongside, if using.

Quick Cherry Soufflés

Washington and Oregon both commercially grow cherries, most of which end up canned or frozen for distribution to other parts of the country. This is a quick dessert using a can of pitted dark sweet cherries. Keep this recipe in mind when you suddenly have company for dinner and no dessert.

Makes 6 servings

2   16-ounce cans pitted dark sweet cherries

3   tablespoons cornstarch

6   tablespoons powdered sugar

2   tablespoons kirsch or brandy

3   large egg whites

¼   teaspoon cream of tartar

Preheat oven to 400°.

Drain cherries, reserving syrup. In a medium saucepan, combine cornstarch and 1 tablespoon powdered sugar. Add reserved syrup and bring mixture to a boil over medium heat, stirring constantly. Reduce heat and simmer 1 minute. Remove from heat and stir in kirsch and drained cherries. Transfer mixture to six 1-cup soufflé dishes or ramekins.

Beat egg whites and cream of tartar until they form soft peaks. Gradually add remaining 5 tablespoons powdered sugar, beating until stiff peaks form. Transfer the beaten egg whites to a pastry bag fitted with a large decorative tip. Pipe onto the top of the cherries in each dish, starting in the center, then around the edges, completely sealing the cherries. Bake until golden brown, about 5 to 10 minutes. Cool slightly; serve warm.

Roasted Red Pears
with Mascarpone Cheese

About 25 years ago, pears with totally brilliant red skins first appeared in western markets. Grown primarily in Wenatchee and Yakima, Washington; Medford and Hood River Valley, Oregon; and Placerville and the Santa Clara Valley, California, red pears are now available nationwide. Red pears taste the same as non-red pears of the same variety. I love them, simply for their dramatic color. Roasting intensifies the flavor of pears.

Here they're roasted with fresh ginger and a little balsamic vinegar to serve with a scoop of mascarpone cheese mixed with orange and pistachios for a simple, but luscious, dessert. Add a grinding of black pepper for a grand finish.

Makes 4 servings

- 2 large red pears
- 2 tablespoons fresh lemon juice
- 1 tablespoon minced fresh ginger
- 3 tablespoons dark corn syrup
- 1 cup water
- 1 tablespoon balsamic vinegar
- 4 ounces mascarpone cheese
- 2 tablespoons fresh orange juice
- 1 teaspoon grated orange rind
- ¼ cup coarsely chopped pistachios
- freshly ground pepper

Preheat oven to 500°. Position rack in the middle of the oven.

Cut pears in half from stem through blossom end; core. Do not peel. Brush all cut surfaces with lemon juice. Place pears, cut side down, in a medium-size metal roasting pan. In a small bowl, whisk together ginger and corn syrup. Using a pastry brush, paint pears with the mixture. Using 2-inch squares of aluminum foil, make a little cap to place over the top of each pear. Roast for 10 minutes.

Combine water and balsamic vinegar. Pour into the baking pan, swishing it around with the pastry brush to mix it with the pear juices. Brush pears with this mixture, then replace foil caps. Turn the pan a quarter turn every 15 minutes for even browning, again brushing each pear with the pan juices and replacing foil caps. Depending on the pear variety, the pan juices should start to thicken in about 20 minutes. After 45 to 55 minutes total roasting time, test the pears with a skewer. Pears should be soft and easy to pierce. If done, remove from oven and discard foil caps. If not, replace caps and roast another 5 to 10 minutes. Remove from oven and again paint pears with the pan juices.

In a small bowl, combine mascarpone, orange juice, and orange rind. Place a pear on each of four dessert plates. Using a small scoop, place an equal portion of mascarpone mixture alongside each pear. If any pan juices remain, drizzle over the pears. Sprinkle with pistachios and a generous grinding of black pepper. Serve warm.

Note: You may need to add additional water to the pan. There should be no less than about ½ cup liquid at any time.

Tropical Fruits in Ginger Sauce

Litchis are one of many uncommon fruits grown in California and Hawaii. Once the hard red shell is removed, the creamy white flesh is delicately sweet and juicy. Fresh litchis are available from June to mid-July. Other times, canned litchis can be substituted.

In Texas I can get both the yellow-fleshed (Solo) and the pink-fleshed (Sunrise) papayas so I use both in this pretty compote. The Sunrise papayas tend to be much larger, so you'll have plenty left for breakfast the next morning.

1   pound fresh litchis, peeled
1   cup cubed yellow-fleshed papaya
1   cup cubed pink-fleshed papaya
1   ripe mango, peeled, pitted and cut into slices
2 to 3 ripe kiwifruit, peeled and sliced
    grated rind of 1 orange
1   cup fresh orange juice
1½ tablespoons finely minced fresh ginger
1   large carambola (star fruit), cut crosswise into 6 slices, discarding ends

In a large glass bowl, gently combine litchis, papayas, mango, and kiwifruit.

In a small saucepan, whisk together orange rind, orange juice, and ginger. Bring to a boil over medium heat. Boil for 2 minutes. Remove from stove and let cool to room temperature. Pour over fruits and gently mix. Cover and let steep, at room temperature, for 30 minutes.

Spoon fruits and juice into individual dessert bowls. Garnish each serving with a slice of carambola (star fruit). Serve at once.

Citrus Tips

Lemons, limes, and oranges will keep at room temperature for 2 to 3 days or up to a month in the refrigerator. To get the most juice from a lemon, lime, or orange, have the fruit at room temperature and roll it on a countertop under your palm before squeezing.

Grate the rind first, then squeeze the juice. To grate the rind (zest), you can use a special tool called a zester from most housewares shops and many supermarkets or you can use a fine hand-held grater that you would use for finely grated cheese or carrots.

To remove the rind in strips, use a very sharp paring knife, a vegetable peeler, or a zester. Remove only the colored part of the peel, leaving the bitter white pith on the fruit. If necessary, turn strips over and scrape off any white pith with a sharp knife.

Pies & Tarts

Kiwifruit Tart, see pages 220–221.

Different Trims for Pie Crusts

There are many ways to flute the edge of a pie crust once the rim of the crust is high enough to hold in all of the filling.

To flute a one-crust pie or a two-crust lattice-topped pie, fold the edge of the crust under so the rim is doubled in size and even with the outside rim of the pie pan. Place the thumb and index finger of one hand against the outside of the pie dough, pushing the dough from the inside with the thumb of your other hand to make a decorative small "U" shaped curve in the dough. Repeat working around the edge of the pie.

Other trims can be made by crimping the edge with fork markings, pressing the tines of the fork into the dough, keeping the depressions about 1 inch apart around the edge of the pie shell.

Another pretty trim is made by cutting tiny leaves from the pastry scraps with the point of a sharp knife. Mark the leaf veins using the back of the knife. Attach to the edge of the crust with a bit of cold water, overlapping the leaves as you work around the shell.

A braided edge is made by cutting strips of pastry ¼-inch wide. Braid together and attach to the edge of the pie shell with a bit of cold water.

When working with a two-crust pie, do not fold or flute the bottom crust until the top crust is in place, then fold the top and bottom crusts under together so that their edge just meets the edge of the pie pan to seal in the juices. Flute both crusts together as described for the one-crust pie.

In a two-crust pie, a lot of steam will be produced during the baking, which will cause the edges of the pie to burst open and spill out. To prevent this, make equally spaced steam vents by slashing the crust with a sharp knife in five or six places. You can also cut out decorative shapes, using the tip of the knife or small cookie cutter, in the dough before placing it over the filling. This works especially well when baking fruit pies that produce a lot of juice such as cherry or peach.

I sometimes use baked cutouts to place on top of a baked one-crust pie such as leaves on a pumpkin or sweet potato pie. Make the cutouts freehand with the tip of a sharp knife or use a small cookie cutter, dipped in flour. Place the cutouts on a baking sheet and bake in a preheated 425° for about 12 minutes, until golden brown. Cool on a rack and apply to the pie just before serving. To add a crunchy texture, brush the unbaked cutout with milk, then sprinkle with granulated sugar, and bake as directed.

Basic Pie Crust

I've been using this recipe for years. A small amount of vinegar in the recipe weakens the gluten in the dough just enough to make it incredibly easy to roll out a tender, flaky crust. It also helps to prevent shrinkage of the dough during baking. It's one of those fabulous recipes that you'll use again and again.

1⅓ cups unbleached all-purpose flour
½ teaspoon salt
½ cup (1 stick) chilled unsalted butter, cut into bits
1 teaspoon cider vinegar
3 to 4 tablespoons ice water

Makes one 9-inch pie shell

In a food processor fitted with the metal blade, or a large mixing bowl, combine flour and salt. Add the bits of butter and process until mixture forms fine crumbs (or cut in butter with a pastry blender or two knives). With motor running, add vinegar and 3 tablespoons water. (If mixing by hand, sprinkle on vinegar and 3 tablespoons water, tossing mixture with a fork.) Process until mixture masses together, adding the last tablespoon of water, as needed.

With your hands, gather the dough into a ball, then flatten between two pieces of waxed paper. Refrigerate for at least 30 minutes. On a floured work surface, roll out dough into a thin round to fit a 9-inch pie plate. Trim and crimp the edges. Fill as directed.

To make a two-crust 9-inch pie, double the recipe.

To make a 10-inch one-crust pie, make 1½ recipes.

Apple-Quince Pie

Quince is not as well known as a homegrown fruit as it was when our grand-mothers were baking quince pies and making quince jelly. Today, quince are commercially grown in California and shipped nationwide. Looking somewhat like an overgrown ripe pear, quince are available from October through December. I like the flavor combination of apple and quince.

Makes 6 to 8 servings

¼ *cup packed light brown sugar*
¼ *cup granulated sugar*
3 *tablespoons unbleached all-purpose flour*
1 *teaspoon ground cinnamon*
3 *large Granny Smith apples, peeled, cored, and thinly sliced*
2 *ripe quince, peeled, cored, and thinly sliced*
1 *tablespoon fresh lemon juice*
3 *tablespoons unsalted butter, melted*
1 *9-inch pastry shell (page 173), unbaked*

Streusel Topping

½ *cup packed light brown sugar*
1 *cup unbleached all-purpose flour*
½ *cup (1 stick) unsalted butter, melted*
½ *cup sliced almonds*

Preheat oven to 350°. Adjust rack to the lower third of the oven.

In a small bowl, mix sugars, flour, and cinnamon. In a large bowl, combine apples and quince. Sprinkle with the sugar mixture and gently toss. Sprinkle with lemon juice and melted butter. Toss again to combine. Pile filling into pastry shell, mounding slightly higher in center.

TO PREPARE STREUSEL TOPPING

Combine brown sugar, flour, and butter, mixing until coarse crumbs form. Top apple-quince mixture evenly with streusel topping. Bake for 25 minutes. Sprinkle with sliced almonds and continue to bake for another 10 to 15 minutes, until crust is golden and fruit is tender. Remove from oven to a rack to cool. Serve warm or at room temperature.

Avocado Pie

One doesn't usually think of avocados as an ingredient for dessert. Our last home in Southern California was in the midst of avocado country where during the peak of the season you could buy them a dollar a dozen. My housekeeper Maria made a pie with a couple of avocados in which she used beaten egg whites. The pasteurized dried egg whites available today work wonderfully, eliminating any possible problem of eating uncooked egg whites.

2   ripe avocados
1   14-ounce can sweetened condensed milk
1   teaspoon finely grated lime rind
½   cup fresh lime juice
    dash salt
2   tablespoons pasteurized dried egg whites, reconstituted in 6 tablespoons warm water, or ½ cup pasteurized liquid egg whites
1   9-inch pie shell (page 173), baked and cooled
⅓   cup sliced almonds

Makes 6 to 8 servings

Peel and pit avocados. Mash pulp thoroughly and whisk in condensed milk, lime peel, lime juice, and salt.

Stir the powdered egg whites into the warm water or pour the liquid egg whites into a metal bowl. Beat with an electric mixer until mixture forms stiff peaks. Gently fold into avocado mixture, then turn into cooled baked pie shell. Chill for at least 4 hours. Just before serving, sprinkle top with almonds. Cut into wedges to serve.

Buttermilk Pie

Buttermilk Pie is a Texas favorite, especially amongt those of us with Southern connections. Lighter than flan, the filling is sweet and smooth—comfort food perfected. For a tasty variation at another time, add 1 tablespoon fresh lemon juice and 2 teaspoons grated lemon rind to the filling before baking. A word of caution: this pie will disappear quickly, so you might want to bake two.

When we were testing this recipe, we baked several pies and sent them to our fire fighter "volunteer tasters." They sent back a note, saying "Now, this is a man's pie!" Women and children will love it, too.

*Makes
6 to 8
servings*

2   *large eggs*

1   *cup sugar*

3   *tablespoons unbleached all-purpose flour*

½   *cup (1 stick) unsalted butter, melted*

1   *cup buttermilk*

2   *teaspoons pure vanilla extract*

1   *9-inch pie shell (page 173), unbaked and well chilled*

Preheat the oven to 425°.

In a large bowl, beat eggs until frothy. Beat in the sugar and flour. Stir in melted butter, buttermilk, and vanilla extract. Mix well.

Pour into the chilled pie shell. Bake for 10 minutes. Reduce oven temperature to 350° and continue to bake for another 35 minutes, or until a toothpick inserted near the center comes out clean. Let pie cool thoroughly before slicing into wedges.

California Orange
Meringue Pie

Lemon meringue pie has always been a favorite of the West, but other kinds of citrus fruits can also be used. Here I've used the juice and grated rind of thin-skinned Valencia oranges to create a delectable pie. Garnish each slice with a thin orange slice. Another time, try using tangerine juice or grapefruit juice.

1½ cups superfine sugar

5 tablespoons cornstarch

½ teaspoon salt

4 large eggs, at room temperature, separated

½ cup fresh squeezed Valencia orange juice

2 cups cold water

1 tablespoon grated orange rind

5 tablespoons cold unsalted butter, cut into 5 pieces

1 9-inch pie shell (page 173), baked and cooled

1 large egg white, at room temperature

*Makes
6 to 8
servings*

Garnish

1 Valencia orange, thinly sliced (optional)

In a large heavy saucepan, combine 1 cup of the sugar, cornstarch, ¼ teaspoon of the salt, 4 egg yolks, and the orange juice. Whisk in cold water. Place over medium heat and cook, whisking constantly, until mixture comes to a full boil. Boil for 1 minute.

Remove from heat and whisk in orange rind. Add butter, 1 tablespoon at a time, whisking after each addition until butter melts. Set aside to cool.

Preheat oven to 350°.

TO MAKE MERINGUE

In a large bowl, combine 4 remaining egg whites plus the additional egg white with the remaining ¼ teaspoon salt. Using an electric mixer, beat egg whites until soft peaks form, then gradually add the remaining ½ cup sugar and beat until stiff peaks form.

TO ASSEMBLE PIE

Transfer cooled orange mixture to the cooled baked pie shell. Top with meringue, spreading to slightly overlap and seal the edges of the pie crust. If desired, make decorative swirls with the back of a spoon.

Bake until meringue is pale golden, about 10 minutes. Remove from oven and cool to room temperature on a rack, then refrigerate until filling is set, about 2 hours. Slice with a sharp knife that has been dipped in hot water. If desired, garnish each piece with a thin slice of orange which has been cut halfway through and twisted to form a spiral.

Deep-Dish Peach Pie

I've tried lots of peach pies over the years, but this recipe I developed for a baking class I taught at a gourmet shop in California is one of the best. Sight and smell are the most trustworthy guides to buying fresh peaches. Don't buy a hard, unyielding peach that looks green beneath its blush and don't buy a peach that doesn't smell like a peach. Serve this pie warm with a scoop of Cinnamon Ice Cream (page 252).

Deep-Dish Crust

1½ cups unbleached all-purpose flour

1½ tablespoons granulated sugar

½ teaspoon salt

½ cup (1 stick) cold unsalted butter, cut in small pieces

1 large egg yolk

4 to 5 tablespoons cold half-and-half

Makes 8 to 10 servings

Peach Filling

8 cups sliced, peeled peaches, about 2½ pounds peaches

3 tablespoons fresh lemon juice

1 cup granulated sugar

pinch ground nutmeg

3 tablespoons quick-cooking tapioca

Topping

¾ cup unbleached all-purpose flour

¾ cup light brown sugar

1 teaspoon ground cinnamon

¼ teaspoon salt

⅛ teaspoon ground nutmeg

2 tablespoons peach liqueur or brandy

¼ cup (½ stick) unsalted butter, cut in small pieces

In a large bowl, combine flour, granulated sugar, and salt. Using a pastry blender or two knives, cut in butter until coarse crumbs form. Whisk together egg yolk and half-and-half. Gradually add to flour-butter mixture, tossing with a fork until dough comes together. Wrap the dough in plastic wrap and refrigerate for 30 minutes.

Preheat oven to 425°.

On a lightly floured surface, roll the dough out to ⅛-inch thickness. Place in a 10-inch deep-dish pie plate; trim and crimp edges. Line the dough with aluminum foil and fill with dried beans, raw rice, or pie weights. Bake for 10 minutes. Lower oven temperature to 375°. Continue to bake until crust is lightly browned, about 5 minutes. Remove from oven and carefully remove aluminum foil and beans.

In a large bowl, toss peaches with lemon juice. Add the sugar, nutmeg, and tapioca. Gently toss again. Pile into baked pie shell.

In a medium bowl, combine flour, brown sugar, cinnamon, salt, and nutmeg. Using your fingers, rub the peach liqueur and butter into the flour mixture until well mixed. Sprinkle mixture over peaches and bake until filling is set and browned, about 30 minutes. Serve warm.

Double-Crust Lemon Pie

My sister-in-law Gloria Giedt of Rancho Palos Verdes, California, faxed me this recipe. She got the recipe from her Auntie Dutch, whose California family has been making the pie for generations. Meyer lemons, which Gloria grows by her pool, offer the mildest lemon flavor, but the more familiar Eureka or Lisbon commercial variety sold at every supermarket will also do.

Of the fresh lemons produced in the United States, more than 95 percent are grown in the deserts of Arizona and California, with smaller groves near the coastal region of Southern California.

1¼ cups sugar

2 tablespoons unbleached all-purpose flour

¼ teaspoon salt

¼ cup (½ stick) unsalted butter, at room temperature

3 whole eggs minus 1 teaspoon egg white for brushing the top crust

1 teaspoon grated lemon rind

1 extra-large lemon, washed

⅓ cup water

pastry for double crust 9-inch pie (page 173)

granulated sugar and ground cinnamon for sprinkling

Makes 6 servings

Preheat oven to 400°.

In a large bowl, combine sugar, flour, and salt. Beat in butter and eggs (remember to reserve 1 teaspoon egg white for brushing the top crust). Add rind. Using a thin-bladed knife, slice the lemon paper thin, but collect all the juice and remove and discard any seeds. When you get to the end, stop slicing and discard end pieces. Add lemon slices, any collected juice, and water to the bowl. Pour mixture into the bottom crust of an 9-inch pie shell.

Cover with top crust, trim pastry edges and crimp to seal. Cut several decorative vents in the top crust to allow steam to escape. Beat reserved egg white with a fork. Brush over top crust and sprinkle with sugar and cinnamon. Bake for 30 to 35 minutes, until crust is golden and filling bubbling. Cool pie on a rack for at least 2 hours before serving.

Eileen's Lemon Pie

My sister Eileen Ryberg grows lemons in her Phoenix, Arizona, backyard. So prolific are the trees that she gives lemons away to anyone who comes to visit. On my last trip, she made this luscious pie. Her lemons are so huge, she only used one. With store-bought lemons, you'll need two. The lemons need to macerate in sugar for at least 6 hours or overnight, so plan ahead.

Makes
6 to 8
servings

2   *large lemons*
⅔   *cup sugar*
2   *large eggs*
1   *tablespoon grated lemon rind*
1   *9-inch pie crust (see page 173), unbaked*

Working over a large bowl, peel the lemons removing all white pith. Slice the lemons crosswise into ⅛-inch-thick slices, removing any seeds. Place lemon slices in boiling water to cover for 1 minute. Drain well. Make two or three layers of the lemon slices, each layer sprinkled with sugar, in a large bowl. Pour on any lemon juice collected from the peeling and slicing. Cover with plastic wrap and let stand at room temperature for at least 6 hours or overnight.

When ready to bake the pie, preheat oven to 375°. Carefully line the pie crust with aluminum foil, pressing it into the corners and edges. Weigh down with dried beans, raw rice, or aluminum or ceramic pie weights. Bake for 10 to 12 minutes. When pastry begins to color around edges, remove the foil and weights. Continue to bake just until pastry dries out and turns light golden. Let cool completely on a wire rack before filling. Maintain oven temperature.

Using a slotted spoon, carefully lift lemon slices from the bowl. Set aside. Reserve lemon juice.

In a medium bowl and using an electric mixer on medium speed, beat the eggs. Gradually beat in lemon rind and reserved juice. Pour mixture into cooled pie shell and gently place the lemon slices on top, overlapping them slightly. Bake for 25 to 30 minutes at 375°, until the filling is set and the top of the pie is lightly browned. Let cool completely before serving.

Fresh Coconut Cream Pie

A family favorite and very popular in most western homes, this pie is made extra special with the use of fresh coconut. If you don't want the bother of cracking and grating the coconut, buy unsweetened coconut from a natural foods store.

Makes 6 to 8 servings

1   9-inch pie shell (page 173), unbaked
1   cup sugar
½   cup plus 2 teaspoons unbleached all-purpose flour
3   cups milk
2   large egg yolks
2   tablespoons butter
2   teaspoons pure vanilla extract
¾   cup plus 2 tablespoons grated fresh coconut

Meringue

4   egg whites, at room temperature
⅓   cup sugar
⅛   teaspoon salt
½   teaspoon pure vanilla extract

Preheat oven to 425°. Prick the bottom and sides of the pie shell with the tines of a fork. Bake for 10 to 12 minutes, until lightly browned. Set aside to cool.

In a large saucepan, combine sugar and flour. Stir in milk and cook over low heat, stirring constantly, until thick. Add the egg yolks and continue cooking, stirring constantly, for 3 minutes. Remove from heat and blend in butter, vanilla, and ¾ cup coconut. Let cool for 15 minutes, then pour into baked pie shell.

TO MAKE MERINGUE

Using an electric mixer on high speed, beat egg whites until frothy. While beating, add the sugar in a slow, steady stream and continue to beat until whites form stiff peaks. Fold in salt and vanilla. Mound the meringue on top of the pie filling, making sure to seal the edges. Sprinkle remaining 2 tablespoons fresh coconut on top of the meringue.

Turn the oven temperature to broil. Place the pie under the broiler, watching closely, until meringue is lightly browned and coconut is toasted.

How to Open a Coconut

Opening a fresh coconut can be quick and easy. First puncture the eyes at the end of the coconut and drain off the liquid. If you're intending to use the coconut milk, strain the liquid through cheesecloth; otherwise discard the liquid. Then place the coconut in a preheated 350° oven for about 30 minutes. The heating will cause the coconut meat inside to pull away from the shell. Next, place the hot coconut on a hard surface and hit hard with a hammer. Once cracked, you can remove the meat in large pieces that are easy to dice or grate.

Fresh Thimbleberry Pie

Among the most aromatic and intensely flavored of the western berries, raspberries are most plentiful from May through November, although overnight air freight brings them to us from other parts of the world year-round. Unlike blackberries, raspberries will pull away from their core when ripe, creating a hollow center in the berry and making them very fragile. This characteristic explains why raspberries are often nicknamed "thimbleberries." Be careful when handling them because even a quick rinse under water running too fast can damage the fragile berries.

You'll love working with this pastry dough. Half-and-half replaces the traditional water, making the dough easier to handle, a feature particularly helpful when weaving the lattice crust.

Cream Pastry

2⅔ cups unbleached all-purpose flour

½ teaspoon salt

1 cup (2 sticks) cold unsalted butter, cut into small bits

7 to 8 tablespoons very cold half-and-half

Makes 6 to 8 servings

Raspberry Filling

1⅓ cups plus 1 tablespoon sugar

7 tablespoons cornstarch

1 tablespoon grated lemon rind

6 cups fresh raspberries

⅛ teaspoon ground cinnamon

In a large bowl, combine flour and salt. Using a pastry blender or two knives, cut in butter until mixture resembles coarse crumbs. Add the half-and-half, 1 tablespoon at a time, tossing mixture with a fork, just until dough clumps together. Gather the dough with your fingers. Divide in half and form each half into a ball. Wrap in plastic wrap and chill for at least 30 minutes.

Preheat oven to 375°.

On a lightly floured work surface, roll out a pastry ball to form a 12-inch circle. Press pastry circle into a 9-inch pie plate. Roll out remaining pastry ball to ⅛-inch thickness and using a pastry wheel or sharp knife, cut as many lattice strips as possible.

In a large bowl, combine 1⅓ cups sugar, cornstarch, and lemon zest. Add the raspberries and lightly toss to mix. Pile mixture in the prepared bottom crust. Weave lattice strips over the filling and secure the ends by pasting them to the bottom crust with a bit of water. Crimp the edges to seal and bake for 50 to 60 minutes, until pastry is nicely browned and juices bubble. Transfer pie to a rack to cool. Combine remaining 1 tablespoon sugar and cinnamon. Sprinkle over hot pie. Cool before serving.

Lemon Chess Pie

Long revered by Southerners, Lemon Chess Pie is a favorite in Texas for the Thanksgiving to New Year's holidays. The bakery department of grocery stores are filled with pies to purchase and you're sure to be served the pie at least once at holiday parties. My recipe comes from my late aunt Kathleen Towner, a grand lady, born and bred in Dallas, after whom I got my middle name.

1   10-inch pie shell (page 173), partially baked
6   large egg yolks
¾   cup sugar
6   tablespoons (¾ stick) unsalted butter, at room temperature
¼   cup heavy cream
1   tablespoon fresh lemon juice
1   teaspoon finely grated lemon rind
    whipped cream (optional)

Makes 8 servings

Preheat oven to 325°. Cool partially baked pie shell. Set aside.

In a large bowl, beat the yolks, sugar, and softened butter until smooth. Beat in the cream, lemon juice, and lemon peel. Pour batter into prepared pie shell.

Bake for about 30 minutes, until filling is set and golden brown. Watch carefully during the last of the baking period. If top becomes too brown, cover with a loose sheet of aluminum foil. Cook in pan on a rack. Serve warm or at room temperature with whipped cream, if desired.

Mango Meringue Pie in Coconut Crust

Mangoes are a Texas favorite—often on special at the supermarket, five for a dollar. Mango tarts often appear on the dessert carts at Hawaiian restaurants. Here I've used them in a lush pie topped with meringue and baked in a coconut crust.

Coconut Crust

Makes 8 to 10 servings

½   *cup (1 stick) cold unsalted butter, cut into 8 pieces*
¼   *cup superfine sugar*
1   *cup unbleached all-purpose flour*
¼   *cup flaked unsweetened coconut*
⅛   *teaspoon salt*
1   *large egg, lightly beaten*

Mango Filling

2   *tablespoons cornstarch*
¾   *cup water*
2   *tablespoons fresh lemon juice*
2   *large eggs*
4   *large egg yolks*
3   *large ripe mangoes, peeled and diced*
¼   *cup (½ stick) unsalted butter*
½   *cup superfine sugar*

Meringue

5   *large egg whites, at room temperature*
½   *cup superfine sugar*
    pinch cream of tartar
    pinch salt

In a food processor fitted with the metal blade, pulse butter and sugar for about 10 seconds, until the sugar disappears. Add the flour, coconut, and salt. Pulse until small particles form, about the size of tiny peas. Add half of the beaten egg (about 1½ tablespoons) and pulse until just incorporated, about 5 seconds. Discard unused egg.

Transfer mixture to a large self-sealing plastic bag (at this point, the dough will still be quite crumbly). Close the bag and, using your fingers, press the dough together until it forms a smooth dough. Form into a 6-inch disk and put in freezer for 10 minutes.

Preheat oven to 400°. Using your fingers, pat and press the dough evenly over the bottom and sides of a 9-inch pie plate, bringing the crust up and over the outer edge of the pie plate. Prick the bottom and sides with the tines of a fork. Line the pie shell with aluminum foil and fill with pie weights, dried beans, or raw rice. Bake for 15 minutes. Carefully remove pie weights and foil. Continue to bake until crust is golden, about 10 to 15 minutes. If dough puffs up, prick again with a fork. Remove from oven and cool in the pan on a rack. Reduce oven temperature to 375°.

TO MAKE FILLING

In a medium bowl, whisk together the cornstarch, ¼ cup water, and lemon juice. Whisk in eggs and egg yolks. Set aside.

In a food processor, puree mango and remaining ½ cup water to a smooth puree. Transfer mango puree to a heavy nonreactive saucepan and bring to a boil over medium heat. While whisking, add ½ cup of the hot mango puree to the cornstarch-egg mixture. Return the mixture to the saucepan and cook, whisking constantly, over medium heat, until mixture coats the back of a wooden spoon, about 5 minutes. Pour mixture into prepared pie shell and cover with plastic wrap to keep it hot.

TO MAKE MERINGUE

In a large bowl and using an electric mixer, whip egg whites until they form soft peaks. While whipping, gradually add sugar, salt, and cream of tartar. Whip until egg whites form stiff peaks.

Spread meringue over hot filling, making sure the meringue touches the crust to completely seal in the filling. If desired, pull up peaks of the meringue as you work. Bake for 15 minutes, until most of the meringue is golden.

Margarita Pie

In the West, we love margaritas and are always looking for ways to incorporate the distinctive flavor into other dishes—chicken and fish, salad dressings, and desserts. This pie is a good example; the pretzel crust adds the necessary kick of salt. A food processor makes quick work of preparing the pretzel crumbs.

Pretzel Crust

Makes 8 to 10 servings

1   *cup plus 2 tablespoons pretzel crumbs*
½   *cup (1 stick) unsalted butter, melted*
1½ *tablespoons packed light brown sugar*

Margarita Filling

¾   *cup fresh lime juice*
1   *envelope unflavored gelatin*
3   *large egg yolks*
⅔   *cup plus 3 tablespoons granulated sugar*
¼   *cup gold tequila*
2   *tablespoons Triple Sec, Cointreau or other orange liqueur*
½   *tablespoon grated lime rind*
2   *tablespoons pasteurized dried egg whites, reconstituted in 6 tablespoons warm water or ½ cup pasteurized liquid egg whites (see page 6)*
½   *cup heavy cream*

In a small bowl, combine 1 cup pretzel crumbs, melted butter, and brown sugar. Toss with a fork. Press the crumbs into a 10-inch pie plate. Refrigerate until firm.

Meanwhile, place ¼ cup lime juice in a small bowl. Sprinkle gelatin over juice and let stand for 5 minutes to soften. In a heavy saucepan, combine remaining lime juice, egg yolks, ⅔ cup sugar, tequila, Cointreau, and lime rind. Bring to a simmer over medium-low heat, stirring constantly. Remove from heat and add the gelatin-lime mixture, stirring until gelatin is dissolved. Chill mixture in the refrigerator for about 20 minutes, stirring occasionally, until syrupy and just starting to set.

In a mixing bowl, stir dried egg whites into warm water until completely dissolved, about 2 minutes, or pour in the liquid egg whites. Beat with an electric mixer on medium-high speed until egg whites form soft peaks. Gradually add remaining 3 tablespoons sugar and beat until stiff but not dry. In a large bowl, whip cream to soft peaks. Stir one-fourth of the lime mixture into the cream to lighten it. Carefully fold in remaining lime mixture and whipped egg whites. Spoon mixture into chilled crust.

Refrigerate until set, at least 3 hours. Just before serving, sprinkle top with remaining pretzel crumbs. Cut into wedges to serve.

Mile-High Apple Pie

Although more than half of the apples grown in the United States come from Washington, apple orchards thrive in scattered areas in all of the western states, from Oregon to the western plains of Texas. I love this pie with its loads of apples and a fragrant hint of orange.

Serve the pie warm with a wedge of Tillamook cheese, an aged cheddar from Oregon. Since Tillamook is sometimes hard to find outside of the West, you can substitute a Wisconsin, Canadian, or English cheddar.

Orange-Scented Pastry

Makes 8 to 10 servings

2	cups unbleached all-purpose flour
½	teaspoon salt
¼	teaspoon sugar
2	teaspoons grated orange rind
½	cup (1 stick) cold unsalted butter, cut into 8 pieces
	up to 5 tablespoons ice water

Apple Filling

3	pounds apples—Granny Smith, Jonathan, McIntosh, Winesap, or Golden Delicious
2	teaspoons grated orange rind
1	tablespoon fresh orange juice
¾	cup sugar
⅓	cup unbleached all-purpose flour
1	teaspoon ground cinnamon
1	teaspoon ground nutmeg
1	tablespoon unsalted butter
1	large egg
	Tillamook cheddar cheese, cut into thin wedges for garnish (optional)

In a food processor fitted with the metal blade or in a mixing bowl using a pastry blender, combine flour, salt, sugar, and orange rind. Cut butter into flour mixture, using the pulse motion or pastry blender. Add water, 1 tablespoon at a time, tossing with a fork, until dough just holds together. Divide the dough into two discs, one slightly larger than the other. Wrap in plastic wrap and refrigerate for at least 1 hour.

When ready to bake, preheat oven to 375°. Adjust oven rack to the middle position.

Peel, core, and slice the apples into a large bowl. Add orange rind and orange juice. Sprinkle the apples with the flour, sugar, cinnamon, and nutmeg. Toss to combine.

Working on a lightly floured work surface, roll out the large disc of dough to a 12-inch round and fit it into a 9-inch pie pan. Pile the apple filling into the pie crust, mounding slightly in the center. Dot apples with butter.

Roll out the remaining dough and place over the apples. Trim pastry to within ½ inch of pan rim and fold edges under, flush to the rim. Flute edges to seal or press together, then scallop with the bottom side of a teaspoon.

Combine pastry scraps and roll out. Cut into decorative shapes. In a small bowl, beat egg with a fork to blend well. Brush egg lightly over top of the pie, place decorative pastry pieces on pie, and brush them lightly with the egg. Slash pastry in several places so steam can vent. Bake until crust is a rich golden brown, about 45 to 55 minutes. Cool on a rack, then serve warm with a thin wedge of cheese.

Millionaire Pie

This is a recipe that dates back to the 1950s when the Wyatt Cafeterias in Fort Worth served this luscious, creamy dessert to the after-church crowds that swamped the cafeteria each Sunday. Most of the cafeterias have since closed, but the memory of the pie lives on.

Makes 6 to 8 servings

1   8-ounce package cream of cheese, softened
½   cup plus 3 tablespoons sugar
1   8-ounce can crushed pineapple, with juice
1   cup grated coconut
1   cup chopped pecans
2   cups cold heavy whipping cream
1   10-inch graham cracker crust (page 33), unbaked

In a large bowl and using an electric mixer, cream together the softened cream cheese and sugar. Beat on high speed for 3 to 4 minutes. Using a wooden spoon, stir in crushed pineapple, coconut, and pecans. Mix well.

In a metal bowl, beat whipping cream with an electric mixer until foamy. Gradually add sugar and continue to whip until cream holds soft peaks. Stir one-third of the whipped cream into the cream cheese mixture to lighten it. Fold in remaining whipped cream. Transfer mixture to prepared pie crust, smoothing the top with the back of a spoon. Chill for at least 4 hours before serving.

Ninnie's Fried Pies

A grand Texas lady, now approaching her 100th birthday, Ninnie Sanders greeted afternoon callers in her Texas parlor with these sweet pies and a steaming pot or iced pitcher of tea. The origin of these pies comes from the canning season when fresh peaches were put up for canning. As tradition has it, nothing was wasted. The peelings were cooked and used to make these pies while the peaches were canned for using during the winter. Here, I've used fresh apples; for variety at another time, use fresh peaches (but I'd toss the peelings). To keep the fat grams down, I've baked the pies, instead of frying them in hot vegetable oil or melted lard.

Crust

3   cups sifted unbleached all-purpose flour

2   tablespoons sugar

1   teaspoon salt

1   cup solid shortening

6 to 7 tablespoons ice water

Makes 8 small pies

Filling

½   pound tart cooking apples, peeled, cored, and diced

½   cup sugar

1   tablespoon flour

½   cup water

grated rind of 1 lemon

¼   cup coarsely chopped walnuts

¼   cup raisins (optional)

1   teaspoon ground cinnamon

whole milk

Preheat oven to 400°. Lightly grease a large baking sheet.

In a medium bowl, combine flour, sugar, and salt. Using a pastry blender or two knives, cut in shortening until mixture resembles small crumbs. Add ice water, 1 tablespoon at a time, stirring with a fork just until mixture forms a ball. Divide dough into eight equal portions. Place each portion on a well-floured work surface and press or roll out to form a 6-inch circle.

Meanwhile, in a large saucepan, combine apples, sugar, flour, and water. Bring to a boil, reduce heat, and simmer for 5 minutes. Remove from heat and stir in lemon rind, walnuts, raisins (if using), and cinnamon. Moisten the edge of each circle with a little milk. Place about 2 heaping tablespoons of the apple mixture near the enter of each circle of dough. Fold dough over filling making a half circle. Press edges of dough together and seal, marking the edge with the tines of a fork. Place the filled pies on the prepared baking sheet. Brush the top of each pie with additional milk. Cut a small vent in the top of each pie.

Bake 20 minutes, until crust is golden brown. Let cool for at least 15 minutes before serving.

Oatmeal Pie

This unusual pie recipe comes from Billie Brown, a native Texan from Kennedale. She's been making this pie for almost 40 years, and up to now, wouldn't give out the recipe, even to family members. Try it—it tastes very much like pecan pie.

⅔ cup sugar

½ cup (1 stick) unsalted butter, at room temperature

⅔ cup dark corn syrup

2 large eggs, lightly beaten

⅔ cup rolled oats

1 teaspoon pure vanilla extract

1 9-inch pie shell (page 173), unbaked

Makes 6 to 8 servings

Preheat oven to 325°.

In a large bowl, cream together sugar and butter until mixture is light and fluffy. Beat in corn syrup and eggs, mixing well. Stir in rolled oats and vanilla. Pour into pie shell.

Bake for 40 minutes, until filling is set. Remove from oven and cool on a rack. Serve at room temperature.

Strawberry-Rhubarb Pie

This is a delicious pie to make during the all-too-short fresh rhubarb season. Commercially, rhubarb is grown in Oregon and Washington. Hopefully, when rhubarb is in the stores, the first of the fresh spring strawberries from California are also available.

Makes 8 to 10 servings

1	*10-inch pie shell (page 173), partially baked*
1	*large egg white, lightly beaten*
4	*large eggs*
1	*cup sugar*
2	*teaspoons pure vanilla extract*
1	*tablespoon cornstarch*
4	*cups sliced fresh strawberries*
1	*pound fresh rhubarb, peeled, halved lengthwise and sliced*
⅓	*cup red currant jelly*

Preheat oven to 375°. Brush inside of partially baked pie crust with egg white. Set aside.

In large bowl, whisk together eggs, sugar, vanilla extract, and cornstarch. Stir in strawberries and rhubarb. Transfer mixture to prepared pie shell and bake 45 to 50 minutes, until filling is set.

Remove from oven and cool on a rack.

While pie is still warm, heat jelly in a small saucepan, stirring until jelly melts. Brush over top of the pie filling. Serve warm.

Note: If using frozen rhubarb, thaw and drain well. Increase cornstarch to 2 tablespoons.

Sweet Cherry-Almond Pie

California's climate in the San Joaquin and coastal valley regions of Hollister and Gilroy produces bountiful harvests of sweet cherries—Bing, Rainier, Lambert, and Vans—making California one of the top three cherry producing states. Here, I've combined plump Bing cherries with California almonds in a pie that's sure to satisfy everyone's "sweet tooth."

The cherries are easily pitted with an inexpensive gadget called a cherry (or olive) pitter, available at most cookware stores and some supermarkets.

⅔ cup blanched almonds

⅓ cup sugar

¼ cup (½ stick) unsalted butter, at room temperature

2 large eggs

1 tablespoon unbleached all-purpose flour

1 tablespoon brandy

2½ cups pitted Bing cherries, about 1¼ pounds

1 9-inch pastry shell (page 173), unbaked and chilled

Makes 8 servings

Cherry Sauce

½ cup currant jelly

1½ tablespoons brandy

Vanilla Ice Cream (page 252)

Preheat oven to 400°.

Place the almonds and sugar in the workbowl of a food processor fitted with the metal blade. Process until almonds are finely ground. Add the butter, eggs, flour, and brandy. Process until smooth.

Pour the mixture into the chilled pastry shell. Set aside ½ cup pitted cherries. Arrange remaining cherries on top of the almond filling. Bake until filling is set, about 40 minutes. Remove from oven and place on a rack to cool.

Just before serving, heat the jelly in a small saucepan until melted and bubbly. Stir in reserved cherries and brandy. Cook, stirring, for 1 minute. Serve the pie at room temperature, topped with a scoop of ice cream and some of the hot cherry sauce.

Sweet Potato Pie

Golden, Texas, is in the middle of sweet potato land and each fall celebrates the new harvest with a Sweet Potato Festival. This pie, made by the mother-daughter team of Sheila and Amanda Parker, has been a blue-ribbon winner in their baking contest. It's different from other sweet potato pies because it has beaten egg whites baked in, giving the pie a light texture and a delicious, mild flavor.

Makes 6 to 8 servings

4   tablespoons (½ stick) unsalted butter
½   cup sugar
3   large eggs, separated
½   teaspoon ground cinnamon
2   cups mashed cooked sweet potatoes
1   cup whole milk
1   9-inch pie shell (recipe, page 173), unbaked

Preheat oven to 350°.

In a large bowl, cream together butter and sugar. Beat in egg yolks and cinnamon. Stir in sweet potatoes and milk.

In a separate bowl, beat egg whites until they form stiff peaks. Gently stir one-third of the beaten egg whites into the sweet potato mixture to lighten it. Fold in remaining beaten egg whites and pour mixture into unbaked pie shell. Bake for 40 minutes, until done when a tester is inserted near the middle comes out clean.

Sweet Tamales
with Crème Fraîche

While tamales are a staple in many Texas homes, during the Christmas season Sweet Tamales are often served at holiday parties and pot luck suppers. Although a diehard tamale maker would never use anything but lard, I've found that butter also works well, giving the tamale a rich, buttery flavor.

1	8-ounce package dried corn husks
1	pound masa harina
1	teaspoon baking powder
1½	teaspoons ground cinnamon
¼	teaspoon salt
½	cup (1 stick) butter or lard, softened
½	cup sugar
½	cup milk, at room temperature
¼	cup dark raisins
¼	cup chopped dried figs
¾	cup coarsely chopped pecans
	Crème Fraîche (page 156)

Makes 6 servings

Rinse corn husks and soak in warm water for several hours until completely flexible.

In a large bowl, combine masa harina, baking powder, cinnamon, and salt. In another large bowl and using an electric mixer, cream butter until light and fluffy, about 1 minute. Add the sugar and half of the masa mixture. Beat well. Add remaining masa mixture, alternating with milk, beginning and ending with masa mixture. Continue to beat until mixture has the consistency of thick batter.

Lay 12 of the largest, most perfect corn husks on a work surface (or overlap 2 or 3 smaller ones to form a surface about 3 inches wide). Pat the husks dry with a kitchen towel. Cut a few of the husks into strips to makes ties for the tamales. Using the back of a spoon, spread about ⅓ cup of the batter in the center of each husk. For each tamale, scatter 1 teaspoon of the raisins and 1 teaspoon of the dried figs on the spread batter. Top with 1 tablespoon pecans. Fold sides of each husk over the filling, then fold the ends of each husk to enclose the filling. Tie closed with the prepared husk strips. (May be made ahead to this point and refrigerated.)

TO STEAM TAMALES

Use a tamale steamer or large pot with a rack or colander in the bottom. Fill the pot with water to a depth of 1 inch (water should not touch rack). Line the rack with some of the remaining corn husks. Arrange the tamales on the husk-covered rack. Top with more corn husks or a clean kitchen towel. Steam over simmering water for about 2½ hours, until the husks can be easily pulled away from the filling and the tamales retain their shape.

Let cool slightly, then serve two to a person with a dollop of Crème Fraîche.

Note: Tamales may be steamed ahead of time and refrigerated. Reheat in a steamer or wrap in aluminum foil and reheat in a 300° oven for 25 to 30 minutes.

Terrific Pecan Pie

Pecan pie is a family tradition at holiday dinners and special celebrations. For years, I've made the traditional recipe on the back of the bottle of corn syrup. But last year, alas, I forgot to buy the needed syrup so used maple syrup instead. The results were spectacular, proving that old adage that great things *can* come out of adversity. Of course, the Texas-grown pecans from my neighbor's grove also had a lot to do with the end result.

Whole pecans look lovely arranged on the top, but they make it difficult to cut a pretty slice. I chop most of the pecans, using 12 whole pecans arranged equidistant apart around the outer edge of the pie so that the slice cuts nicely with a whole pecan in the center of each piece.

4	large eggs
¾	cup pure maple syrup
1	cup packed light brown sugar
1	teaspoon vanilla extract
½	cup (1 stick) unsalted butter, melted
1½	cups chopped pecans
1	10-inch pastry crust (page 173), unbaked and chilled
12	whole pecans
	Vanilla Ice Cream (page 252) or whipped cream (optional)

Makes 12 servings

Preheat oven to 350°.

In a large bowl, whisk the eggs. Add maple syrup, brown sugar, and vanilla extract. Whisk to combine well. Gradually whisk in butter. Stir in chopped pecans. Pour mixture into prepared pastry crust. Garnish the top with whole pecans arranged around the edge.

Bake for 50 to 60 minutes, until filling is set and a knife inserted near the center comes out clean. Cool on a rack before slicing. Serve warm with ice cream or at room temperature with whipped cream.

Tiny Mincemeat Pies

The Hill Country of central Texas was predominately settled by Germans. Particularly in Fredericksburg and New Braunfels, German bakeries abound, filled with luscious pies, tarts, cookies, and cakes. Especially during the Thanksgiving to New Year's holiday, many of these bakeries offer tiny mincemeat pies, reflecting the influence of the English who also immigrated to the area. A spicy relish made from fruits, spices, and other savory ingredients, today's mincemeat no longer contains any form of meat. You can buy jars of excellent commercially prepared mincemeat in most supermarkets.

*Makes
12 pies*

2½ cups unbleached all-purpose flour
½ teaspoon salt
⅓ cup cold butter, cut into small pieces
⅓ cup cold solid shortening
6 to 7 tablespoons whole milk
2 cups prepared mincemeat
2 tablespoons bourbon, brandy, or fresh orange juice
  powdered sugar

In a medium bowl, combine flour and salt. Using a pastry blender or two knives, cut in butter and shortening until mixture resembles coarse crumbs. Add milk, 1 tablespoon at a time, tossing mixture with a fork, until dry ingredients are evenly moistened.

On a lightly floured work surface, roll out dough to ⅛-inch thickness. Cut into 24 circles using a 3-inch cookie cutter. Press half of the circles into 12 lightly greased 2-inch tart pans and trim edges.

In a bowl, combine mincemeat and bourbon. Spoon mixture evenly into prepared pie shells. Using a tiny canapé cutter or a sharp knife, cut a tiny star or other decorative shape in the center of the remaining pastry circles. Top each pie with a pastry circle, crimping the edges to seal. Place pies on a baking sheet.

Preheat oven to 400°. Bake for 20 minutes or until pastry is golden. Loosen pies from pans and cool on a rack. Using a fine sieve, sprinkle powdered sugar over pies just before serving.

Walnut Raisin Pie

I've been fond of raisin pie since my early childhood, but it wasn't until I had a slice of a raisin pie made with walnuts in the Fredericksburg area of the Texas Hill Country that I knew what my mother's raisin pie recipe was lacking. Raisins and walnuts are fine by themselves, but together, they are a taste from heaven.

1 cup dark raisins

1 cup coarsely chopped walnuts

1 9-inch pie shell (page 173), unbaked

5 large eggs

1½ cups sugar

1 teaspoon ground cinnamon

½ teaspoon ground allspice

½ teaspoon ground nutmeg

¼ teaspoon ground mace

3 tablespoons fresh lemon juice

3 tablespoons half-and-half

1 teaspoon finely grated lemon rind

Makes 8 servings

Preheat oven to 350°.

Evenly spread raisins and walnuts in the bottom of the unbaked pie shell.

In a medium bowl, whisk eggs until light and lemon-colored. Whisk in sugar and spices. Stir in lemon juice, half-and-half, and lemon rind. Pour mixture over the raisin-walnut mixture. Bake for 50 minutes, until a tester inserted in the center comes out clean.

Cool on a rack before cutting into wedges. Serve warm.

Warm Pineapple Pie with Butter-Rum Sauce

On our first day in Honolulu, we took a taxi to the Aloha Tower, where we dined on locally caught fish at a superb restaurant. Dessert was a delicious lattice-crust pie made with fresh pineapple and a buttery rum sauce. In a hurry to meet our pilot for a helicopter ride over the island, I neglected to get the recipe, but this is close to that fabulous pie.

Makes 8 servings

Cream Pastry for a 2-crust pie (pages 185–186)

1   medium fresh pineapple, peeled, cored, and cut into ½-inch chunks
¼   cup packed light brown sugar
3   tablespoons cornstarch
2   tablespoons unsalted butter, melted
⅓   cup chopped macadamia nuts
½   teaspoon ground cinnamon
¼   teaspoon ground nutmeg
1   teaspoon grated orange rind
1   tablespoon dark rum

Butter-Rum Sauce

½   cup (1 stick) unsalted butter
1   cup packed light brown sugar
½   cup dark rum
⅛   teaspoon ground allspice
⅛   teaspoon ground cinnamon
⅛   teaspoon ground nutmeg

Preheat oven to 375°.

On a lightly floured work surface, roll out a pastry ball to form a 12-inch circle. Press pastry circle into a 9-inch pie plate. Roll out remaining pastry ball to ⅛ inch thickness and using a pastry wheel or sharp knife, cut as many lattice strips as possible.

In a large bowl, toss the pineapple chunks with the brown sugar, cornstarch, melted butter, macadamia nuts, cinnamon, nutmeg, orange rind, and rum. Pile mixture in the prepared bottom crust. Weave lattice strips over the filling and secure the ends by pasting them to the bottom crust with a bit of water. Crimp the edges to seal and bake for 50 to 60 minutes, until pastry is nicely browned and juices bubble. Transfer pie to a rack to cool.

TO MAKE SAUCE

In a small saucepan, cook butter, sugar, rum, and spices over medium heat, stirring constantly until butter is melted and sugar dissolves. Reduce heat and simmer, uncovered for about 10 minutes, stirring occasionally, until sauce thickens and coats the back of a wooden spoon. Keep warm.

To serve, slice the still-warm pie and spoon some of the sauce over one side of the pie. Serve at once.

Yakima Valley Apple Pie with Cinnamon-Scented Crust

The beautiful Yakima Valley, nestled in Washington's Cascade Mountain range, has the ideal growing conditions for exceptional apples: sunny days and cool nights, plenty of irrigation water, and rich volcanic soil.

Here, a delicious cinnamon-scented crust encloses a splendid apple filling with currants, another Yakima crop. The currants should soak overnight, so plan ahead.

Makes 6 to 8 servings

½   cup dried currants, soaked in 3 tablespoons Cognac, brandy, or orange juice

Cinnamon-Scented Pastry

2½ cups unbleached all-purpose flour

¼   cup firmly packed light brown sugar

1   teaspoon ground cinnamon

1   teaspoon salt

½   cup (1 stick) chilled unsalted butter, cut into 8 pieces

½   cup chilled solid vegetable shortening, cut into pieces
     about 6 tablespoons ice water

Apple and Currant Filling

9   medium-size firm baking apples such as Granny Smith, Golden Delicious, Rome Beauty, or Winesap, peeled, cored, and thinly sliced

2   tablespoons unbleached all-purpose flour

⅓   cup granulated sugar

1   tablespoon grated lemon rind

2   tablespoons unsalted butter, cut into small pieces

The night before, combine the currants and Cognac. Cover and refrigerate overnight or for at least 6 hours. Set aside.

FOR PASTRY

Blend flour, sugar, cinnamon, and salt in a food processor fitted with the metal blade. Add the butter and solid shortening and process for about 10 seconds, until mixture resembles coarse crumbs. While motor is running, add water through the feed tube, 1 tablespoon at a time, until mixture forms moist clumps. Gather dough into a ball; divide in half. Form each half into a flattened disk. Wrap in plastic wrap and chill for a least 1 hour or overnight.

Preheat oven to 400°. Lightly flour a work surface and roll out one disk to a 12-inch circle. Transfer dough to a 9-inch pie plate. Roll out the remaining pastry and with a very sharp knife, make three small X-shaped vents. Place the top pastry on a parchment-lined baking sheet and chill.

TO MAKE FILLING

In a large bowl, combine the soaked currants with their liquid and the apples. Combine the flour, sugar, and lemon zest. Add to the apple mixture and stir gently to combine.

Transfer the apple mixture to the prepared bottom crust. Dot the apples with the butter. Carefully cover the apples with the top crust, trim the overhang, and crimp the edges to seal.

Bake for 45 to 50 minutes, until pastry is nicely browned and the juices in the pie are bubbling. Let pie cool slightly on a wire rack before cutting into wedges to serve.

Apricot and Berry Tart

Simple fruit desserts often end a western meal, especially when the meal before has been substantial. When fresh apricots are in the stores, I can't resist them, despite their sometimes high price. Here apricots are teamed with fresh berries—whatever's "best in the market"—for a simple, homey dessert. As common with many western cooks, I've replaced some of the flour for the tart with yellow cornmeal for an interesting change in flavor and texture.

To be at their best, apricots must be picked when ripe, and thereby when most fragile, which is why less than ten percent of the 24,000 acres of apricots grown in California's San Joaquin Valley is shipped fresh. Apricots should be plump and fully colored. Gently squeeze one or ask your produce man to let you sample one before buying.

Makes 6 servings

1   pound fresh apricots, pitted and cut into quarters
1   cup berries—raspberries, blueberries, blackberries, or a mix
½   cup sugar
¾   cup unbleached all-purpose flour
½   cup yellow cornmeal
¼   teaspoon salt
6   tablespoons (¾ stick) cold unsalted butter, cut into 6 pieces
1   large egg yolk
½   teaspoon almond extract
     softly whipped cream for garnish (optional)

Preheat oven to 400°. Lightly butter an 8-inch square baking pan.

In a medium bowl, toss the apricots, berries, and 2 tablespoon of the sugar. Set aside.

In a food processor fitted with the metal blade, combine flour, cornmeal, 5 tablespoons of the sugar, salt, butter, egg yolk, and almond extract. Pulse until dough begins to clump together. Using your fingers, press dough evenly onto the bottom and up the sides of the prepared pan. Bake until golden and slightly puffy, about 15 minutes. Remove from oven and gently flatten the dough against the bottom and sides of the pan with the back of a spoon. Reduce oven temperature to 350°.

Pile apricot-berry mixture in the partially baked crust. Bake 35 to 40 minutes, until apricots are tender. Remove from oven and immediately sprinkle with remaining tablespoon of sugar. Cool in pan on a rack until ready to serve warm.

If desired, serve with a spoon or two of softly whipped cream.

Blood Orange Tart

Once imported from Europe, these bright red-fleshed, sweet-tart oranges are now being grown commercially in southern Texas. Thinly sliced, they make a beautiful tart.

4	large eggs, lightly beaten
1	cup sugar
⅔	cup fresh blood orange juice
⅓	cup fresh lemon juice
1	teaspoon finely grated blood orange rind
1	teaspoon finely grated lemon rind
¼	cup heavy cream
2	whole blood oranges
1	9-inch pie shell (page 173), partially baked

Makes 6 to 8 servings

Preheat oven to 375°.

In a large bowl, whisk together the eggs and sugar until light and fluffy. Whisk in blood orange juice and lemon juice. Stir in citrus rind and cream. Set aside.

Peel blood oranges, removing peel and all white pith. Using a serrated bread knife, thinly slice the oranges crosswise into almost transparent slices. Drain thoroughly on paper towels for at least 20 minutes, turning over once.

Pour egg-cream mixture into pie shell. Top with the blood orange slices arranged in concentric circles. Bake for 25 to 30 minutes, until filling is set and pastry golden brown. Cool before serving.

Buñuelos with
Vanilla Ice Cream and Cajeta

Buñuelos, pieces of fried dough formed into the shape of small baskets, often appear on the menu of a Texas barbecue, reflecting the strong Mexican influence of much of Texas' traditional foods. Here, the rich buñuelos are served with Vanilla Ice Cream and Cajeta, a Mexican caramel sauce made from goat's milk. Most health food stores sell goat's milk, or you can use heavy cream for a slightly milder flavor.

Makes 12
servings

2   *cups unbleached all-purpose flour*
½   *teaspoon baking powder*
½   *teaspoon salt*
2   *large eggs, lightly beaten*
¼   *cup (½ stick) butter, softened*
¼   *cup hot water*
2   *cups canola oil for deep-fat frying*
¼   *cup sugar*
½   *tablespoon cinnamon*
1   *quart Vanilla Ice Cream (page 252)*
    Cajeta (pages 149–150, 212)

Onto a piece of waxed paper, sift together flour, baking powder, and salt. In a large bowl, combine eggs, butter, and water. Stir in as much of the flour mixture as can be absorbed to form a stiff dough. Turn out onto a floured work surface and knead until smooth and silky. Divide the dough into quarters. Then divide each quarter into 6 balls the same size. Roll each ball out to a circle 4 to 5 inches in diameter. Cover dough circles with plastic wrap to prevent drying out.

In a large pot, slowly heat oil to 365° on a deep-frying thermometer. Meanwhile, combine the sugar and cinnamon. Fry each buñuelo until crisp and golden brown, about 30 to 45 seconds, turning once. Lift buñuelos out of the oil with tongs, allowing excess oil to drip back into the pot. Drain buñuelos on several layers of paper towels and lightly dust with cinnamon sugar. Repeat until all dough is fried. Keep warm.

To serve, arrange two still warm buñuelos on each of 12 dessert plates. Add a scoop or two of Vanilla Ice Cream and top with Cajeta.

California Dried Fruit Tart

When fresh fruit is not in season, creative western cooks substitute dried. Here, the best of the dried harvest is served in a luscious tart over a lemon-scented cream cheese base.

Sweet Tart Pastry

1½ cups unbleached all-purpose flour

¼   teaspoon salt

3   tablespoons sugar

10 tablespoons (1¼ sticks) chilled unsalted butter, cut into 10 pieces

1   large egg yolk

1½ to 3 tablespoons water

Makes 8 to 10 servings

Filling

½   cup dried apricots, cut into thin strips

½   cup dried figs, sliced

½   cup golden raisins

¼   cup dried currants

1   tablespoon granulated sugar

3   tablespoons fresh lemon juice

1   cup coarsely chopped walnuts, toasted

¼   cup apple jelly

8   ounces cream cheese, at room temperature

3   tablespoons sugar

2   large eggs

1   teaspoon grated lemon rind

2   tablespoons powdered sugar

In a food processor fitted with the metal blade, combine flour, salt, and sugar. Add butter and pulse with rapid on/off motion until mixture resembles coarse crumbs. In a small bowl, whisk together the egg yolk and 1 tablespoon water. With motor running, add the egg mixture through the feed tube. Stop the machine and gather dough into a clump. If too dry to hold together, add additional water, ½ tablespoon at a time, until dough forms a ball.

Using your fingers, pat the dough evenly into the bottom and up the sides of a 10-tart pan, leaving no gaps and making it as even as you can. Chill tart shell until ready to fill.

In a bowl, combine apricots, figs, raisins, currants, sugar, and 2 tablespoons lemon juice. Cover and let sit at room temperature overnight. Next day, stir in walnuts.

Preheat oven to 350°.

In a small saucepan, stir jelly over low heat until it melts. Brush over the bottom and inside sides of the prepared tart shell.

In a medium bowl and using an electric mixer, beat together cream cheese and sugar. Beat in eggs, remaining tablespoon lemon juice, and lemon rind. Fold in reserved fruit-nut mixture. Pour the mixture into the prepared tart shell and bake for 10 minutes. Sift powdered sugar over the tart and continue to bake for another 10 to 15 minutes, until filling is set. Serve warm.

Date and Pecan Tart

Date palms thrive in the hot deserts of Southern Arizona and Southern California, brought to the region from the Middle East at the turn of the century. This tart is particularly rich, so a small slice will suffice. However, don't neglect to spoon a puff of whipped cream onto each slice to hold a perfect date.

8   ounces pitted dates, coarsely chopped
6   tablespoons (¾ stick) unsalted butter
¾   cup packed light brown sugar
1   teaspoon ground cinnamon
¼   teaspoon ground ginger
⅓   cup fresh orange juice
1   teaspoon grated orange rind
2   cups pecan halves, toasted
2   tablespoons cornstarch
3   large eggs
¼   cup evaporated milk
1   9-inch pie shell (page 173), unbaked

Makes 10 to 12 servings

Garnish

sweetened whipped cream (optional)
10 pitted dates for garnish (optional)

In a small saucepan, combine dates, 2 tablespoons butter, 2 tablespoons brown sugar, cinnamon, ginger, orange juice, and orange rind. Bring to a boil; reduce heat and simmer, uncovered, until very thick, about 15 minutes. Set aside to cool.

Preheat oven to 350°. In a food processor fitted with the metal blade or nut grinder, process pecans to a fine powder. Set aside.

In a large bowl, cream together remaining butter and remaining brown sugar until light and fluffy. Beat in cornstarch. Add eggs, one at a time, beating well after each addition. Stir in the milk, ground pecans, and the cooled date mixture.

Pour mixture into pie shell. Bake for 35 to 40 minutes, until filling is set. Remove from oven and cool on a rack for at least 20 minutes before slicing. If desired, top each slice with a dollop of whipped cream and a date.

Dried Peach Turnovers

A lot of the California commercial peach crop ends up being canned or dried. Here I've used dried peaches (they're available at many supermarkets and natural food stores) in a sweet filling for small dessert turnovers, similar to the *empanaditas,* the little filled pies sold by vendors in the Mexican border towns of Texas, Arizona, and California.

Peach Filling

Makes about 2 dozen

- 1 pound dried peaches, coarsely chopped
- 1 cup water
- ½ cup sugar
- ¼ teaspoon ground cinnamon
- ⅓ cup chopped pine nuts

Crust

- 2 cups unbleached all-purpose flour
- 1 teaspoon salt
- ⅔ cup chilled solid vegetable shortening
- 4 to 5 tablespoons cold water
- 1 large egg, separated

Place peaches, water, and sugar in a medium saucepan. Place over medium-high heat and bring to a boil. Stir until sugar dissolves. Reduce heat and simmer until peaches are very soft and start to break down, 20 to 25 minutes. If necessary, add a little more water. Remove from heat, and stir in cinnamon and pine nuts. Allow mixture to cool to room temperature.

Preheat oven to 400°. Line a large baking sheet with parchment paper.

TO MAKE CRUST

In a large bowl, combine flour and salt. Using a pastry blender or two knives, cut shortening into flour mixture until it forms coarse crumbs. Add water, 1 tablespoon at a time, tossing mixture with a fork, until dough holds together. Gather dough into a ball. Wrap in plastic wrap and chill for 15 minutes.

Meanwhile, beat egg yolk with 1 tablespoon water. Set aside. In a separate bowl, beat egg white.

Working on a floured surface, roll dough out to ¼ inch thickness. Using a cookie or biscuit cutter, cut into circles that are 2½ inches in diameter. Place a heaping teaspoon of the peach filling just off center of each pastry circle. Brush the edge of the pastry with the beaten egg white, fold dough in half, enclosing the filling, and crimp the edges with the tines of a fork.

Brush the filled turnovers with beaten egg yolk and bake 10 to 12 minutes, until golden brown. Transfer turnovers to a rack to cool before serving. Serve warm or at room temperature.

Fig and Goat Cheese Tarts in Walnut Crust

Figs were brought to the United States from Europe by the Spanish Franciscan missionaries who planted the first fig tree at the San Diego Mission in 1759. Fig trees were then planted at each succeeding mission, as the missionary fathers moved north through California. Fresh figs are available from June through October. Otherwise, use dried figs that are sold year round, using three dried figs per tart, plumping them in a little warm water for 5 minutes, then draining them and carefully blotting with a paper towel.

Walnut Crust

Makes 6 tarts

¼ cup finely chopped walnuts

1½ tablespoons sugar

2 cups unbleached all-purpose flour

⅛ teaspoon salt

1 cup (2 sticks) cold unsalted butter

2 to 3 tablespoons ice water

Fig and Goat Cheese Filling

1 pound fresh goat cheese

4 large eggs, lightly beaten

¾ cup sugar

6 large fresh figs, quartered

¼ cup honey

   freshly ground pepper

In a medium bowl, combine walnuts, sugar, flour, and salt. Using a pastry blender, cut in butter until mixture forms fine crumbs. Add 2 tablespoons of the water, tossing with a fork. If necessary, add remaining tablespoon water until mixture comes together. Form into a ball, cover with plastic wrap and chill for 30 minutes.

Divide dough into six equal portions and working on a floured surface, roll out each dough piece to form an 8-inch circle. Fold in half and place in six tart pans that are 4½ inches in diameter with removable bottoms. Unfold the dough and press into the tart pans. Trim the pastry to within 1 inch of the edge and tuck in the excess pastry to reinforce the edge.

Preheat oven to 300°.

TO MAKE FILLING

In a large bowl, whisk together the cheese, eggs, and sugar. Pour the mixture into the prepared tart shells. Top each tart with four fig quarters. Bake for 35 to 45 minutes, until filling is set, figs are tender, and crust is golden. Remove from oven and drizzle honey over the figs in each tart. Grind a few grains of pepper onto each tart. While still hot, loosen the edges and slide each tart onto a rack to cool. Serve at room temperature.

Kiwifruit Tart

Frieda Caplan, founder of a pioneering Los Angeles-based specialty and exotic produce company, first introduced kiwifruit to Americans as an import from New Zealand. Since 1980, kiwifruit have become a major crop in California with more than 400 commercial growers and a favorite backyard tree in mild western climates.

Behind the woolly skin is a green sweet-sour flesh, speckled with tiny edible black seeds, that some say tastes like strawberries, others say lime and pineapple. If used when fully ripe, the kiwifruit slices make a lovely topping for a quick tart.

*Makes
8 to 10
servings*

1   *9-inch Sweet Tart Crust (pages 213–214)*
½   *cup whole milk*
2½ *tablespoons sugar*
2   *large egg yolks*
½   *tablespoon cornstarch*
½   *tablespoon unbleached all-purpose flour*
1   *teaspoon unsalted butter*
½   *teaspoon pure vanilla extract*
½   *cup heavy cream, whipped*
5   *large firm, ripe kiwifruit, peeled and thinly sliced*
⅓   *cup strawberry preserves, melted and strained*
¼   *cup fresh blueberries, rinsed and drained*

Preheat oven to 375°. Carefully line the tart shell with aluminum foil in which a few holes have been poked. Weight down with dried beans, raw rice, or aluminum or ceramic pie weights. Bake for 15 to 18 minutes. When pastry begins to color around the edges, remove the foil and weights. Continue to bake just until the pastry dries out and turns golden brown. Let cool completely in the pan on a rack.

In a small saucepan, scald milk and stir in 2 tablespoons sugar. Set aside. In a separate bowl, whisk egg yolks with the remaining ½ tablespoon sugar until thick. Sprinkle with cornstarch and flour and continue whisking until well combined.

Beat half of the scalded milk mixture into the egg yolk mixture, then whisk this mixture into the remaining hot milk. Quickly bring to a boil over medium-high heat, whisking constantly to prevent scorching. Remove from heat and pour into a bowl to cool. Whisk in butter and vanilla extract. Fold in whipped cream.

TO ASSEMBLE TART

Spoon the cooled custard into the cooled tart shell and arrange the kiwifruit slices on top in overlapping rows. Brush top of kiwifruit with the melted strawberry preserves. Arrange blueberries between and on top of the kiwifruit slices. Chill before serving.

Papaya Tart

For years I tried to grow papayas in my Southern California fruit orchard. The seedlings were supplied by my neighbor's father, then head of the Agronomy Department at the University of California at Davis. Actually a large, fast-growing, woody herb, the papayas produced waxy, slightly fragrant flowers, but never any fruit. Fortunately papayas are commercially grown in Hawaii and readily available in the supermarket. Here, I've used their sweet flesh in a free-form tart. Serve the still warm tart with Crème Fraîche or softly whipped cream, garnished with a sprinkling of chopped pistachios.

Makes 8 to 10 servings

1   sheet frozen puff pastry dough, defrosted
2   large ripe Hawaiian (deep yellow-skinned) papayas, peeled, seeded, and sliced
2   tablespoons sugar
1   tablespoon unsalted butter, cut into tiny bits
    water

Glaze

¼   cup guava jelly
1   tablespoon water

Garnish

Crème Fraîche (page 156) or softly whipped cream
⅓   cup chopped pistachios

Preheat oven to 400°. Line a large baking sheet with parchment paper.

Working on a lightly floured surface, roll out dough to about ⅛-inch thickness. Using a sharp knife, cut a 12-inch circle. Transfer dough circle to the parchment paper. Discard scraps.

Arrange the papaya slices, overlapping slightly and leaving a 2-inch border around the edge of the pastry. Sprinkle the papaya with 1 tablespoon of the sugar and dot with butter. Using your fingers, fold the dough up and over the papaya, letting the dough pleat as you work your way around the circle. Brush pastry edge with water and sprinkle with remaining tablespoon of sugar. Bake for 35 to 40 minutes, until pastry is puffed and golden brown.

Transfer tart to a rack to cool. In a small saucepan, heat the jelly with water until melted and bubbly. Immediately brush over papaya. Serve warm with Crème Fraîche or softly whipped cream. Sprinkle with chopped pistachios.

Sweet Potato and Pecan Tart

Candied pecans piled high on top of this tart are lovely to look at, but the flavor combination of the sugary nuts and the spiced sweet potato filling makes this a spectacular dessert. What a wonderful way to combine two of Texas' major food crops.

1 pound small sweet potatoes, scrubbed
½   cup (1 stick) unsalted butter
½   cup packed light brown sugar
2   large eggs, lightly beaten
½   cup heavy cream
1   teaspoon pure vanilla extract
1   teaspoon ground cinnamon
1   teaspoon ground ginger
½   teaspoon ground allspice
½   teaspoon ground nutmeg
    pinch salt
½   cup light corn syrup
3   tablespoons packed light brown sugar
1   cup pecan halves
1   Sweet Tart Crust (pages 213–214), chilled

Makes 8 to 10 servings

TO MAKE FILLING

Cook sweet potatoes in lightly salted boiling water to cover, until sweet potatoes are tender, about 15 to 25 minutes, depending on their size. Drain and peel sweet potatoes.

Preheat oven to 375°.

Puree the sweet potatoes and ¼ cup (½ stick) butter in a food processor. Cool for 15 minutes. In a large bowl, whisk together sweet potato mixture, sugar, eggs, cream, vanilla, and spices. Pour mixture into prepared tart shell and bake for 20 minutes.

Meanwhile, melt remaining butter. Stir in corn syrup, brown sugar, and pecans. Spread over top of partially baked tart. Reduce oven temperature to 350°. Continue to bake another 30 to 35 minutes, until a tester inserted near the center comes out clean.

Ultimate Pear Tarts

It takes just the right combination of warm days, cool nights, rich volcanic soil, and ample water to grow a perfect pear. Thankfully, both Oregon and Washington have large pear-producing areas which grow over 90 percent of the nation's winter pear crop.

Here I've used Bartlett pears in a simple tart, flavor heightened by a bit of raspberry jelly, in a rich tart crust to which I added ground pecans—making a great dessert even better.

Pecan Crust

Makes 6 servings

¼ *cup chopped pecans*

1½ *tablespoons sugar*

2 *cups unbleached all-purpose flour*

⅛ *teaspoon salt*

1 *cup (2 sticks) cold unsalted butter*

2 to 3 tablespoons ice water

Pear Filling

6 *medium Bartlett pears*
    fresh lemon juice

3 *tablespoons sugar*

1 *tablespoon cornstarch*

¼ *teaspoon ground cardamon*

½ *cup red raspberry jelly*
    whipped cream

In a food processor fitted with the metal blade, finely grind the pecans and sugar. Transfer mixture to a medium bowl and stir in flour and salt. Using a pastry blender or two knives, cut in butter until mixture is the size of tiny peas. Add 2 tablespoons water. Mix until dough comes together, adding additional water as needed. Form into a ball, cover with plastic wrap, and chill for 30 minutes.

Divide dough into six equal portions and working on a floured surface, roll out each dough piece to form an 8-inch circle. Fold in half and place in six tart pans that are 4½ inches in diameter with removable bottoms. Unfold the dough and press into the tart pan. Trim the pastry to within 1 inch of the edge of each pan and tuck in the excess pastry to reinforce the edge.

Preheat oven to 350°.

Peel and core pears. Thinly slice, keeping each pear shape intact. Place a pear in each filled tart pan and with the palm of your hand flatten the pear slightly to fan out the slices. Sprinkle each pear with lemon juice. Combine the sugar, cornstarch, and cardamon. Sprinkle evenly over pears.

Bake for 45 to 50 minutes until pears are tender and crust nicely browned. While still hot, loosen the edges and slide each tart onto a dessert plate. In a small saucepan, melt jelly over medium heat, stirring until smooth. Using a pastry brush, coat the pear with the melted jelly. Serve warm with whipped cream.

Western Nut Tart

Nut tarts are very popular in the West with each nut variety adding its distinctive flavor and texture to the tart. Baked in a rich butter crust, the tart is terrific with a glass of western dessert wine such as orange Muscat or late-harvest Gewürztraminer (pages 266–269).

Butter Pastry

Makes 10 to 12 servings

1⅓ cups unbleached all-purpose flour
¼ cup sugar
½ cup (1 stick) cold unsalted butter, cut into small pieces
1 large egg yolk

Nut Filling

⅓ cup hazelnuts, toasted and skins rubbed off
⅓ cup whole blanched almonds, toasted
⅓ cup walnut halves, toasted
⅓ cup pecan halves, toasted
¼ cup (½ stick) unsalted butter, at room temperature
1 cup packed lightly brown sugar
½ cup light corn syrup
3 large eggs
1 tablespoon brandy
½ teaspoon vanilla
   whipped cream (optional)

Preheat oven to 350°. Place an oven rack in the lower third of the oven.

In a food processor fitted with a metal blade, combine flour and sugar. Scatter butter pieces over flour mixture. Process until mixture forms fine crumbs. Add egg yolk and process until dough holds together.

Press dough over bottom and sides of an 11-inch tart pan with removable rim. Distribute toasted nuts evenly over the bottom.

In a large bowl and using an electric mixer, cream together the butter and brown sugar. Blend in corn syrup. Beat in eggs, one at a time. Stir in brandy and vanilla. Pour mixture evenly over the nuts.

Bake until filling is set and crust is golden brown, 45 to 50 minutes. Cool in the pan on a rack. Remove pan rim. Cut tart into wedges and serve with whipped cream, if desired.

Puddings, Custards, Ice Creams, & Sorbets

Texas Ruby Red Grapefruit Sorbet, see page 263.

Baked Blueberry Pudding with Butter Sauce

This recipe, from my sister-in-law Ruth, calls for lots of blueberries—easy for her because she grows blueberries in her backyard and lives within an easy walk of the Overlake Blueberry Farms of Bellevue, Washington. If you don't want to bother with the Butter Sauce, the pudding's great with Vanilla Ice Cream (page 252). You can, of course, use unsweetened frozen blueberries with good results.

Makes 9 servings

2 cups unbleached all-purpose flour
1 cup sugar
2½ teaspoons baking powder
  dash salt
3 tablespoons butter, melted
⅔ cup whole milk
1 large egg, lightly beaten
3 cups fresh blueberries
  Butter Sauce (recipe follows)

Preheat oven to 350°. Butter a 9-inch square baking pan.

Into a large bowl, sift together flour, sugar, baking powder, and salt. Make a well in the center and stir in melted butter, milk, and egg. Mix just until dry ingredients are evenly moistened. Stir in blueberries.

Transfer mixture to prepared pan. Bake 35 to 40 minutes, until a tester inserted in the center comes out clean. Cool slightly before cutting into 3-inch squares. Serve with Butter Sauce.

Butter Sauce

½ cup (1 stick) unsalted butter
1 cup sugar
¾ cup heavy cream

Melt butter in the top of a double boiler or in a saucepan that will fit into a large pan of gently simmering water without the smaller pan actually touching the water. Stir in sugar and cream. Cook, stirring constantly, until thickened, about 5 minutes. Serve hot over blueberry pudding.

Buttermilk Lemon Custard
with Raspberry Sauce

A fifth generation Californian, my sister-in-law Gloria Giedt gave me this family recipe, along with the recipe for the Double-Crust Lemon Pie (page 181). This is a dessert that tastes as good as it looks, and it's so easy to make.

grated rind of 2 large lemons

⅓ *cup fresh lemon juice*

3 *tablespoons butter, melted and cooled*

1 *cup sugar*

3 *large eggs, separated*

⅓ *cup unbleached all-purpose flour*

1½ *cups buttermilk*

Makes 6 to 8 servings

Raspberry Sauce

1 *pint frozen unsweetened raspberries, defrosted*

¼ *cup sugar*

1 *cup fresh raspberries*

Preheat oven to 350°. Lightly butter a 2-quart casserole. Place the casserole in a large baking pan.

In a bowl, mix together lemon rind, lemon juice, melted butter, sugar, and egg yolks. Beat well. Stir in flour and buttermilk, whisking until well blended. Pour into prepared casserole.

Fill the baking pan with boiling water to come halfway up the side of the casserole. Bake 30 minutes, until custard is firm. Cool on a rack to room temperature.

TO MAKE RASPBERRY SAUCE

Meanwhile, in a food processor fitted with the metal blade, puree frozen raspberries. Strain into a small saucepan and stir in sugar. Cook over medium-low heat for 5 minutes, until mixture starts to thicken. Remove from heat and chill.

When ready to serve, stir fresh raspberries into the berry sauce. Transfer mixture to a pretty bowl or pitcher. Spoon custard into individual desserts dishes. Pass raspberry sauce to spoon over custard.

Cream Puffs with Lemon Curd

When the Bonaventure Hotel in Los Angeles first opened its doors, the food and travel writers of the area were feted to a lovely afternoon tea. One of the offerings was diminutive cream puffs filled with a tangy lemon curd. Over the years, I've served these after a heavy meal with a glass of dessert wine or as a special treat for a neighborhood coffee get-together.

Cream Puffs

*Makes
24*

1   cup milk

7   tablespoons unsalted butter

¼   teaspoon salt

1   cup plus 2 tablespoons unbleached all-purpose flour

1   teaspoon pure vanilla extract

2   large eggs

Lemon Curd

2   large eggs

¾   cup granulated sugar

⅔   cup fresh lemon juice

2   teaspoons grated lemon peel

2   tablespoons unsalted butter

   powdered sugar, for dusting

Preheat oven to 375°. Place the rack in the upper third of the oven. Lightly butter twenty-four 3-inch muffin cups.

In a medium heavy saucepan, combine milk, butter, and salt. Bring to a boil. Add flour all at once. Mix quickly with a wooden spoon until a ball forms on the spoon and the flour is evenly moistened. Remove from heat and beat in vanilla extract and eggs, one at a time, beating well after each addition.

Place about 1 tablespoon of the dough into each of the prepared muffin cups. With moistened fingers, press dough partway up the side of the muffin cups and make a small indentation in the center. Bake for 5 minutes. Remove from oven and prick the centers of each cream puff with a fork. Return to the oven and bake another 15 to 20 minutes, until shells are puffed and golden. Loosen shells from muffin cups with a small knife and transfer to a wire rack to cool. (May be made ahead, and stored in an airtight container for up to 2 days).

TO MAKE LEMON CURD

Fill a medium saucepan ⅓ full of water. Bring water to a slow boil. In a medium stainless-steel bowl, whisk together the eggs and sugar. Stir in lemon juice and zest. Set the bowl over the pot of boiling water, making sure the water doesn't touch the bottom of the bowl. Cook the mixture, stirring occasionally, until thick, about 10 minutes. Whisk in butter. Transfer the lemon curd to a bowl, cover, and refrigerate (will keep for up to 2 days).

TO ASSEMBLE CREAM PUFFS

Spoon 1 tablespoon of the lemon curd into each puff pastry shell. Place on a serving plate and dust with sifted powdered sugar. Serve within 1 hour of filling.

Crème Brûlée
with Raspberry Sauce

Dean Fearing, one of Texas' most celebrated chefs, shares his recipe for a stunningly innovative Crème Brûlée. It's a favorite dessert at the renowned Mansion on Turtle Creek in Dallas where Dean is executive chef.

6   extra large egg yolks

1¼ cups sugar

3   cups heavy cream

1   vanilla bean, split

1   cup raspberries

6   frozen puff pastry shells, thawed and baked

    Raspberry Sauce (recipe follows)

Combine egg yolks and ½ cup sugar in the top of a double boiler over very hot water. Whisk (or beat with a hand mixer) until lemon-colored and the consistency of mousse. Remove from heat and set aside.

Place cream and vanilla bean in a heavy saucepan over medium heat. Bring to a boil and immediately remove from heat. Strain through a fine sieve. Discard vanilla bean. Slowly pour into egg yolks, whisking rapidly as you pour.

Return double boiler to heat and cook, stirring constantly, for about 10 minutes, or until mixture is quite thick. Remove from heat and place in a bowl of ice. Stir occasionally while crème cools until it reaches consistency of a very thick custard.

Spread a single layer of fresh raspberries over the bottom of six baked puff pastry shells. Spoon cooled crème over raspberries to top of shells. Refrigerate for at least 3 hours (or up to 8 hours). When chilled, preheat broiler.

Sprinkle 2 tablespoons sugar over each filled shell and place about 6 inches away from broiler flame for about 3 minutes or until sugar caramelizes. Do not overcook or crème will melt. Immediately remove from heat.

Pour Raspberry Sauce over the bottom of each of six dessert plates. Place a Crème Brûlée in the center and serve immediately.

Raspberry Sauce

    1   *cup fresh raspberries*
    ¼   *cup Simple Syrup (recipe follows)*

Puree raspberries in a blender or food processor. When smooth, strain through an extra-fine sieve to remove all seeds. Stir simple syrup into raspberry puree until well blended.

Simple Syrup

    1   *cup sugar*
    1   *cup water*

In a small heavy saucepan, combine sugar and water over high heat. Bring to a boil, and boil, stirring constantly, for about 3 minutes, or until sugar is dissolved. Remove from heat and cool. May be stored, refrigerated, tightly covered, for up to 3 months.

Flan with Cinnamon-Sugared Pecans and Kahlua Cream

Texans love flan (caramel custard), and at times it seems almost every restaurant in the state that makes their own dessert, offers its version of this rich, smooth custard. Since all flan recipes are pretty much the same, unless you add nontraditional ingredients like pumpkin, sweet potatoes, or fruits, it's the final presentation that will make your flan a stand-out dessert.

Flan

Makes 6 servings

¾ cup sugar
6 large eggs, lightly beaten
pinch salt
1 teaspoon pure vanilla extract
1 quart whole milk, scalded

Cinnamon-Sugared Pecans

¾ cup sugar
½ teaspoon ground cinnamon
pinch cream of tartar
3 tablespoons water
1 cup pecan halves
¼ teaspoon pure vanilla extract

Kahlua Cream

1 cup heavy cream
1 teaspoon sugar
2 tablespoons Kahlua liqueur

Preheat oven to 350°. Set six ¾-cup custard cups in a baking pan.

Caramelize ½ cup of the sugar by heating it in a heavy-bottom skillet over very low heat, stirring constantly, until sugar melts and turns brown. Immediately pour into the custard cups, dividing evenly.

In a medium bowl, whisk beaten eggs, remaining ¼ cup sugar, salt, and vanilla. While whisking, slowly add the scalded milk. Pour over the caramel in each custard cup. Fill the baking pan with hot water to come halfway up the sides of the cups.

Bake for 20 to 30 minutes, until a knife inserted into the center comes out clean and the custard is set. Remove from baking pan and chill.

TO MAKE CINNAMON-SUGARED PECANS

Meanwhile, in a small saucepan, combine sugar, cinnamon, cream of tartar, and water over medium heat. Stir constantly, cooking until mixture comes to the soft ball candy stage or registers 240° on a candy thermometer. Remove from heat and stir in pecans and vanilla. Spread pecans evenly onto a parchment-paper-lined cookie sheet. Allow to cool; if necessary, break pecans apart.

When ready to serve, make the Kahlua Cream. Whip the heavy cream and sugar until the mixture forms soft peaks. Whip in Kahlua. Unmold custard cups (if necessary, run a thin knife around the edge of each cup to loosen) and invert onto individual dessert plates. Garnish with a drift of the Kahlua Cream and sprinkle with the Cinnamon-Sugared Pecans. Serve at once.

Frozen Key Lime Mousse with Candied Lime Slices

I used to make this luscious dessert with fresh Persian limes grown in my exten-sive Southern California backyard orchard. Nowadays, bottled key lime juice is readily available at supermarkets. Used here, it's the basis of a delectable frozen dessert much like the key lime pie one increasingly finds in western restaurants, from posh to roadside diner. Without the crust, the dessert is lighter and so good for hot summer meals. The candied lime slices must be made a day ahead, but they're worth the effort.

Candied Lime Slices

*Makes
8 to 10
servings*

2   *fresh limes*

1   *cup water*

⅔   *cup sugar*

Key Lime Mousse

powdered sugar

1   *tablespoon unflavored gelatin*

1   *cup key lime juice*

6   *large egg yolks*

1½ *cups sugar*

1   *cup evaporated milk*

2   *tablespoons grated lime rind*

¼   *cup pasteurized dried egg whites, reconstituted in ¾ cup warm water, or 1 cup plus 1 tablespoon pasteurized liquid egg whites (see page 6)*

¾   *cup warm water*

1   *cup heavy cream*

Thinly slice the limes; discard the end pieces. In a saucepan, bring water and sugar to a boil. Reduce the heat and add the lime slices. Slowly simmer, uncovered, for about 2 hours. Transfer the syrup and lime slices to a bowl, cover, and refrigerate overnight.

Securely fasten a 12-inch wide band of double thick aluminum foil around a 1 ½-quart soufflé dish with adhesive tape. Lightly butter the dish and inside of the collar. Dust both with powdered sugar and set aside.

Sprinkle gelatin over lime juice to soften. In a heavy saucepan, beat egg yolks with sugar until thick and light yellow. Add evaporated milk, whisking constantly. Place over medium heat and cook, stirring constantly, until mixture thickens and begins to coat the back of a wooden spoon. Do not let mixture boil. Remove from heat and add gelatin-juice mixture, stirring until gelatin is completely dissolved. Chill until cool and thick, but not set. Stir in grated lime rind.

In a metal bowl, stir dried egg whites into warm water until completely dissolved, about 2 minutes, or pour in liquid egg whites. Beat with an electric mixer on medium-high speed until egg whites form firm peaks. In a separate bowl, beat heavy cream until it forms soft peaks. Gently stir one-third of the whipped egg whites into the lime mixture to lighten it. Carefully fold in remaining egg whites and whipped cream. Transfer mixture to the prepared soufflé dish, smoothing the top with the back of a spoon. Freeze for 6 hours, or until firm.

When ready to serve, remove and discard foil collar. Remove the lime slices from the syrup and arrange on the top of the mousse, following the edge of the mousse. Let stand at room temperature for about 10 minutes before serving.

Lemon Pudding
with Fresh Blackberries

One of the several lemon trees in my California backyard orchard was a Meyer lemon—actually a cross between a lemon and an orange—and, to my thinking, the most delicious lemon of all. If you (or your neighbor) don't have access to Meyer lemons, use freshly squeezed juice and rind from the more common Eureka or Lisbon lemon sold in the supermarket. To make up for the difference in taste, you can replace one tablespoon of lemon juice with a tablespoon of freshly squeezed orange juice. This pudding is best served warm.

Makes 4 servings

- 3 tablespoons unsalted butter
- ¾ cup sugar
- 3 large eggs, separated
- ⅛ teaspoon salt
- 1 tablespoon finely grated Meyer lemon rind
- ¼ cup unbleached all-purpose flour
- 3 tablespoons freshly squeezed Meyer lemon juice
- ¾ cup whole milk
- 1 cup fresh blackberries

Preheat oven to 325°. Using 1 tablespoon of the butter, lightly butter four ¾ cup custard cups. Coat each with ½ tablespoon of the sugar. Position cups in a baking dish that is at least 3 inches deep.

In a mixing bowl and using an electric mixer, cream together remaining 2 tablespoons butter and ½ cup of the sugar until light and fluffy. Add egg yolks, one at a time, mixing well after each addition. Stir in salt and lemon rind. Mix in flour, then the lemon juice and milk.

In a small bowl, beat egg whites until stiff. Gently whisk whites into the lemon mixture. Pour into prepared cups and fill baking pan with boiling water to fill pan halfway up the sides of the custard cups. Bake 20 to 25 minutes, until filling is set. Remove from oven and transfer cups to a rack to cool. Immediately run a sharp knife around the outside rim between the cup and the filling. Continue to cool for another 30 minutes.

Toss the blackberries with remaining 2 tablespoons sugar. Set aside.

To serve, invert the still-warm puddings onto individual dessert plates. Scatter berries and their juice over and around the puddings. Serve warm.

Mango Brûlée

Mark Miller offers imaginative contemporary Southwest food at his Coyote Café in Santa Fe, New Mexico, and for all too briefly, Austin, Texas. I've always been especially intrigued with Mark's desserts, combining classic recipes with Southwestern ingredients for a fabulous ending to an already superb meal. Because I can buy beautiful mangos, sometimes five for a dollar, at my local produce store most of the year, I make my version of his crème brûlée frequently.

Mark sometimes adds fresh raspberries or blueberries to his recipe, but I love the taste of just the mango. Should you wish to use berries, substitute half of the mango with either fresh raspberries or fresh blueberries.

5	large egg yolks
2	cups heavy cream
⅔	cup half-and-half
⅔	cup sugar
½	teaspoon pure vanilla extract
2½ cups finely chopped fresh mango (about 2 large)	

Makes 6 servings

Preheat oven to 325°. Lightly butter six 6-inch ramekins or soufflé dishes. Set ramekins in a large baking pan.

In a large bowl, beat the egg yolks until thick and lemon colored. Add the cream, half-and-half, ⅓ cup plus 1 tablespoon sugar, and vanilla. Blend well.

Distribute the mango evenly in the bottom of the prepared ramekins. Pour the custard evenly over the mango. Fill the pan with hot water until it reaches halfway up the sides of the ramekins. Bake for 30 to 40 minutes, until custard is set and a tester inserted in the center comes out clean. Remove ramekins from the water bath and cool on a rack. Refrigerate until ready to serve.

TO SERVE

Preheat broiler. Sprinkle the remaining sugar evenly over the tops of the ramekins and place under broiler until sugar caramelizes. Rotate the ramekins as necessary to ensure even browning.

Mexican Bread Pudding

Called *Capirotada* by our neighbors to the south, this old-fashioned Mexican dessert has made its way into the recipe repertoire of many Southwestern cooks, particularly in the border towns. The first time I tasted the pudding, it was made with sharp cheddar cheese. Another time it was made with Mexican Cotija Cheese, and yet again with Monterey Jack cheese. Either way, it's a delicious concoction of bread, sweets, fruits, cheese, and spices. Since the pudding is nonacidic, you can safely bake it in your colorful glazed Mexican pottery.

Makes 6 servings

1 cup sugar

2 cups water

1 teaspoon ground cinnamon

pinch salt

¼ cup (½ stick) unsalted butter

6 slices day-old French bread, cubed

1½ cups shredded cheese—sharp cheddar, Mexican Cotija, or Monterey Jack

½ cup golden raisins

1 large apple, peeled, cored, and shredded

⅓ cup pine nuts, toasted

softly whipped cream

Preheat oven to 350°.

In a small saucepan, place sugar over medium heat. Cook, stirring constantly, until sugar melts and turns amber-colored. Remove from heat and stir in water, ground cinnamon, and salt. Return to low heat and cook, stirring, until caramel dissolves and smooth syrup is formed. Set aside.

In a large skillet, melt 2 tablespoons butter over medium-high heat. Add bread cubes and toast them, occasionally tossing the cubes to evenly toast. Transfer half of the toasted bread cubes to a shallow 2-quart casserole, spreading evenly. Top evenly with half of the cheese, half of the raisins, half of the grated apple, and half of the pine nuts. Repeat for second layer with remaining bread cubes, cheese, raisins, apple, and pine nuts. Dot top with the remaining 2 tablespoons butter and pour the hot syrup over all. Bake for 30 minutes, until syrup is absorbed.

Mexican Rice Pudding

A particular favorite throughout the Southwest, Mexican pudding is usually made without raisins, relying on cinnamon and vanilla to supply the flavor. Toasted pine nuts, the tiny nut of the Southwest, garnish the top.

½	cup raw rice
½	cup water
½	cinnamon stick
4	cups whole milk
4	large eggs, separated
⅓	cup sugar
¼	cup unbleached all-purpose flour
	pinch salt
½	tablespoon pure vanilla extract
1	teaspoon ground cinnamon
¼	cup pine nuts, toasted

Makes 6 to 8 servings

In a small saucepan, combine rice, water, and cinnamon stick. Bring to a boil, reduce heat, cover, and simmer until rice absorbs the water, about 10 minutes. Discard cinnamon stick. Set aside.

In a heavy saucepan, heat milk. Beat egg whites until stiff peaks form. Set aside. In a bowl, whisk together egg yolks, sugar, flour, salt, and ½ cup of the hot milk. Whisk egg mixture into the remaining hot milk. Add reserved rice and simmer until pudding has thickened, about 10 minutes. Remove from heat and stir in vanilla and cinnamon. Immediately fold in reserved egg whites. Chill.

To serve, sprinkle top of pudding with cinnamon and toasted pine nuts.

Persimmon Steamed Pudding with Hard Sauce

Many Californians prefer a persimmon pudding to the traditional plum pudding for gala holiday meals—partly because persimmon pudding is just as festive, but lighter in character. To some extent, it's also because persimmons are frequently grown in yards as an ornamental tree, and people are overwhelmed with the amount of persimmons their trees produce each fall.

Persimmon pudding is sometimes baked, but my version is steamed and full of plump Texas pecans. Serve it with Hard Sauce or softly whipped cream. You can use a pudding mold, sold at gourmet cookware shops, or as I do, an old crockery bowl. If the bowl is quite thick, the pudding may take up to an extra half hour to steam.

Makes 6 to 8 servings

3 to 4 very ripe persimmons
1 cup granulated sugar
½ cup (1 stick) butter, melted
1 teaspoon pure vanilla extract
1 cup unbleached all-purpose flour
1½ teaspoons baking powder
¼ teaspoon baking soda
¼ teaspoon ground cinnamon
¼ teaspoon ground nutmeg
¼ teaspoon salt
1 cup coarsely chopped pecans
¾ cup golden raisins
¼ cup brandy or fresh orange juice
2 large eggs, lightly beaten
Hard Sauce (recipe follows)

Peel persimmons and slice into a food processor or blender. Blend to a puree. Measure out 1 cup of puree, freezing any remaining puree for another use. Combine the 1 cup puree, sugar, butter, and vanilla extract.

Onto waxed paper, sift together flour, baking powder, baking soda, cinnamon, nutmeg, and salt. In a bowl, combine pecans and raisins. Sprinkle with a tablespoon or two of the flour mixture and toss to coat well. Add remaining flour mixture to persimmon mixture all at once and stir until smooth. Stir in brandy and eggs; mix well. Add pecan and raisin mixture.

Transfer batter to a well-buttered 6-cup heat-proof pudding mold or crockery bowl. Cover tightly, using aluminum foil tied with kitchen string if mold does not have a cover. Place a rack in a large kettle with boiling water reaching halfway up sides of the mold. Cover kettle and steam 2 to 2½ hours, until a tester inserted near center comes out clean. Let pudding cool slightly on a rack, turn out, and serve hot with Hard Sauce.

Hard Sauce

½   *cup (1 stick) butter*
2   *cups powdered sugar*
    brandy or fresh orange juice
    pinch ground cinnamon
    pinch ground nutmeg

Melt butter; stir in sugar. Add brandy until mixture can be stirred. Stir in cinnamon and nutmeg. Fluff with a fork just before serving.

Raisin Rice Pudding

I first made this not-too-sweet pudding for a television appearance I did in San Diego for the California Raisin Board. Back then, jasmine rice, a long-grain aromatic rice primarily grown in Thailand, wasn't yet readily available. Long prized for its wonderful aroma and nutty flavor, jasmine rice is now grown around the Houston area in Texas. Because the snowy white grains cook up very soft and tender, the pudding has a wonderful creamy texture.

Makes 6 to 8 servings

6 cups whole milk
1 cup sugar
¼ cup (½ stick) unsalted butter
1 cup Jasmati® or other long-grain rice
2 3-inch cinnamon sticks
1 3-inch piece of vanilla bean
2 large egg yolks
2¼ cups water
1 cup dark raisins
ground cinnamon

In a large heavy pot, bring milk, sugar, and butter to a boil, stirring until sugar dissolves. Add rice, cinnamon sticks, and vanilla bean. Return to a boil; reduce heat to medium-low and cook, stirring occasionally, for 10 minutes (25 minutes if using regular long-grain rice). In a small bowl, whisk together egg yolks and ¼ cup water. While stirring, slowly add the egg mixture to the rice mixture. Continue to simmer for 10 minutes. Transfer mixture to a bowl, cover, and refrigerate for at least 6 hours.

Meanwhile, in a small saucepan, bring remaining 2 cups water to a rapid boil. Add raisins and cook for 3 minutes. Drain raisins completely, transfer to a bowl, cover, and cool completely.

Remove and discard cinnamon sticks and vanilla bean. Stir raisins into chilled pudding. Spoon into dessert dishes and dust each serving with cinnamon.

Tangerine Mousse
with Blackberry Puree

California groves ship many different varieties of tangerines from October through April, with the most distinctive flavor coming from honey tangerines, which are very juicy and perfect for making this dessert.

Tangerine Mousse

Makes 6
servings

1   cup sugar

4   large eggs

4   large egg yolks

1   cup fresh, strained honey tangerine juice (6 to 8 tangerines)

1   tablespoon fresh lemon juice

½   cup plus 2 tablespoons (1¼ sticks) unsalted butter

1   tablespoon grated tangerine rind

½   cup heavy cream

Blackberry Puree

2   cups blackberries

    up to 2 tablespoons sugar (optional)

    fresh mint for garnish (optional)

In the top of a double boiler or a stainless steel bowl, whisk together ¾ cup sugar, eggs, and egg yolks. In a small saucepan, bring tangerine juice, lemon juice, and butter come to a boil. Gradually whisk the hot tangerine mixture into the egg mixture.

Set pan over a pot of simmering water (do not allow water to touch bottom of the pan) and cook, stirring, until mixture thickens and coats the back of a wooden spoon. Remove from stove and stir in tangerine rind. Transfer mixture to a clean metal bowl and cover surface with a piece of plastic wrap. Chill for at least 3 hours.

Just before serving, whip cream and remaining ¼ cup sugar until cream forms stiff peaks. Gently fold into tangerine mixture.

TO PREPARE PUREE

Set aside six perfect blackberries. In a food processor or blender, puree remaining berries. Strain through a fine sieve to remove any seeds. Taste and add sugar, a little at a time, to desired sweetness.

To serve, spoon ¼ cup of the blackberry puree in the bottom of each of six stemmed glasses. Carefully spoon tangerine mousse on top of the berry puree. Refrigerate until ready to serve.

If desired, garnish each serving with a small sprig of mint and a reserved blackberry.

Vincent Price's Bread Pudding with Lemon Sauce

Years ago, I attended a fundraising luncheon at the home of the late actor Vincent Price. A delicious bread pudding was served as the dessert and the recipe was printed on the souvenir menu. His recipe called for a Creme Anglaise sauce, but I prefer it with tangy lemon.

¼ cup dark raisins

¼ cup packed light brown sugar

8 slices day-old French bread, crusts trimmed

4 large eggs, lightly beaten

4 cups whole milk

2 teaspoons pure vanilla extract

2 tablespoons sugar

2 tablespoons unsalted butter, diced

Lemon Sauce (recipe follows)

Makes 10 to 12 servings

Preheat oven to 350°. Generously butter a 13-inch by 9-inch baking dish. Evenly sprinkle raisins and brown sugar over the bottom of the baking dish. Top with bread slices.

In a large bowl, whisk eggs until frothy. Whisk in milk and vanilla. Pour over bread slices. Sprinkle top with sugar and dot with butter.

Place dish in a large ovenproof pan and surround with hot water to come halfway up the sides of the pudding baking dish. Bake for 1 hour, until pudding is firm. Cut into squares and serve warm with Lemon Sauce.

Lemon Sauce

1½ cups sugar

1½ cups (3 stick) unsalted butter

3 large eggs

2 teaspoons finely grated lemon rind

¾ cup fresh lemon juice

Makes about 3 cups

In a food processor or blender, combine all ingredients. Transfer to the top portion of a double boiler or to a stainless-steel bowl set a pan of barely simmering water. (Don't let the bottom of the bowl actually touch the water.)

Cook, stirring constantly, until sauce is thick, about 10 minutes. Cool slightly before serving with bread pudding.

Western Trifle

Throughout the West, soft custards layered with fresh fruits and sponge cake are a popular dessert, varied by the harvest of backyard fruit trees or the local produce stands. This trifle is made with fresh raspberries and raspberry jam; another time try stewed apricots and apricot jam or fresh blackberries and blackberry jam. It's also terrific made with strawberries and strawberry jam.

Makes
8 to 10
servings

2   *cups whole milk*
⅓   *cup plus 3 tablespoons sugar*
⅛   *teaspoon salt*
¼   *cup unbleached all-purpose flour*
2   *large eggs plus 1 egg yolk*
2   *tablespoons dark rum*
2   *cups heavy cream*
2   *tablespoons red raspberry preserves*
1   *10-inch sponge cake*
¼   *cup brandy*
¼   *cup dry sherry*
1   *pint fresh raspberries, rinsed and drained on paper towels*

In a heavy saucepan, combine milk, ⅓ cup sugar, and salt. Place over low heat and cook, stirring, until sugar dissolves. Transfer ½ cup of milk mixture to a small bowl to cool. Once cool, sprinkle flour over the mixture and whisk in eggs and egg yolk. Pour this mixture back into the hot milk mixture in the pan, whisking constantly, until a soft custard forms and coats the back of a wooden spoon. Stir in rum and cool.

In a large bowl, whip cream with remaining 3 tablespoons of the sugar until cream forms stiff peaks. Fold half of the whipped cream mixture into cooled custard.

Using a pastry brush, brush the inside of a deep 10-inch glass bowl with raspberry preserves. Slice cake horizontally into quarters. Place top slice, crust side up in the bottom of the bowl. Combine brandy and sherry. Evenly sprinkle cake with 2 tablespoons of the brandy mixture. Spread one-third of the pudding mixture over the cake. Top with a second cake layer, sprinkle with 2 tablespoons of the brandy mixture, and top with another one-third of the pudding mixture. Repeat third layer. Place last cake layer on top and sprinkle with remaining brandy mixture. Spread top with remaining whipped cream mixture.

Chill for at least 2 hours. To serve, top with raspberries and spoon onto chilled dessert plates.

Banana Nut Ice Cream

Wolfgang Puck serves a similar banana ice cream at his famed Los Angeles Spago restaurant. I always have a bowl of bananas on my kitchen counter for snacking. When they start to show brown spots on the skin, the overripe bananas are used for baking or making this luscious ice cream. I like walnuts in this ice cream, but you could leave them out or substitute pecans.

6   large egg yolks
6   tablespoons sugar
1⅓ cups whole milk
1⅓ cups heavy cream
3   very ripe bananas
3   tablespoons sour cream
1   tablespoon honey
½   tablespoon pure vanilla extract
⅔   cup coarsely chopped walnuts (optional)

Makes about 1 quart

In a large mixing bowl, whisk together the egg yolks and sugar.

In a heavy saucepan, bring milk and cream to a boil. Slowly whisk one-third of the hot cream mixture into the egg mixture. Stir in remaining cream mixture. Return to the saucepan and cook, stirring constantly, over low heat until a thin custard forms that coats the back of a spoon, about 8 to 10 minutes. Strain through a fine sieve into a large bowl.

Puree the bananas, sour cream, honey, and vanilla extract in a food processor or blender, adding a little of the egg-cream mixture as needed to liquefy. Stir banana mixture into egg-cream mixture; add the walnuts (if using). Chill thoroughly.

Freeze in an ice-cream freezer, following the manufacturer's instructions.

Cinnamon Ice Cream with Vanilla Ice Cream Variation

Recently it seems most every upscale restaurant in the West is making Cinnamon Ice Cream to serve over pies, cobblers, cakes, and puddings. Likely most everyone's favorite spice, cinnamon makes a wonderful ice cream that's so easy to make at home.

Makes about 1½ quarts

6 large egg yolks
1 cup granulated sugar
  pinch salt
2 cups heavy cream
1½ cups whole milk
2½ tablespoons freshly ground cinnamon

In a medium bowl, whisk together egg yolks, sugar, and salt.

In a medium heavy-bottom saucepan, combine cream and milk. Scald mixture over medium-high heat. Slowly whisk it into the reserved egg mixture. Return the mixture to the saucepan and stir in the cinnamon. Cook over medium heat, stirring constantly, until mixture coats the back of a spoon, about 5 minutes.

Pour the mixture into a clean mixing bowl. Set this bowl into a larger bowl of ice water and cool, stirring occasionally. Refrigerate for 1 hour before pouring into an ice-cream maker. Freeze according to the manufacturer's directions.

Vanilla Ice Cream Variation

Replace the 2½ tablespoons freshly ground cinnamon with 1 vanilla bean, split in half lengthwise, adding the vanilla bean halves at the last, as you would have added the freshly ground cinnamon. Continue to follow recipe. Once mixture has been poured into the mixing bowl to cool, remove the vanilla bean halves and scrape any remaining vanilla seeds into the mixture. Discard empty vanilla bean halves. Continue to chill mixture and freeze as directed.

Date Ice Cream

This ice cream is quite rich, perfect by itself, topped with a chocolate sauce or blended with whole milk to make a date shake. The original recipe comes from Shields Date Gardens in Indio, California.

Makes about 1 quart

2   large eggs
½   cup sugar
1½ tablespoons unbleached all-purpose flour
      pinch salt
3   cups half-and-half
1   tablespoon pure vanilla extract
1¼ cups chopped dates
1   cup heavy cream

Beat the eggs in a mixing bowl until light and foamy. Set aside.

In a heavy saucepan over low heat, combine the sugar, flour, and salt. Gradually stir in 2 cups half-and-half and continue stirring until the mixture is smooth. Cook, stirring, until mixture thickens to a thin custard, about 15 minutes.

Pour about ½ cup of the cream mixture into the beaten eggs. Then pour the egg mixture into the hot custard and cook, stirring constantly, for another 5 minutes. Remove from heat and stir in vanilla and chopped dates. Cover and chill in the refrigerator for several hours.

Stir in remaining half-and-half and heavy cream. Pour mixture into an ice-cream freezer and freeze according to the manufacturer's directions.

Peach Ice Cream

Peach Ice Cream is one of those dishes that simply says "summer" in the West when farm stands offer bushels of ripe, luscious peaches and supermarkets feature peaches on special throughout the week. Until the new models of ice-cream makers were introduced, I always made ice cream the old hand-cranked way, layered with salt and ice. Nowadays, the newfangled machines are a lot less work, and in my opinion, produce an equally fine product.

Makes
about
1 quart

8   *large ripe peaches, about 2 pounds total*
¼   *cup fresh lemon juice*
1½ *cups heavy cream*
1½ *cup whole milk*
¾   *cup superfine sugar*
3   *large egg yolks*

Peel and pit peaches. Cut peaches into large chunks and coarsely puree in a food processor or blender with the lemon juice. Cover and refrigerate.

In the top of a double boiler or metal bowl suspended over simmering water (do not let water actually touch the bowl), combine heavy cream and milk. Bring to a boil over medium-low heat. In a bowl, whisk together sugar and egg yolks. Whisk in ½ cup of the hot cream mixture, then pour the warmed yolk mixture into the saucepan. Cook, stirring, until custard coats the back of a spoon, about 8 minutes. Do not let mixture come to a boil or it may separate. Remove from heat and press a sheet of waxed paper directly onto the top of the custard. Chill.

When chilled, stir in peach puree. Pour into an ice-cream maker and freeze according to the manufacturer's directions.

Persimmon Ice Cream with Chile Pecans

Hachiya persimmons are fully colored when picked for shipping, but are not ripe for eating or cooking until they feel soft to gentle pressure. Here the sweet persimmon pulp is for ice cream. I've sprinkled the ice cream with chile-coated pecans, which frequently show up in Texas restaurants as croutons for salads and toppings for desserts and ice creams.

For an extra-special dessert, split whole ripe persimmons in half lengthwise and top each half with a scoop of the ice cream, then toss on the pecans. The combination of flavors and textures makes it a great dessert for guests.

3 large eggs
1¼ cups sugar
1 teaspoon ground allspice
¼ teaspoon ground cinnamon
    pinch salt
1 cup half-and-half
1 cup heavy cream
1½ cups Hachiya persimmon pulp

Makes 8 to 10 servings

Chile Pecans

1 cup pecan halves
1½ tablespoons unsalted butter, melted
1 teaspoon Ancho or New Mexican chile powder (see Mail-Order Sources, pages 270–271)
2 tablespoons light brown sugar

1 tablespoon brandy, preferably pear brandy

In the top of a double boiler or in a metal bowl suspended over a large pan of simmering water (make sure the bottom of the bowl doesn't actually touch the water), beat eggs with an electric mixer until pale yellow and thickened. Beat in sugar, allspice, cinnamon, and salt. Add half-and-half and heavy cream. Cook, stirring constantly, until mixture forms a soft custard and coats the back of a wooden spoon, 6 to 7 minutes. Do not let mixture boil. Remove from heat and set pan or bowl in a bowl of crushed ice. Stir until cool. Cover and refrigerate for at least 2 hours or overnight. Place ½ cup persimmon pulp in a container, cover, and refrigerate.

When ready to make ice cream, stir remaining 1 cup persimmon pulp into the chilled custard. Transfer mixture to an ice-cream freezer and freeze following the manufacturer's directions.

TO MAKE CHILE PECANS

Meanwhile, preheat oven to 350°. In a bowl, toss pecans with melted butter, then the chile powder and brown sugar. Spread in a single layer on a baking sheet and toast in the oven for 15 to 20 minutes, until nuts are crisp and sugar begins to melt. Cool and store at room temperature until ready to serve.

When ready to serve, place reserved persimmon pulp in a microwave-safe dish. Microwave on MEDIUM (50 percent power) for 45 to 60 seconds until warm, stirring once. Remove and stir in brandy.

Scoop ice cream into individual dessert bowls. Drizzle each serving with some of the warm pulp mixture. Sprinkle with Spicy Pecans.

Praline Ice Cream

Homemade ice cream is particularly welcome during the long hot Texas summers. Because we're not often without pralines in the house, either made from the recipe for No-Fail Pecan Pralines (page 135) or purchased from a local Tex-Mex restaurant or Mexican bakery, I added some chopped pralines to my mother's recipe for vanilla ice cream made from an egg-rich cooked custard. The ice cream is incredible. Serve this alone or piled into Texas Pecan Lace Cookies (page 143).

6   large egg yolks
1   cup granulated sugar
    pinch salt
2   cups heavy cream
1½ cups whole milk
1   vanilla bean, split in half and scraped, or 2 teaspoons pure vanilla extract
2½ cups coarsely chopped No-Fail Pecan Pralines (page 135)

Makes about 2 quarts

Fill a medium bowl one-third full of ice water. Set aside.

In another medium bowl, whisk together egg yolks, sugar, and salt.

In a medium heavy-bottomed saucepan, combine the cream and milk. Add the scrapings of the vanilla bean and scald the cream mixture over medium-high heat. Slowly add the hot cream to the egg mixture, whisking constantly. Return the mixture to the saucepan and cook over medium heat, stirring constantly, until the custard thickens and coats the back of a wooden spoon, about 5 to 10 minutes.

Immediately remove from the stove and strain the custard into a clean bowl. Set this bowl over the bowl of ice water and stir until cool. Pour custard into an ice-cream maker and freeze according to manufacturer's directions. When ice cream is almost frozen, stir in chopped pralines. Continue to churn for another 5 to 10 minutes.

Quince Ice Cream

Quince is an old-fashioned fruit, loved by our grandmothers for making jelly and poaching like a pear. Today, however, quince is lumped into the same "other fruit" category as boysenberries, olallieberries, and jujubes. In fact, California's San Joaquin Valley, the largest area of commercial quince production in the United States, has fewer than 300 acres of quince trees. As an ornamental in the yard, the tree will become a bush and produce little fruit unless it is pruned regularly.

I happen to love the seductive apple-pear flavor of quince and look forward to its September-to-December appearance in high-end supermarkets or Mexican and Korean green markets. Never eaten fresh, here quince is gently simmered before freezing into a scrumptious ice cream. I clipped this recipe from the *Los Angeles Times* back in 1966. The recipe is attributed to the renowned Brown Derby on Hollywood Boulevard. I've adapted the larger recipe for my countertop ice cream machine. Serve this delightful ice cream with Howdy Doody Sugar Cookies (page 128).

Makes about 1 quart

1½ cups whole milk

2 cups heavy cream

1¼ cups sugar

½ teaspoon ground cinnamon

6 large egg yolks

1½ teaspoons pure vanilla extract

3 large quince

¼ cup water

In a medium saucepan, combine milk, heavy cream, ½ cup sugar, and cinnamon. Cook over medium heat, stirring constantly, until mixture is scalded and sugar is dissolved, about 8 minutes. Do not allow the mixture to boil. Remove from heat to cool slightly.

In a large bowl, whisk egg yolks and ½ cup sugar until mixture is thick and pale, about 2 minutes. Gradually whisk in warm milk mixture. Pour entire mixture back into the saucepan. Cook over low heat, stirring, until a thin custard forms, about 12 minutes. Do not allow the mixture to boil. Remove from heat and stir in vanilla extract. Cover surface with a piece of plastic wrap and chill for at least 1 hour.

Meanwhile, peel, core, and dice quince. You should have about 2 cups diced fruit. Place in a small saucepan and stir in remaining ¼ cup sugar and water. Cover and simmer over medium heat until quince is tender and liquid is almost entirely evaporated, 20 to 25 minutes. (Quince will scorch if water evaporates too quickly; check occasionally and add more water if necessary.)

Remove from heat and chill by setting saucepan into a bowl of crushed ice for a few minutes. Stir cooled quince mixture into the chilled custard base. Freeze in an ice-cream maker according to manufacturer's instructions.

Blackberry Sorbet

This is a basic recipe that can be made with other western berries—raspberries, strawberries, boysenberries, loganberries, and so forth. Taste the fruit, adjusting the amount of sugar in the syrup to match the tartness of the fruit. Don't omit the lemon juice; it helps to bring out the berry flavor.

Makes
6 to 8
servings

1½ cups sugar

1½ cups water

3 tablespoons fresh lemon juice

2 tablespoons blackberry liqueur (*change liqueur flavor to suit the berries*)

6 cups fresh blackberries, rinsed and drained

In a heavy saucepan, bring sugar and water to a boil. Cook, stirring, for about 2 minutes, until sugar is completely dissolved. Remove from heat and transfer to a large metal bowl. Stir in lemon juice and blackberry liqueur. Thoroughly chill.

Set aside six perfect blackberries for garnish. Puree the remaining blackberries in a food processor, then strain through a fine sieve to extract the seeds. Pour into chilled syrup and stir well to combine. Process in an ice-cream maker, following the manufacturer's directions, or freeze in a shallow metal cake pan until almost solid. Break into chunks and process in a food processor until mixture forms a thick slush. Transfer to a freezer container and freeze until firm.

Let soften in the refrigerator for 10 to 15 minutes before scooping into dessert dishes. Garnish each serving with a whole blackberry.

Cantaloupe Sorbet

Years ago, I was privileged to work with Gayelord Hauser, a leader in the Southern California health-food movement, on his last book, for which I developed a series of recipes for fruit sorbets. I originally called for honeydew melon and fresh lime in this recipe, but since then I've found cantaloupe to be particularly pleasing in flavor and its pale color lovely when sprinkled with a few fresh blueberries or blackberries. The original recipe called for honey, but I prefer the texture when it's made with sugar.

⅓ cup sugar

2 tablespoons finely grated lemon rind

⅓ to ½ cup fresh lemon juice

4½ cups diced cantaloupe (from about 3½ pounds melon)
    fresh blueberries or blackberries, washed and drained

Makes about 1 quart

In a small bowl, mash sugar and lemon rind with a fork to release the citrus oil. Set aside for 10 minutes.

Meanwhile, process cantaloupe in a food processor or blender to a smooth puree. Stir ⅓ cup lemon juice into sugar mixture and add to cantaloupe. Process for another 30 seconds. Taste, adding more lemon juice, if needed. Transfer mixture to a bowl and nest in a larger bowl of crushed ice. Stir often until mixture is quite cold, about 10 minutes.

Pour mixture into a 1-quart or larger ice-cream freezer. Freeze, following the manufacturer's instructions. Or, freeze in a shallow metal cake pan until almost solid. Break into chunks and process in a food processor until mixture forms a thick slush. Transfer to a freezer container and freeze until firm. Let soften in the refrigerator for 10 to 15 minutes before scooping into dessert dishes. Garnish each serving with a few fresh blueberries.

Sangria Sorbet

Wine has been a part of the Texas culture since 1662 when the Franciscan priests first produced Texas wines. With 29 wineries now producing premium varietal and table wines, Texas wines are starting to win national and international recognition.

For this sorbet, I would use Llano Estacado Signature Red, a Texas wine that was just voted into the prestigious Meritage Association in the company of other wines handcrafted in the Bordeaux tradition from renowned wineries as Kendall Jackson, Chateau St. Michelle, Geyser Peak, and Mondavi. Its berry and red cherry flavors blend beautifully with the other fruits to produce an excellent sorbet. Serve this after a spicy Tex-Mex meal. If Texas wine isn't available where you live, ask for a Bordeaux-style red wine with similar berry flavors.

Makes 6 servings

2   cups Llano Estacado Signature Red or dry Bordeaux-style red wine
2   cups ginger ale
1   large orange, peeled with all white pith removed, chopped
2   large peaches, peeled, pitted, and chopped
⅓   cup fresh tangerine juice
⅓   cup fresh lime juice
⅓   cup honey
3   tablespoons tequila
    fresh mint sprigs for garnish (optional)
    fresh lime slices for garnish (optional)

Working in two batches, place all ingredients except mint and lime slices in a food processor or blender. Process until smooth. Pour into an ice-cream maker and freeze according to the manufacturer's directions. Or, freeze in a shallow metal cake pan until almost solid. Break into chunks and process in a food processor or beat with an electric mixer until it forms a thick slush. Transfer to a freezer container and freeze until firm.

To serve, scoop into dessert bowls. Garnish each serving with a sprig of mint and a thin slice of lime, if desired.

Texas Ruby Red Grapefruit Sorbet

California and Arizona also grow wonderful grapefruits, but I'm particularly partial to the sweet Ruby Red grapefruits grown in Texas. The deep pink color of the grapefruit gives a lovely, delicate hue to the sorbet. Serve this alone or with slices of Pistachio Pound Cake (page 80).

2   cups sugar
1   cup water
2½ cups fresh Ruby Red grapefruit juice with some pulp
1   tablespoons finely grated Ruby Red grapefruit rind
½   cup fresh lime juice
⅓   cup tequila

Makes about 1 quart

In a saucepan, bring sugar and water to a boil. Reduce heat and cook, stirring constantly, until sugar crystals are dissolved. Remove from heat and chill.

In a large bowl, combine sugar mixture, grapefruit juice, grapefruit peel, lime juice, and tequila. Pour into an ice-cream freezer and freeze according to the manufacturer's instructions. Or, freeze in a shallow metal cake pan until almost solid. Break into chunks and process in a food processor or beat with an electric mixer until it forms a thick slush. Transfer to a freezer container and freeze until firm.

Scoop into stemmed dessert glasses to serve.

Appendix

The Dessert Cheese Tray

Westerners love cheese and produce a variety of cheeses that rival those of Europe. Any of the recipes presented in this book become an extra-special dessert when followed with or accompanied by a variety of different flavored and textured cheeses. If choosing cheese is a daunting task for you, visit a good local cheese shop or department at your local supermarket. Its staff should be knowledgeable about the various cheeses available, eager to answer questions, and even let you sample before you buy.

Basically, western cheeses are produced in two categories:

Soft and Soft-Ripened. Soft, creamy cheese such as Brie, Camembert, and Schloss, with their edible white rinds and smooth, running centers, are produced in cheese factories in Marin County, north of San Francisco. Teleme is a popular soft-ripened cheese, excellent with dessert, and a California original. There is also a wide range of goat cheeses, made in California, Texas, and New Mexico. Usually sold in logs or rounds and sometimes coated with herbs, goat cheese is prized for its rich, tangy flavor.

Semihard and Hard. Usually produced in large wheels to be cut into wedges, these firm cheeses range from barely aged to those aged up to several months or more. Monterey Jack and Cheddar are the most popular western cheeses in this category. Each comes in a wide range of styles and textures. Names like Colby, Longhorn, and Tillamook, a specialty of Oregon, describe different types of Cheddar. Jack cheese is usually semi-firm and creamy, although some cheesemakers age it many months to make a firm, dry Jack, which can also be enjoyed with or after dessert. Western cheese also includes a range of Italian-style cheeses such as Fontina, Provolone, and Mozzarella, as well as Edam, Gouda, and feta. There are also a number of firm and semi-firm Hispanic-style cheeses, such as Manchego and Oaxaca. Very hard cheeses such as Parmesan, Romano, and Cotija, a dry Hispanic-style white cheese, also fall within the dessert cheese category.

Although the variety of dessert cheeses available is vast, limit your choices to two or three for a dinner party and no more than five for a gala event. Even a single offering of a perfect cheese can be a wonderful counterpart to your dessert.

To present the cheeses, I have several china, small marble, and woven basket trays chosen to go along with the theme and formality of the occasion, on which I display the cheese. I line the surface with fresh grape leaves or printed paper grape leaves and include appropriate cutting instruments for each of the cheeses. Let the cheeses soften at room temperature for 30 minutes before serving to make it easy for your guests to help themselves. Tray garnishes could include edible flowers such as pesticide-free nasturtiums, pansies, scented geraniums, or violets.

If you feel you must offer crackers for the soft and soft-ripened cheese, always use water-based crackers so as to not interfere with the flavor of the cheese.

Dessert Wines
of the West

New Mexico claims to have been the first major wine producing state of the West, beginning in the early 1500s when the first Spanish explorers and settlers brought their European wine grape cuttings with them, finding the sunny, fertile Rio Grande Valley in New Mexico for their first plantings. Texas followed in 1662 when the Franciscan priests first produced Texas wines. The founding of the California missions began in 1769, but state historians differ on when and where the first rootstocks were planted. It is known that in 1798, ten California missions were growing grapes and making wine. The first grape rootstocks were brought to Oregon by those braving the Oregon Trail in the 1860s, and Washington dates the birth of its wine industry to a few years later.

Dessert wines are among the most alluring and delicious, yet the least understood products of the vintner's art. A quality dessert wine is a harmonious balance of rich, deep flavors, natural sweetness, and clean crisp acidity that can easily stand alone as an encore to a fine meal. By following a few simple pairing guidelines, anyone can choose a dessert wine that will transform a good dessert into a special occasion. When pairing wines with desserts, a wine should be chosen that is somewhat sweeter than the dessert itself in order to accentuate the flavors of the wine and to keep the wine from seeming too tart.

Dessert wines feature a wide range of flavors. The peach, honey, and apricot of the muscats; apple, pear, and spice of the Rieslings and Gewürztraminers; and cherry, cinnamon, and vanilla found in Port are just a few choices that enable a cook to either echo the flavors of a dessert in the wine or to choose flavors that are complementary.

Of the hundreds of western wineries, several have produced outstanding dessert wines that stand above the rest in quality. Because selecting a wine is a matter of personal taste, your dessert wine preferences may differ greatly from the results of my personal wine tastings and that of my wine consultant Chesley Sanders, a wine expert who writes and lectures on wine and matching wine with food. I have also included recommendations from the various vintners of the major wine-producing states with whom I consulted. All wines listed have won wine competitions, so you're likely to enjoy them.

Gewürztraminer

(Tularosa Vineyards, Tularosa, New Mexico)

Described as having a wonderful spicy nose, with hints of fig, nutmeg, some cinnamon, and a crisp finish, its sweet and sour type characteristics make it an excellent choice after a spicy meal. It pairs well with any kind of dessert made with a hint of cinnamon such as Pear Dumplings with Red Currant Sauce (pages 112–113), Pear Fluden (pages 78–79), and Prune Spice Cake (pages 84–85). It's also a perfect match with desserts made with figs, such as Dried Fig Cake with Pine Nuts (page 61) and Fig and Goat Cheese Tarts in Walnut Crust (pages 218–219).

Llano Estacado Cellar Select Port

(Llano Estacado Vineyards, Lubbock, Texas)

This dessert wine from the Texas High Plains is a rich, ruby red port fortified with grape spirits. Full of cherry and vanilla flavors with a smooth sweetness and satisfying finish, it would be an excellent choice with any chocolate dessert such as Bittersweet Chocolate Mini-Cakes (page 2), Chocolate Pie with Hazelnut Meringue (page 31), Mocha Chocolate Chunk Brownies (page 23), or Raspberry Chocolate-Pecan Torte (page 13).

Messina Hof Glory

(Messina Hof Vineyards, Bryan, Texas)

A late harvest Muscat Canelli, this silky wine has delicious honeyed peach flavors, and a wonderful fruit-filled aroma. Glory, which took a Gold Medal at the International Taster's Guild competition in 1998, owes its sweet richness to grapes left on the vine until they are fully ripened and beginning to lose moisture. This dessert wine would be a perfect choice with Deep-Dish Peach Pie (pages 179–180), Old-Fashioned Peach Cobbler (pages 106–107), Baked Peaches with Cream (page 152), or a scoop of Vanilla Ice Cream (page 252).

Moscato d'Oro

(Robert Mondavi Winery, Napa Valley, California)

This wine made from Muscat Canelli grapes is redolent of the fragrances of honeysuckle and gardenia, leading to a combination of fruit flavors, including guava, ripe peaches, and citrus. Moscato d'Oro is an elegant accompaniment to lightly sweet desserts, such as Hazelnut Cheesecake (page 68), Maui Macaroons (page 21), Kiwifruit Tart (pages 220–221), or Chocolate Hazelnut Truffles (page 14).

Muscat Canelli

(Tularosa Vineyards, Tularosa, New Mexico)

This Muscat maintains its traditional Italian heritage with a wonderful floral aroma with bountiful honeysuckle and honeydew melon finish. It can be paired with desserts with a strong fruit taste such as Apple Blackberry Crisp (pages 90, 92), Strawberry Cobbler (page 115) or Hot Peach Crepe Soufflé (pages 162–163). Muscat Canelli is also excellent with desserts made with pecans such as Date and Pecan Tart (page 215), Sweet Potato and Pecan Tart (page 223), and Terrific Texas Pecan Pie (page 203).

Muscat Vin De Glaciere

(Bonny Doon, Santa Cruz, California)

This dessert wine is made with Muscat Canelli, Malvasia Bianca, and Orange Muscat grapes that are flash frozen after they are picked. This method, pioneered at Bonny Doon, concentrates the sugars, flavors, and acid in the juice, leaving behind much of the water as ice. Vin De Glaciere has bright fruit flavors of apricot and tangerine, with enough acid for a clean, fresh finish. *Wine Spectator* magazine has rated it as one of the world's top 100 wines three years in a row. This wine and the Mango Brûlée (page 241) and Tangerine Mousse with Blackberry Puree (pages 247–248) are matches made in heaven.

New Mexico Port

(La Chiripada Winery, Dixon, New Mexico)

Fortified with the finest oak-aged brandy, this vintage Port is harvested from Leon Millot French hybrid grapes from the Rio Embudo Valley. This results in a Port filled with concentrated fruit that displays richness and depth. The fine balance of sweetness, spice, and high alcohol make this the perfect choice to enjoy with any chocolate dessert such as Chocolate Bread Pudding (page 36), Chocolate Mousse Tostadas (pages 39–40), Fallen Chocolate Soufflé Cake (pages 5–6), as well as any fresh fruit and dessert cheese (page 265).

Vino Gelate
(Ponzi Vineyards, Beavertown, Oregon)

Oregon is fast establishing itself as one of America's premium wine growing regions. It is home to some of this countries best Rieslings, and Ponzi Vineyards' Vino Gelate is one of the finest. Vino Gelate is made from sweet ripe Riesling grapes that are frozen and pressed immediately after harvest, resulting in a dessert wine with crisp green apple and pear flavors. With its clean finish, this wine would be a natural with Baked Bosc Pears with Hazelnuts (page 151), Baked Winter Western Fruits (page 153), Roasted Red Pears with Mascarpone Cheese (pages 167–168), or any sliced fruit and light dessert cheese (page 265).

White Riesling Sweet Select
(Chateau Ste. Michelle, Woodville, Washington)

From the Columbia Valley vineyards that lie deep in the rain shadow of the Cascade Mountains comes a late-harvest Riesling whose generous sweetness, according to Chateau Ste. Michelle's PR department, is expressed in a "luscious, viscous mouthfeel." The wine offers nectar-like aromas of apricots, honey, and flowers while sweet flavors of ripe peaches and apricots explode on the palate. Serve this dessert wine with any fruity dessert such as Grilled Peaches with Goat Cheese and Raspberry Sauce (page 161), Peach and Mixed Berry Cobbler (pages 110–111), Apricot Kuchen (page 98), or Apricot and Berry Tart (page 210).

Mail-Order Sources

Bell's Farm to Market
navel oranges,
ruby red grapefruit, pecans
16 S. Ware Road
McAllen, TX 78501
(800) 798-0424
www.bellsfarm.com

Bite-Size Bakery
traditional New Mexican
cookies and crackers
410 Camino Oriente
P.O. Box 1549
Moriarty, NM 87035
(505) 832-5158
www.bite-size.com

Buchanan Hollow Nut Company
almonds and pistachios
6510 Minturn Road
Le Gran, CA 95333
(800) 532-1500
www.bhnc.com

Coyote Café General Store
dried chiles and
Southwestern products
132 West Water Street
Santa Fe, NM 87501
(800) 866-HOWL
www.interart.net/food/coyote.cafe

Frieda's, Inc.
exotic fruits such as
persimmons and quince
4465 Corporate Center Drive
Los Alamitos, CA 90720
800-421-9477
www.friedas.com

Laura Chenel's Chevre
goat cheese
c/o Williams-Sonoma Catalog
(800) 541-2233

Mozzarella Company
goat cheese, crème fraîche,
and mascarpone
2944 Elm Street
Dallas, TX 75226
(214) 741-4072
www.mozzco.com

Pendery's
dried chiles, vanilla beans, and
pine nuts
1221 Manufacturing Street
Dallas, TX 75207
(800) 533-1870
www.penderys.com

Taxco Produce Company
dried chiles and Southwestern
produce and products
1801 S. Good Latimer
Dallas, TX 75226
(214) 421-7191

Timber Crest Farms
dried fruits, nuts
4791 Dry Creek Road
Healdsburg, CA 95448
(707) 433-8251
www.sonic.net/tcf

Vanilla Saffron Imports
vanilla beans
949 Valencia Street
San Francisco, CA 94110
(415) 648-8990
www.saffron.com

White Egret Farms
goat cheese
15704 Webberville Road, FM 969
Austin, TX 78724
(512) 276-7408
www.whiteegretfarm.com

Williams-Sonoma
cookware and gourmet foods
P.O. Box 7456
San Francisco, CA 94120
(415) 421-4242

Zoria Farms
dried apricots, dried cherries, dried
peaches, dried nectarines, dried pears,
dried apple rings, dried plums,
almonds, pecans, pistachios, walnuts
234 N. Capitol Avenue
San Jose, CA 95127
(408) 258-2900
www.zoria.com

Metric Conversion Table

Liquid Measurements

¼ teaspoon = 1.25 milliliters
½ teaspoon = 2.5 milliliters
1 teaspoon = 5 milliliters
1 tablespoon = 15 milliliters
2 tablespoons = 30 milliliters
¼ cup = 60 milliliters
⅓ cup = 80 milliliters
½ cup = 120 milliliters
⅔ cup = 160 milliliters
¾ cup = 180 milliliters
1 cup = 240 milliliters
1 pint (2 cups) = 480 milliliters
1 quart (4 cups) = 960 milliliters (.96 liters)

Equivalents for Dry Measurements

Amount	Fine Powder (flour)	Grain (rice)	Granular (sugar)	Granular (sugar)
1 cup	140 grams	150 grams	190 grams	200 grams
¾ cup	105 grams	113 grams	143 grams	150 grams
⅔ cup	93 grams	100 grams	125 grams	133 grams
½ cup	70 grams	75 grams	95 grams	100 grams
⅓ cup	47 grams	50 grams	63 grams	67 grams
¼ cup	35 grams	38 grams	48 grams	50 grams
⅛ cup	18 grams	19 grams	24 grams	15 grams

Oven Temperatures

	Fahrenheit	Celsius	Gas Mark
Freeze water	32°F	0°C	
Room Temperature	68°F	20°C	
Boil Water	212°F	100°C	
Bake	325°F	160°C	3
	350°F	180°C	4
	375°F	190°C	5
	400°F	200°C	6
	425°F	220°C	7
	450°F	230°C	8

Equivalents for Weight

1 ounce = 30 grams
4 ounces = 120 grams
8 ounces = 240 grams
12 ounces = ¾ pound = 360 grams
16 ounces = 1 pound = 480 grams

Equivalents for Length

1 inch = 2.5 centimeters
6 inches = ½ foot = 15 centimeters
12 inches = 1 foot = 30 centimeters
36 inches = 3 feet = 1 yard = 90 centimeters
40 inches = 100 centimeters = 1 meter

Index